THE NANCY WHO DREW THE WAY HOME

A MEMOIR

NANCY WAIT

This book is a sequel to
The Nancy Who Drew; the Memoir That Solved A Mystery

Many of the paintings described in the story can be viewed online at http://nancywait.com/artwork/

Though certain names have been changed to protect their privacy, the events and experiences described here are all true and have been faithfully rendered.

ISBN: 979-8-9910200-0-8

To the one who said,
Do you have something I could read?

And the who said,
Write how you got here.

Home is neither here nor there.
Home is within you,
or home is nowhere at all.

— HERMAN HESSE

You think, that just because it's already happened,
The past is finished and unchangeable?
Oh, no, the past is cloaked in multicolored taffeta
And every time we look at it we see a different hue.

— MILOS KUNDERA

Among the great questions of the human heart,
none is more central than the question,
"Who am I?"

— JACOB NEEDLEMAN

CONTENTS

Beginnings 1

Part I

THE CLEARING GROUND 1977-1981

1. Follow the Light 23
2. What About Me? 28
3. Labyrinth of Shadows 41
4. The Botany 47
5. The Path of Return 53
6. Hades Cave 56
7. Staying in the Light 62
8. The Writing Course 67
9. The Underworld 73
10. Art Was Left 79
11. "Are You an Artist?" 89
12. Art and Marriage 97
13. My Private Guadeloupe 105
14. Marriage and Swinging 114
15. The Age of Reckoning 123
16. Who Are You 135
17. More Light 141
18. Threads of Fate 146
19. The Dreamer 156
20. The Key 160
21. Aftermath 172

Part II

JOURNEY TO THE DEEP 1982-1986

22. First Connections 181
23. Bowling Green 193

24. An Empty Vessel 198
25. Safe Harbor 203
26. Daylight Time 212
27. The Drafting Room 221
28. The Plunge 234
29. The Way Out is the Way In 250
30. Light in the Water 259
31. The Kingdom of Heaven 272
32. A Departure 288
33. The Last Fish 293

Part III
A GATEWAY 1986-1987

34. Gene the Genie 305
35. The Obstacle 318
36. A Cleansing 331
37. Double Vision 340
38. A Quickening 348
39. The Commission 352
40. To Bear 366
41. Perilous Passage 375
42. July 4, 1987 385
43. How I Got Here? 393
44. Aftermath II 403
45. Finding 'Here' Again 422

Epilogue 432

About the Author 441

BEGINNINGS

I was in some kind of holding area, a cavernous undefined space, waiting my turn with dozens of others by an opening where the slide was. The light was dim but I could see we all looked the same, plump little cherubs as if we had just stepped out of a Renaissance painting with nothing to do but hang out by the opening. Some were milling about while others stood still or sat quietly on the floor. No one made a sound. Neither was there any sense of urgency or impatience. Suddenly I made a dash for the opening. I don't remember hearing anything so it must have been a silent call that caused me to make a run for it, jumping down the slide as if there wasn't a moment to lose.

What a hurry to get here, yet how unprepared I'd been for skin, scratching my face up so badly as an infant they had to cover my hands with mittens. Had I forgotten there was skin? Growing up I thought there had been a mistake and I had been sent to the wrong family. Had I jumped the queue, come out of turn? Should I have waited? I wondered if that was why I was born into the Wait family. Then one day I looked up 'wait' and found it meant to be in constant readiness. It wasn't passive it was active, like waiting in the wings for your cue to go on. Now, as I look back after a long life, I believe the cue was love. Despite what happened, and maybe the reason why it happened, had everything to do with love.

I used to think God must have hated me and wondered what I had done that was so wrong. It was a mystery until I began putting it all down on paper, my early life at least. I called it, *The Nancy Who Drew, the Memoir That Solved a Mystery,* because at least one mystery was solved. Though it came through the pictures I drew and painted, the book ended before I became an artist. This story is the 'how' of it all. The story behind the pictures that seemed to come from a place of knowledge inside. The inner life I could only access through drawings. First I had to stop wanting to leave this place though—this 'veil of sorrow,' because there was no getting out once I was here. Not even death would free me. Only love would melt the bars. Only then would I remember the holding area, and how it had been my choice to come down the slide.

* * *

Until I was eight I was just one of a brood of five in 1950s America. Then one night when our parents were having a fight that was more virulent than usual, my mother came to check we were all in bed and found me still in the bathroom brushing my teeth. First she was angry at my slowness, then angry I existed at all and cried, 'I wish you'd never been born!' The words stung but I didn't think she meant it. Her face was red and streaked with tears. I knew it was my father she was really angry with. I didn't know that if she hadn't been pregnant with me, she wouldn't have had to marry him in the first place. She had yet to tell me that he wasn't my real father.

Still, I must have gone to sleep wondering where I would have been if I hadn't been born, because that night I dreamed I was trapped in a steel box with water pouring in from a hole in the corner. It rose higher and higher and I was frantic to get out. I felt around in the dark for some kind of crack to suggest there was a door, but found nothing. When the water reached my nose and I knew I was going to drown, I woke up in a cold sweat, relieved to find myself in a warm dry bed at home. But I dreamed it again the next night, and so many nights afterwards that I give it a name, the No Exit dream, which was the name of a book on the coffee table in the living room with a picture of a brick wall on the cover. It was Sartre's *No Exit*, a play about hell, but I didn't know that then. Neither did I know that it was the beginning of something else, the fear of never getting out.

It must have preyed on my mind because some years later I drew a picture of a girl who looked like me when I was eight, and she was being taken home. A man was carrying her up a path to a little house set among the trees. I saw them from the back, his head down, his shoulders bent with grief. Her head hung limply over one of his arms,

her legs with shoes and socks hung over the other. Whether or not I was remembering the No Exit dream, it would have been typical of me to want to see her being taken home so she wouldn't have to stay drowned in the steel box all alone. If not exactly a happy ending, I was making the best of things.

I fretted over the lack of a door though. I was too young at the time to think the steel box with smooth sides could have been the walls of the womb and the fear was never being be born, never getting out alive. What worried me was how could I have gotten in there in the first place if there wasn't an opening. It bothered me almost as much as the problem of getting out. It may have been the reason why around the same time I did the drawing, I attempted a story about a door that *was* there. I began with a boy and a girl, Andy and Andrea who went for a walk and came to a house, but it only brought up more questions. Should they knock? Try the handle? What if no one was home? Or what if they were, what would happen then? Simply providing a door was no answer at all. If I had known that Andy was for Andrew and that Andrea and Andy had the same name, I might have known they were two aspects of the same person. But not knowing that then, all I could do was leave them on the threshold and give up the idea of writing stories.

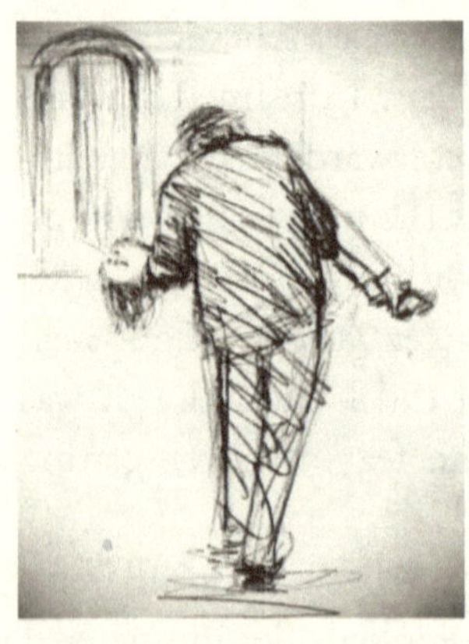

Partial replica from memory of a drawing, age 13.

Then I gave up art too and decided to be an actress, acting out other people's stories. We lived in New York and I was going to Performing Arts High School. It was to please my father, but it was also a chance to imagine I was someone else. Someone not me, having a totally different life. By the age of sixteen I was picturing myself in my own play, becoming an actress in England, going to Rada, the Royal Academy of Dramatic Art in London. Meanwhile, I was glad to be getting as far away as college in Pittsburg. But before I was able to leave I had to live through a scene that was far worse than the No Exit dream because this time I was trapped for real.

My mother had decided her boyfriend should teach me about sex before I left for college and took me to his apartment on the pretext he wanted to give me a farewell party. Then she left me there and went home. It was as awful and as bizarre as it sounds. There was a door but it was barred, so there was no escape. And though I wasn't consciously thinking of the No Exit dream, I seemed to know that death was the way out because I pretended I was drowned at the bottom of a pool. I was a good actress and very convincing, but part of me did die that night. It also left me with the knowledge that whenever things got really bad there was always drowning, which I thought to do for real when I was twenty-six.

The problem was not knowing what love was. If I thought my mother didn't love me that would have been one thing. But I knew that she did. She'd said she was sorry afterwards, so again I had no choice but to think she didn't know what she was doing, and I went on with my life as if nothing had changed. This was made easier when the day after I arrived in Pittsburgh I met a boy with the same dream as mine, studying at Rada and becoming an actor in England. He went over there first, and before I could join him, another layer of confusion was added to the question of love.

I was nineteen that summer, working at Bloomingdales to save up for a ticket to London. My mother didn't want me to go. She called acting "a bee-in-my-bonnet" and thought I was only doing it to please my dad, so she told me he wasn't my real father. She hadn't stayed in touch with Milton, the man she'd had an affair with twenty years ago, yet she managed to locate him in Houston. When he came to New York to meet me she hoped he'd take an interest, encourage me to go back to college in the states at least, maybe even pay the tuition. But Milton, an elderly bachelor in poor health who worked as a photographer of weddings, bar mitzvahs and aspiring models, was as set in his ways as I was set in mine. The only thing we seemed to have in common was an undeniable physical resemblance. Until then I hadn't really noticed I didn't particularly look like anyone else in my family, but it only added to the guilt and bewilderment I felt not being Dad's natural daughter. Having two fathers was like having none at all, and the answer seemed to be in having my own life, be who *I* wanted to be, and I couldn't leave the country fast enough.

I called Milton my 'other father' or my Jewish father, and he remained on the periphery of my life while I stayed safely away from it all in London. By the time I was twenty-five, if I wasn't playing a part, I was playing out the dream of myself I'd cooked up at sixteen when I read Isadora Duncan's autobiography. I wanted to be like her, a great artist who lived by her own rules. And though I came up short with what can only be described as a watered-down version at best, there was the romance of not only working as an actor in a foreign country, but living eighty-seven steps high in an attic bedsit in South Kensington. Though the furniture was old and battered it had an air of faded glamour. I fed coins into the little gas fire to keep warm and dined on bread and cheese at a table by the dormer window. And when I slept on a narrow bed under the eaves, it didn't matter that I hadn't had any parts for a year because offstage I was living out the part I'd created for myself. Lately it even included being the mistress of a wealthy man like Isadora, which was why I could afford to go to a shrink when Milton died and I thought I'd lost the key to my soul.

I had never thought of Milton that way when he was alive, and now it was too late. What did I even know about the soul anyway? When I studied acting at Carnegie-Mellon in Pittsburgh, they told us to bare our soul on stage, but that was when we were pretending to be someone else. They didn't mention baring your soul when I went to Rada, but it was on my mind because when I was offered a film where I had to take off my clothes, I wondered if baring my soul and my body at the same time would lead to great acting. Instead, it led to almost being expelled from school and a reputation I thought I'd never live down. But I stuck it out until Milton died and I realized I'd lost the chance to discover the part of me that was part of him.

Thinking I'd lost the key to my soul may have been overly dramatic, but at twenty-five I wasn't prepared for such finalities. When I turned to a shrink for help he only made it worse. Dr. Shields seemed to want the impossible, telling me to visualize a bridge over the abyss, seeing the new me on the other side. The first bridge that came to mind was Thornton Wilder's *Bridge Over the San Luis Rey*, the rope bridge in Peru that broke and sent five people to their death in the gorge below. I replaced it immediately with Monet's wooden bridge over a lily pond, but it was no good. The self on the other side was supposed to be authentic and real, a woman in control of her life, and I kept seeing myself falling into that murky slimy pit below and never being able to climb out.

Outwardly, I didn't appear headed for the abyss. I was impeccably groomed and had a confident, worldly manner, especially after Toshi, short for Toshikazu, offered me a job so I could quit working as a hostess in the Japanese night club between parts. The salary was generous and all I had to do was research copyright information for the British and

American films he sold to Japanese television stations. He lived in Japan and only came to London for a few weeks a few times a year, and then we'd be off to Paris or Rome, visiting places I'd only dreamed about before. Suddenly my time was free for learning how to play tennis and drive a car when I wasn't riding in Hyde Park or brushing up on my French at Berlitz. I thought I had it made. When Toshi put me on a plane back to London, I'd climb the eighty-seven steps up to my attic room and think how lucky I was. Then I got the call that Milton died of a heart attack and it was three days before anyone found him.

Toshi thought buying me a car and a new flat to furnish would take my mind off sadness and loss, and after sessions with Dr. Shields I'd drive home in my new car to the newly renovated three-bedroom duplex in Kensington that was beautifully decorated but didn't look lived in, and find myself missing the attic bedsit that felt more like the real me, even if I didn't have my own loo. I had two bathrooms all to myself now and a terrace to rattle around in, but no one to share them with. My life felt like a sham.

Then a play came out of the blue and Dr. Shields was put on hold while I went on tour playing the cockney maid in a Restoration comedy. Doing a play had once felt like the answer to everything. When I fell in love with one of the actors before we even finished rehearsals in London, he felt like the answer to everything. By the end of the six-week-run when Hamish was talking about marriage and a baby, settling down and having a regular life—a real life with no more play-acting—I was so happy at being rescued from the loneliness of House Beautiful that I ignored the signs it may have only been a tour-romance. Sensitive, poetic-looking Hamish who wore denim the color of his eyes, said he needed space. Then he called with the news he had a part in a film shooting in Ireland and didn't know when he'd be back. If Milton's death had unmoored me, I was now adrift, latching onto a passing ship to keep my self-esteem afloat.

I knew I shouldn't have gone off to the South of France with another man instead of being home for Toshi's arrival. But before Hamish disappeared, I had been planning to end it with Toshi anyway. Not this way, but in a reasonable, sensible way so that we could remain friends. But reason had deserted me along with my heart's desire. The story I told to cover up my absence didn't fly because Toshi had hired a detective. "I know all about you!" he shouted. This gentle soft-spoken older man with Old World manners and never a hair out of place ranted for hours, saying in Old Japan he could have had me killed and no one would blame him. I was relieved when he left the following day. Everything was all up in the air about the flat and my allowance, but things might still turn out alright. When I went to my regular appointment with Dr. Shields I was already looking on the bright side. "Toshi will surely give me a settlement of some kind," I said. "And Hamish will be back. We might still get married."

Dr. Shields seemed to consider this for a moment before he said, "But are these men with an uppercase M or a lowercase m?"

This seemingly innocuous question was the end of me. I didn't have to know that regardless of its case, M was the 13th letter of the alphabet, a number so unlucky we didn't have a 13th floor in the building where I grew up. I didn't have to know that Death was the 13th card of the tarot in order to hear a death knell. Nor did I have to recall Hitchcock's *Dial M for Murder*, or know that in Fritz Lang's film *M,* the *M* was for *Mörder* in German, 'murderer' in English. I didn't have to know or recall these things to know that whether it was M or m, or even if it was M for Milton, the father who died and took the key to my soul with him, I was finished. Dr. Shields may have only been saying that I didn't know how to choose men, but I had been seeing him for a year by then and could hear so much more.

The session was over and Dr. Shields said kindly, "Have a nice weekend." I was already crying when I got in the car, but I consoled myself with the thought of a Valium when I got home. All I had to do was get home, but what with it being a Friday at the end of May, everyone trying to get an early start on what looked to be a glorious weekend, traffic moved at a crawl on Park Lane. I was boxed in on all sides thinking about my failure at love. Losing the key to my soul may have started it, but that was nothing compared to my botched attempts to find love. I told myself just get to Hyde Park Corner, just get past the roundabout, then you'll be on Kensington High Street and it will be clear sailing, but all I could think about was how I didn't know how to find love. By the time I parked and hurried up the stairs, it had come down to how could I ever find love if I didn't even know what it was?

What it was was the anniversary of Milton's death. Whether I was aware of it or not, the earth had come round again to that place of sadness and loss and nothing had changed. Nothing had worked. Going to a shrink made it worse because he made me look at things I didn't want to see. Coming home was a reminder that I once thought material things would make me happy. Even the thrill of doing a play had quickly worn off. The pain was more than a low-dosage pill could handle and I took another and tried to wash it down with a glass of white wine from the fridge, but the floodgates had opened and I couldn't hold the glass steady or calm myself enough to take a sip. I wanted to fall asleep and not have to think anymore until I remembered I'd only wake up again tomorrow and nothing would have changed. Unless I didn't wake up.

The idea of driving my car off a cliff probably came from the close call I'd had last winter when I took a solo trip to Cornwall to celebrate passing the driving test on my fourth try. I set out under a cloudless blue sky, then caught up with the rain on a winding road in Devon. I didn't know you weren't supposed to brake on a wet road while making a turn and I lost control of the wheel. The car began to spin. My life started flashing before me and I thought I was done for. But the wheels got stuck on a low stone wall and I didn't go plunging into the ravine. Now I thought, what if there wasn't a wall. There wasn't a wall on the cliffs overlooking the Channel. All I had to do was get myself to the coast to sink peacefully into the abyss of oblivion.

I took out a map and sat at my desk to plan a route, but thinking of death brought on a fresh bout of tears. I sobbed all the more when the map became too blurry to read and I stood up in despair to wail at my helplessness. Then a voice in my head said, *You'll only have to come back again, and it will be harder next time.*

I went suddenly quiet. Having to repeat this life was unthinkable. I couldn't come back again. The idea terrified me. It was out of the question. I couldn't even imagine it being harder next time. If a moment ago I'd been in a panic to have done with it, I was now in a panic to stay, and with a calmness I wouldn't have known I was capable of I called my GP for antidepressants. The nurse said he was at the clinic, but I could come by to pick up a prescription. I had never taken them before and was glad I asked how long they took to work because she said, "Two or three days." I told her I didn't have that long, I needed something right away, and she gave me the address of the clinic. The tranquilizer must have started to kick in by then because I drove slowly and carefully and kept checking the map so I wouldn't get lost. The doctor only said to pack a bag, I was going for a rest somewhere. That was a relief. I had no idea I'd be taken to a psych ward, but it took me so long to pack a suitcase I thought I'd already lost my mind. I hadn't wanted to think anymore, and now I had to think about everything. What went with toothbrush? Toothpaste. What went with robe? Slippers. Nothing was automatic. The world had slowed down and taken me with it.

Though they didn't give me anything more than a mild sleeping pill, the slowness continued all through the week in hospital. It was the shock of course. Suddenly being told there was no way out of this. If I tried to escape I'd only be sent back. This wasn't the world I thought I lived in where death was the end, and it made me feel I didn't know anything anymore. When I woke up that first morning at St. Mary Abbots Hospital I didn't know where I was and silently called out, *Don't leave me here!* Who did I think I was calling to? The voice that warned me I'd be sent back? I hardly knew who I was or what was what anymore. When I got back into bed and another patient came in and walked off with my toiletry case, I didn't say anything because maybe that's the way things were around here. The nurse brought it back later and scolded me for not looking after my belongings, but that was the least of it. I forgot I didn't like ants. When I saw them parading around the sink, crawling over my soap and toothbrush, instead of shooing them away I watched in fascination thinking what amazing creatures ants were. I was like a child again, with no memory how to write in script and barely able to read. I remembered Ophelia's lines though. That warm sunny afternoon when we were allowed into the garden and I sat on the grass, one of the social workers joined me. But when he wanted to talk and ask questions I grabbed a fistful of grass and held it out saying, *There's rosemary, that's for remembrance. There's rue for you, and here's some for me.* Then I stood and floated off, the Ophelia who made it to the nunnery rather than drowning herself.

Rather than floating down the stream I floated down the hallway in a long white silk kimono from Japan. When I looked down to see where my feet were taking me I saw a floor of black and white squares. They were repetitive and colorless but there was an order to that grid of straight lines. I had lost my way, and now here was a floor made of squares to lead me through space. I was soothed by its uniformity, the unchanging pattern clearly marked. And so I kept going, putting one foot in front of the other, black-white, dark-light. It seemed to keep me intact when nothing else felt certain.

Black and white squares had come to my aid another time when my world fell apart. I had done a film over term break at Rada, not knowing it was against the rules. Aside from the challenge of baring my body along with my soul, I needed the money for school fees. When the principal threatened to expel me, saying I'd do anything for the "All-American dollar," I cried to be so misunderstood and he shouted, "Don't play the tragedy queen with me!" It had taken me two years and four auditions to get in, and whether I was expelled or not, it was over. This time it wasn't just school that was over, it was the life I'd been living. At Rada I made it to the end of the hallway by focusing on the black and white checkered linoleum until I got to the Ladies Room. At St. Mary Abbots the squares got me to the end of the week when they said I could go home.

Maybe the checkerboard pattern was a reminder to check myself. I had veered off course and it provided an orderly predictable pattern to follow that might set me straight. I know the squares made an impression because practically the first thing I noticed when I came home was that the sofa was a rectangle, the matching club chair and side tables were square, and the throw pillows were both square and rectangular. I'd never had reason to take this into account before and can only assume that in lieu of the grid of black and white linoleum since the entire flat was carpeted in solid brown, my eye must have settled on whatever geometric shapes were at hand. I wonder now if I was honing in on some kind of inner map I'd lost sight of.

The world outside was just as strange when I took a walk up to Gloucester Road for bread and milk and found myself looking around at the neat little houses and shops as if I'd never really seen them before. When the Launderette sign in pink script came into view across the street, I stopped to study it. Launderette, a place to wash your clothes. The meaning was in the word launder-ette, launder-it. The word *was* the meaning. I don't recall thinking anything else at the time, but I've come to see it as a premonition of the dream I was going to have that night. The one I called the Dream of '76 because that was the year, 1976. The year I relived a death that hadn't disappeared in the wash between lives.

I went to bed early, glad for the peace and quiet after the hubbub of the ward. The dream came shortly before dawn. I saw myself sitting at my desk in the study when I heard someone coming up the stairs. Toshi was the only other person with a key, but when I called out his name there was no answer. Now I was frightened and slipped into the next room to hide in the closet but I wasn't quick enough. The detective he'd hired shot me from five feet away. I knew I was dying when I fell to the floor, but it felt blissful. Then the floor opened up and I kept falling. An endless fall amidst a deafening rumble and shaking until I landed at the bottom of the sea and a door appeared. A massive wooden door like the door to a castle opened by itself, pushing against the water with a terrifying roar. I came up and stood on the threshold, but all I could see through the doorway was more water, more sea. A shimmering wall of an inner sea. I stood riveted in place, unable to move forward or back, and suddenly I was returned to the study. The gunman was there too, only now he was a frail old Mongolian. We sat together and I comforted him, and when he held out a crushed pack of cigarettes to offer me one, I took out my Bensons that came in a box. Then I couldn't find a match and Sharon, an actress I knew from Rada, appeared out of nowhere and held out a light.

The light woke me up. The dream was so real I threw off the covers and leapt up saying, *I'm alive! I'm alive!* Then I drank a glass of water—I couldn't believe how thirsty I was —and sat at my desk in the study to write it all down. In my excited state I smoked one cigarette after another until I came to the fifth and quickly put it back. I couldn't say why but it had nothing to do with smoking. Maybe it had to do with being shot from five feet away because it was the number five that felt scary.

It was getting light out when I finished, and when I looked at the cold gray light of dawn and heard the birds singing, it struck me that I knew something inside. That I had some kind of knowledge or information I'd never be able to learn from a book or hear from anyone else because it was *in me*. And just as I knew that, I knew I would only find it through painting or writing what was inside.

I would need both as it turned out. Art could take me a

long way, but until I wrote the story behind the pictures I wouldn't be able to see what I had done. The pictures were a kind of sign language that seemed to come from a place I had no words for. The day I'd be able to describe the signs and what led to them would be a long time coming. But by then I will know the castle door under water that opened by itself really *was* the door to a kingdom. The Fifth Kingdom of Soul. If there was a key, it was a vibration. If anything had been lost, it was the memory that I was a soul. The light I'd been given at the end of the dream was the light that would guide me back.

I know that now, but all I knew then was that I had woken up from some kind of death experience that scared me, and I put the fifth cigarette back. I couldn't say why four was okay, but when I thought about it I realized that we live in a world of four. Rooms have four walls and windows and doors have four sides. There are four points on a compass, four seasons of the year. There are four quarters to a dollar, four quarters in an hour and four corners of the earth. I know where I am with four. My mother used to cut our sandwiches into quarters to be chewed one at a time, and when I'd eaten them all I knew I had eaten the whole.

I will have to wait a long time before I come to know that four also signifies the Fourth Kingdom of Humanity and five is the Fifth Kingdom of Soul. To find the key I thought was lost when Milton died I will have to become a detective like the one Toshi hired to follow me, and follow myself as I make my way back to the shimmering wall of water I saw in a dream at twenty-six. It will take almost another twenty-six years before I learn that the gunman shot me from five feet away because the dream occurred on June 5, 1976, five days after the thirty-third anniversary of a British civilian aircraft called *Ibis* was shot down by the Luftwaffe over the Bay of Biscay on June 1, 1943. No wonder five was scary. It wasn't just a dream; it was a memory entrained in my soul.

One day I will realize the Mongolian was dream-speak for 'mon-gol.' My goal of seeing through the veil of water across the threshold at the bottom of the sea. That he was old and frail may have signified that the goal of seeing into the 'inner-see' was an old one. But I was given a light. Then a few weeks later I was given a clue. A vision of roses encased in a cube of ice, moisture dripping down the sides like tears. The frozen roses hovered in the air for a moment before they disappeared. I'd never had a vision before and I was intrigued. But when it kept coming back I found it unnerving. I associated roses with love, especially red ones, and assumed it was telling me my heart was frozen. I didn't want to believe it and tried to shoo the vision away. When it followed me back to New York I thought to get it out of my head by putting it on canvas. It was the first painting I did once I got settled, except I omitted the ice. The bouquet of roses looked so vibrant and alive it seemed a shame to paint ice over them. I didn't know how to paint ice anyway and was afraid I'd ruin the whole thing. Yet simply painting the roses, capturing them in perennial bloom, open forever to the joy of being alive seemed enough because I never saw the vision again.

There was actually more to the roses than that. For along with learning about the *Ibis* decades later, I discovered that among the passengers on that ill-fated journey was an eleven-year-old English girl called Petra which means rose-red after the ancient city of Petra known for its rose-red sandstone. I knew then that the vision of frozen roses signified a memory on ice preserved in my heart. I could say that this is the story of how I melted the ice and opened my heart so that I would know what love was. Except it never would have happened without the willingness to surrender and ask for help. Asking for help gave me a reprieve. What I called the Dream of '76 opened me to the inner life. An inner life that one day would me lead to the *Ibis.*

But before I can begin making connections to the memory of a past life, I will have to move through my fears of what happened in this one. I've called the first section the Clearing Ground because of what had to be cleared away before any progress could be made. That it was a 'Clearing Ground' only came to me in hindsight. Like so much else, knowledge came only after the fact.

Maybe I had a sense of what was in store the way I dithered for months whether to stay in London or move back to New York. I knew acting was finished. I cancelled my audition for *Kennedy's Children* at Manchester Rep, a chance I once would have given my eyeteeth for, but it came too late. I was on a different track now, planning to work as a secretary while I studied art or writing. The only question was where. The settlement from Toshi made either city viable, so I went to various fortune tellers and tarot card readers for advice. They all said it was time to go back to New York, and still I delayed until an old gypsy rang the bell when I was over at a friend's house in Chelsea. I never heard of gypsies coming to your house uninvited, and was surprised when my friend let her in. She studied my palms and said, "Leave. You must leave, go across the water. That's where you'll find him." The elusive 'him' meant for me was all I needed to hear.

So it was that in 1977 when I was twenty-seven I returned to New York after having lived abroad for seven years. I sailed back on a Polish cargo ship, fulfilling the last of my girlhood dreams. During those eleven days on the ocean when there was nothing to see but water and sky and unobstructed space, I imagined a secret opening at the horizon line. Some kind of slit or gap between the curtain of sky and the rolling carpet of sea. A hole in the fabric of reality, an opening between worlds like the door at the bottom of the sea. But as the ship kept moving forward, the horizon line remained in the distance, forever out of reach. It will be a long time before I begin looking for it on the inner plane of the inner-see, and it may not have come at all if not for the Clearing Ground.

But sure enough, two days after my arrival I met him, the one who would guide me through my fears. The ship docked on a Wednesday, and that Friday when I went looking for an apartment, I found Lenny in a real estate office in Greenwich Village. He was reading a newspaper as if killing time before I showed up. And it all seemed to happen by chance.

PART I

THE CLEARING GROUND
1977-1981

What is love? said the fish. It is but fleeting.
All the taste is in the eating. What is love?
It's not for Keeping.
Who is sowing, who is reaping?
All those tears and all that weeping.
Fishes swimming, lovers leaping.
What is love? said the fish.

— LOUISE OLIVER

1

FOLLOW THE LIGHT

If light is in your heart,
You will find your way home.

— RUMI

I wasn't planning to look for an apartment in the Village. Uptown was cheaper, and because my family still lived on the Upper West Side where I grew up, I was thinking of the East Side that morning when I took the crosstown bus through the park to Gardner Realty on Lexington. Oddly enough, Lenny would be working at Gardner the following year. Meanwhile, a broker named Joel took down my information. He seemed surprised I couldn't afford a doorman building or one with an elevator, or even one that had central air-conditioning. I wasn't dressed as if I had money, just ordinary jeans and a blouse with a navy sweater vest. I didn't need a jacket. Though it was the middle of March, still officially winter, the weather was mild. It must have been my English accent. No one would have guessed I was originally from Skokie, Illinois.

Joel said he would check what was available in my price range and get back to me later. This was disappointing as I had been hoping to see some apartments right away. I stood on the corner of Lexington and 86th and wondered what to do with myself. I didn't relish going back to my mother's residential hotel to wait for Joel to call. Her room faced a dark courtyard and it seemed a shame to be inside on such a beautiful day. Why not go down to the Village, I thought. I hadn't walked around the Village since high school when a bunch of us shopped for dangly earrings and drank cappuccinos at Café Figaro on Bleecker Street. I wondered if it was still there. The Village had been on my mind since reading *The Diaries of Anais Nin* on the ship. I would have loved to live in the Village like Nin. No matter it had changed since the bohemian days she wrote about in the 1940s and '50s, the streets wouldn't have changed. And just being there, breathing the air, would make me feel more like the artist or writer I wanted to become.

I rode the train down to Forty-Second and took the Shuttle to the West Side where I caught the local to Sheridan Square. It was already noon by the time I came up from the station and squinted in the bright sunlight. While I stood wondering which way to Bleecker, I spotted a bookstore across the street. Maybe they had a copy of Rimbaud. Anais Nin raved about Rimbaud. The bookstore wasn't much more than a hole in the wall, packed to the gills with shelves all the way up to the ceiling, but they had a poetry section and a copy of Rimbaud's *Illuminations.* I told the cashier not to bother putting it in a bag, and began reading before I was out the door. When the glare of the sun hit the page and the words disappeared, I looked up, shading my eyes with my hand, and saw a sign on the other side of the Square. A huge banner stretching across the entire second floor said, "Apartments for Rent." I slipped Rimbaud into my purse and made my way over. They probably wouldn't have anything I could afford, but there was no harm in asking.

I came up the stairs into a large airy room filled with empty desks except for the one nearest the door where a man sat bent over a newspaper. When he looked up and smiled, his whole face seemed to light up. He had dark hair and warm brown eyes, and while I wouldn't have said he was good looking, the warmth of his manner and the softness of his voice was so appealing I couldn't help feeling drawn to him even when I saw him looking me up and down, lingering a moment too long on my chest. He told me to have a seat and we chatted about apartments while he flipped through the rolodex. Then out of nowhere he said, "Are you an actress?"

I wondered how he knew and said, "I used to be, but I've given it up."

He said he was in the theater himself, that he'd been an actor and now he was directing a play. He thought I would be right for the lead. "Would you like to try out for the reading at the backer's audition?" he said.

"Really?" I was so surprised that I forgot I had sworn off acting. While Lenny called his partner Wally to set up an audition, I was thinking maybe I only had to give up acting in London. I could still follow my plan of becoming a secretary, but look for temporary jobs instead of something permanent.

Lenny said, "Wally can see you, but you have to go now."

I hurried out the door in a flurry of excitement and headed back uptown thinking how incredibly lucky to arrive back in New York and two days later be invited to read for a part. Wally was a short unassuming man who put me at ease, so that even though I hadn't done any performing for a year, the wheels kicked in as soon as he handed me the script. It was like old times, showing up for a cold reading with a stranger and turning on the emotional taps. When we finished the scene Wally thanked me and said they would let me know. They always said that. But Lenny thought I'd be right for the part and he was the director.

Lenny did not find me an apartment. Along with Wally's address, he had given me the address of a place in the Village I could see that night, and when I went back downtown, my heart leapt at the quaint little building set back from the street with ivy crawling up the brick. Lenny said there was a fireplace too. What a perfect setting for the romantic, bohemian sort of life I would have liked to have had. But no one answered the bell. I rang the other bells too, hoping someone would let me in, but the door to that particular dream remained shut. Maybe it would have been asking too much to have met Lenny, auditioned for a play, and found the apartment of my dreams all on the same day.

Joel, the tall lanky broker at Gardner, asked me out before Lenny did. It was just for coffee. Afterwards we went for a walk by the East River. Though the moon was full and there was a lovely breeze off the water, the walk was anything but romantic. Joel said his goal was to make a lot of money as quickly as possible, then do what he wanted, or at least find out what it was. Make a lot of money to find out what you wanted? I told him I'd had to give up having money in order to go after what I wanted. I had given him the short version in the coffee shop, how I'd been a mistress in London and tossed it all away, the luxurious flat, the new car and fancy trips abroad, so that I could come back to New York and be a secretary.

Joel was aghast. "How could you not be happy when you had thousands of pounds lavished on you?" Poor Joel. As we walked along the river he complained about the "rat race," calling New York a "concrete jungle," the people no more than animals in their cages. Joel didn't find me an apartment either. I ended up finding a place on my own from an ad in the paper and didn't have to pay a broker's fee.

A few weeks after the reading with Wally, Lenny called to offer me one of the smaller parts for the backer's audition. This could have been a disappointment since I'd auditioned for the lead, but I was busy fixing up my new place and no longer cared. Lenny said when they raised the money for the play, he wanted me to try out for the lead again. That was him all over, never wanting to let anyone down. I said no thanks. I was going to secretarial school as soon as I made the apartment livable.

Though I didn't know it yet, the place I found in midtown was only a five-minute walk from where Lenny lived. Nor did I know that meeting Lenny would end up being more important than any apartment or secretarial job. How strange it all was, Anais Nin leading me to the Village which led to Rimbaud's *Illuminations* that guided me to Lenny's office. If the sun had not been so painfully bright that day, I could easily have continued reading with my head down and never looked up at the sign stretched across his windows. It was the light that caused me to look up, but it was the desire for illumination that kept me with Lenny, no matter how dark the places he led me.

2

WHAT ABOUT ME?

I guess I'm lucky, I smile a lot
But sometimes I wish for more than I've got.

— SONG BY *MOVING PICTURES*

It was just as well Lenny took his time asking me out because fixing up the fifth-floor walkup in the rundown tenement on East 53rd needed all my attention. Aside from a bathtub in the kitchen, this relic from the 1890s had a loo down the hall, separate from my apartment, with a tank near the ceiling and an antique pull-chain that reminded me of my bedsit days in London. But I couldn't complain when the rent was only $185 a month for three light and airy rooms with high ceilings.

First there was getting the roach problem under control. After I rolled up the grungy old carpet and wrestled it down the five flights to the courtyard in back, I set off a roach bomb. When the air cleared I put traps in the corners and cupboards and took my brother's advice about sealing up cracks in the wall under the sink. I had never heard of spackle, or tried to fix up a place before, and I was proud that I could spend hours on my hands and knees under the sink getting all hot and sweaty. It made me feel I was getting a grip on my life. I had always been fastidious with my appearance, and now I savored this new way to be in my skin. The first few days I was too exhausted to bathe and too tired to care. I fell asleep in my clothes and told myself I'd have a bath first thing in the morning. Then morning came and I thought why bother since I was only going to get dirty again. It was days before I finally filled up the deep porcelain tub with claw feet and had a long hot soak in a bubble bath while I admired the job I'd done with the kitchen. All it took was a can of tangerine paint and a roll of contact paper with an orange and white pattern to match the color of my London things. The pots and pans, tea towels, dishes, canisters and the wall clock, all had an orange theme. My New York kitchen with a bathtub was a far cry from the shiny modern one I had in Kensington, but it was bigger, and there was a large window with a view of the sky. The view made up for the lack of quiet in this teeming section of midtown where it was never silent or still. Though I was on a side street and faced the back, I could hear the rumble of trucks and buses down Second Avenue at all hours, not to mention the horns and sirens. But I could also hear birds chirping in the morning, and in the afternoon the joyful shouts of children from a playground nearby.

Hanging a leafy green plant in the window was a testament to my willingness to change. Only a year ago I had allowed the evergreens on the London terrace to wither and die. I couldn't help noticing the trees were turning brown during that unusually hot dry summer, but I didn't feel I could alter their fate any more than I could alter my own. When my mother came to visit and saw the dead trees, she said, "Didn't you water them?" She was lying back on one of the cushioned garden chairs, drinking scotch and watching me touch the dry soil in one of the barrels when she burst out in an Irish accent, "Get your fingers in the dirt, Katie Scarlet!" Then she laughed. As a Taurus and a mother of five, I'd always thought of my mother as earthy. It shamed me to remember how I thought that since the trees were outdoors, Nature herself would take care of them. I hadn't considered the drought. Nor was I in the habit of nurturing things, least of all myself. I may have been blind to the trees, blind in so many other ways too, but taking care of my new hanging plant felt like a shot at redemption.

Along with the kitchen things and linens, I had been able to ship back lamps and the stereo, but I couldn't use them or even dry my hair until the plugs were changed. My brother had installed the shelving unit in the living room but he didn't know about electrical wiring so he sent his friend Carl over to switch the English plugs to the American ones. I remembered Carl from when they were boys, and though he'd grown tall and had hair down to his shoulders, I knew him right away. He remembered me too, though not in the way I would have liked. He was sitting hunched over the kitchen table with its clutter of lamps and hair-dryer and electric rollers while I perched on the side of the bathtub. We were chatting amiably about this and that when out of nowhere he mentioned he used to have dreams about me. When he shook the hair from his eyes and looked up at me, I was afraid he was having them still. I wanted to order him to stop it immediately, tell him he had no right. In the uncomfortable silence that followed, I felt the old fear and shame. I knew I wasn't thinking straight. I could see Carl was shy, more in awe of me than anything else, and I wished I could have been generous and laughed it off instead of feeling vaguely threatened. But I didn't want to be in his dreams. I didn't want him imagining things without my even knowing. It made me feel I didn't belong to myself.

I had a backlog of feeling I didn't belong to myself. It wasn't that long ago in London that stills from my movie turned up in *Penthouse* without my permission, without my even knowing. I had no idea they could do that. Five years ago when *Au-Pair Girls* came out I had to put up with my face plastered above the marquee on Charing Cross Road. At least my eyes were closed and it could have been any woman in ecstasy. Six months later when the movie disappeared I thought that would be the end of it. Then *Penthouse* wasn't the end of it either because they put me on the cover of *Cinema X.* A friend saw it on a newsstand and bought me a copy. I left it behind in a taxi somewhere. I thought I could leave it all behind when I came back to New York. Except for the stories I wanted to write. Stories where I was going to lay claim to my life.

It wasn't even a year after the dream I called the Dream of '76 and already I'd forgotten it. Forgotten I had some kind of information inside that had to do with death and a doorway under the sea and being given a light. If that was part of my life too it was hanging back in the shadows, waiting for me to catch up to it again.

All I had time for now was the present. The delight in being able to invite my father over for a meal for the first time since I'd grown up. He was amazed when I showed him the still-lifes I'd been working on, and said he never would have encouraged me to go into acting if he knew I could draw. Though I'd become an actress to please him, I brushed aside the thought it had all been for nothing. It had led me to where I was now and that was all that mattered. The here and now where the garden table and chairs that had been on the terrace in London now graced my kitchen. But what gave me the most pleasure was seeing the elegant secretary desk with a glass enclosed bookcase from Harrods in the living room because it was where I was going to write stories. I already had an electric typewriter purchased second-hand so I could practice touch-typing, and after I got a job I was going to take a writing class. Meanwhile I used it for typing upbeat letters to friends in London where I described the loo down the hall and the bamboo screen I found to hide the bathtub in the kitchen. I strove for humor when the tenant upstairs overflowed his bath, causing half the kitchen ceiling to come down, and neglected to mention how the plaster dust lingered for weeks, coating everything with a fine white powder that kept reappearing no matter how many times I cleaned. Neither did I mention the mouse. At least I hoped it was a mouse I heard scratching inside the wardrobe box stored in the spacious loo down the hall. I couldn't bear to think a rat might have been chewing away at what was left of my London finery. I left out the part of being lonely and the worry that at twenty-seven my best years were behind me. And what if I failed at being a secretary. I would be done for if I didn't get a job by June.

Betty Owen, the secretarial school, was an easy ten-block walk from my apartment. They provided the typewriters, tapes and workbooks, and we taught ourselves, as quickly as possible in my case. I was surprised how much I enjoyed it. I loathed the required typing and shorthand class in high school and never thought I'd actually *want* to be a secretary. Or that it would feel like a game, competing with myself to get my scores up. I got used to the deafening noise of the new Selectric machines when three or four of us were pounding away in the tiny classroom, because at least the school was air-conditioned, unlike my apartment where I practiced speed-writing at the kitchen table. If I turned on the fan it ruffled the pages, which was more annoying than a clammy hand sticking to my notebook.

Rimbaud's *Illuminations* lay neglected on the bedside table. I couldn't focus on poetry when my bank account was dangerously low. No one in my family was in a position to help. Yet getting a job meant more than just paying the rent. I craved a routine. A place to go every day and have tasks to perform. Then at five o'clock I would be free to spend the evening writing. I had already sent away for the summer catalogue at the New School.

When I completed the six-week course, Mrs. Payne, the job-placement councilor, called me in. She looked at my resume and shook her head. "Not good," she said. "Your scores are fine, but it seems you've been involved in acting your whole life."

"Oh, that's all in the past," I assured her.

She peered at me over the top of her glasses. "But who is going to believe you?"

This possibility had not occurred to me. I'd heard it called the 'acting bug' as if it was some kind of virus, but didn't she know a person could change?

I milled through the lunchtime crowd on Third Avenue as I made my way home. The oppressive heat added to my feeling of woe. It was only the middle of May and already it felt like August. I'd forgotten how tropical the city became, and it made me long for those cool, cloudy London summers when the air was chilly and damp. Even during the uncommon heat wave the year before, there wasn't the debilitating humidity that frizzed my hair and made me long for sleep. I stared at the woman walking in front of me, envying her crisp white summer suit and stylish shoes. Comfortable shoes were at the top of my list when I landed a job. None of mine were suitable for long walks. It hadn't mattered in London when I zipped around in my little white Honda. But it was no use thinking about that now. I had wanted to come home and here I was.

When I passed Doubleday Books I ducked in to get out of the heat. My spirits rose as soon as I entered the air-conditioned cool and saw tables piled high with books. I needed a new dictionary since my current one had the British spellings. The last thing I needed was to look up a word and still get it wrong. I picked up a shrink-wrapped weighty tome and quickly put it back when I saw the price. Then a title on the lower shelf caught my eye, *Stop, Look, and Write!* It was a slim paperback full of black and white photographs. How strange for a book on writing to be full of pictures. Then I read the captions. *Learning to write is learning to see…that they which see not, might see.* And, *When you look at something, LOOK at it!* It was only ninety-five cents. I took it to the cashier, and while he rang it up I studied his face, wondering if he thought I looked serious enough to be a writer, or if he assumed I was buying it for a friend. Then I thought how dare he think I couldn't be a writer, and how dare Mrs. Payne think I hadn't given up acting!

But all that was forgotten when I got home and the bulletin from the New School tumbled from the mailbox. There was a picture of a doorway on the cover, opening into the light. It reminded me of the door in the Dream. But I liked this one better. Instead of opening under the sea into more sea, it opened into the light. Golden light at the bottom giving way to pale green, then pale blue followed by pink, and finally a violet light at the top. The color of enlightenment I wondered? I think best of all was knowing the door on the bulletin wasn't a dream; it was about making a dream come true. That I should have received it right after buying a book on writing seemed confirmation that I was on the right track. Becoming a secretary was just the means to an end. What I really wanted was to take a writing course. Art could wait. I painted and drew as a child, and the prospect of going back to it wasn't as new or exciting as becoming a writer. Then it seemed writing had to wait too, at least until the fall, because despite Mrs. Payne's doubts, the first interview she sent me to led to a job offer, and working full-time took all my energy. Except for seeing Lenny.

Living so nearby made it easy to pop over to his place in the evening and dash back to my apartment in the morning to change before work. Of course it was more than just the convenience. It was his effortless warmth, his almost feminine softness, and the way he focused his whole attention on me as if there was no one in the world he would rather be with. Lenny had asked a lot of questions when we met, and the first time he invited me over to his apartment he asked a lot more, giving me the impression he was genuinely interested in who I was as a person. Though he only drank Perrier, he poured me a glass of wine and I settled back comfortably in the red beanbag chair. I couldn't remember the last time I'd sat in a beanbag chair, hearing it crunch whenever I moved. Lenny sat on a chair opposite me so my eyes were level with his knees, but I didn't feel at a disadvantage because when he looked down at me, his chin a little to the side, he was the least threatening man I'd ever known.

Unlike Joel, the first broker I met, Lenny already considered himself a success. "A successful human being," was how he put it. His studio apartment was spacious, but aside from the stereo and some original artwork in conté crayon beautifully framed, he didn't appear interested in material things. I didn't quite know what to make of him. The framed drawings were of couples having sex, but Lenny's interest in me seemed more friendly than sexual. If he had asked me to dinner that night I would have said yes, but he didn't ask, and then I didn't hear from him for a while. He confided to me later that despite his probing questions, I gave little away, and he didn't know what to make of me either.

We were already a couple when I called him at the office to tell him the good news about my job offer. He wasn't in, and I didn't ring him at home because calling him at home was off limits for a couple of weeks while he was with Marcy, his other girlfriend. Lenny told me from the beginning he wanted to be close yet free, which left me free to date other people too. I didn't think of Lenny as someone long-term anyway. He didn't look it, but he was almost fifty with an ex-wife and two teenage children. I didn't think of Marcy as a rival. She was married and Lenny was trying to get her to an AA meeting. He was in AA himself, and though he'd been sober for eight years he still went to meetings almost every day. He said it was part of his sobriety. Getting other alcoholics into AA was another part. Lenny took me to a fancy cocktail lounge with a view of the East River to spring the news that Marcy always stayed with him when her husband was out of town on business. "I hope you'll understand," he said.

I stared out the window at the Pepsi sign across the river, its red-light bleeding into the dark rippling water. What I understood was that Lenny thought it was okay to abandon me for two weeks while he was with this married woman. What about me? But I didn't say that. Instead I said breezily, "I'll be busy looking for a job anyway, so it's just as well."

After a few weeks of the never-ending busyness of office work, I was again thinking 'what about me?' Rather than finally being able to relax now I had a paycheck, I was harried with all the demands, flustered when I made a mistake, and depressed to realize how eager I was to please when being a secretary wasn't my real ambition at all. The resumes I had to type up at this employment agency for computer programmers were sprinkled with phrases like DOS and COBAL and umpteen others I can't recall that sounded like gibberish. I would have felt sorry for the frumpy candidates slouching in reception if I hadn't seen their asking salaries. Still I hardly envied them. The people I envied were the recruiters who weren't tied to a desk and were free to slip out for coffee or a snack or a walk around the block because I would be by the phone taking messages on little pink slips printed at the top with, "While You Were Out." I was only allowed out for lunch, and I couldn't go to the bathroom until I got someone to cover for me. But the recruiters worked on commission, and I needed something regular, even if it reminded me of being a waitress, taking orders and being at everyone's beck and call. I wasn't even allowed to keep a plant on my desk. I bought one specially, a Chinese Evergreen that cheered me up in that antiseptic windowless reception area before the boss told me to take it home. Meanwhile, I answered the phone with a cheery, "Target!" Target-Wilson was the name of the company though I never bothered with the Wilson. I liked saying "Target!" and singing it out because I had hit mine, a job by June. I got what I wanted, but some days I pretended I was just playing the role of a secretary. I had played one on the telly once. It was only a couple of lines, but what a lot of money for a day's work—and I didn't even have to type! Sometimes I wondered if I should have become a secretary in London instead of New York. At least I'd had a life there. Then I remembered in London you had to pass a spelling test as part of your application to secretarial school, which would have doomed me from the start. I knew it was the right thing to have come back, but I was reluctant to let go of where I had been, and kept up a stream of long type-written letters stuffed into air-mail envelopes. When the replies became fewer and farther in between, I told myself it was unreasonable to have expected otherwise. My old life, as well as the person I used to be, was slipping away, replaced by something that felt smaller and more confined.

I sought refuge in my journal, writing during my lunch hour when I sat on a bench in Bryant Park behind the library. I had nothing else to do since my sandwich from home was gone by mid-morning. I was too hungry to wait, and hid the sandwich on my lap under the desk, careful to take small bites so my mouth wouldn't be full in case the phone rang. Which it always did. If only Lenny hadn't answered the phone the night I was with him after Marcy left. She had been a phantom till then. The only real thing about her was the air-conditioner she gave him, which made the room more comfortable for me as well.

We were lying naked on the bed, enjoying the cool air and I was feeling loved and cherished until the phone rang and Lenny said *Hiiii,* the same way he said it to me. I put on a robe and went to the fridge for a can of soda, and when I came back to get a cigarette from my purse and heard him call her *Darling*, I went to the bathroom and shut the door. I tried to reason with myself while I sat on the edge of the tub flicking ash into the toilet and sipping a Fresca wishing it was Frascati. I didn't want to be jealous. I always said I hated jealousy. Then from the corner of my eye I saw a huge cock-roach making its way slowly up the shower curtain. Why didn't Lenny do something about the roaches? Why didn't he set traps and bomb them like I did? And why did I have to hide in the bathroom with the roaches? I flushed the cigarette down the toilet and wondered why couldn't I be with someone who loved only me? When I came out of the bathroom and saw Lenny still hunched over the phone, I held out the can of Fresca to offer him a sip and remind him I was still here. He shook his head no without looking up. I lit another cigarette and flung myself down on the bed behind him. He hung up a few minutes later and began stroking my back.

"How do you feel?" he said.

I felt cold. But Lenny kept talking and stroking my back, reminding me he was trying to get Marcy to an AA meeting. She wasn't as healthy as I was, he said. "Marcy needs me in a way that you don't," he said. I began to relax in spite of myself, and when I was relaxed I could afford to be generous. My Ideal Self knew that of course Lenny had to help her. Alcoholics were sworn to help one another. It was part of their creed. Did his attachment to Marcy take anything away from me? She was the one in the unhappy marriage. I was the one he was with now. Marcy meant nothing to me, but if Lenny loved her, shouldn't I find it in my heart to care for her even a little? I prided myself on being open-minded. Anything less had to be squashed by my Ideal Self.

Lenny was the hot poker as well as the balm. The bitter with the sweet. The sweet had come in the first flush of love, enveloping me in a cocoon of safety. A bubble of such pure happiness that one Sunday morning I floated back to my apartment. Lenny had to work that day, but I had all the time in the world to savor the night before. There were so many things I hadn't told him yet. So many feelings I wanted to share, like how no one had ever satisfied me the way he did, and how I was utterly and completely in love, and felt his presence even when we were apart. I thought I might burst if I didn't tell him soon. Then I thought, why not write him a letter?

I sat at my typewriter for hours that morning, telling him things I would have been too shy to say in person, like how I'd been looking for someone like him my entire life. A braver side of me came out when I wrote, and seeing the words on paper made it feel more real. When I finished I read the letter over again several times. There was nothing I wanted to add except maybe a drawing in the margin. The little figure I came up with was supposed to be me, but she looked like a child. A little girl in a pink dress, and I had never even worn pink. I couldn't erase her since I had used colored pencils, and I didn't want to re-type the letter, so I left it the way it was knowing Lenny would understand. I put the letter in an envelope and sealed it, then tore it open again to read it one more time. I still wasn't sure about posting it though. A friend back in London warned me never to write letters to a man. "Or write them if you must," she said, "but for god's sake don't send them. You'll always regret it." I thought I could risk it this time though. Lenny was so accepting. It was one of the things that drew me to him. He kept it folded up in his wallet saying it was the most wonderful letter he had ever received and was proof we were soul mates. "I've always dreamed of the kind of relationship I have with you," he said. Months later he called me at work and read part of it aloud to remind me what I had told him in the letter, because by then I was no longer floating home after a night in his arms, and I didn't want to remember the time when I did.

3

LABYRINTH OF SHADOWS

I am the one I seek; I am the one I fear
In mirrors I see myself
In the labyrinth it becomes so clear

— CRYSTAL BLANTON

Lenny took me on a dizzying round of restaurants, movies and plays, and always in a taxi. But the nights we stayed home were equally special. He'd buzz me in downstairs, then stand in the doorway in one of his white silk Indian shirts to watch me come off the elevator down the hall, and I'd be in his arms before the door was even closed. Inside the curtains were drawn, the candles lit, and Janis Ian or Phoebe Snow would be crooning on the stereo. There would be a plate of fruit and a bowl of granola with two spoons on the table. 'Love food,' he called it. The sliced apples and bananas or grapes and a kiwi would be stored in the refrigerator if we couldn't wait until afterwards. Then we'd talk. I had never known a man so interested in hearing what I had to say. When he lit a joint and drank Perrier or grapefruit juice and I smoked cigarettes and sipped wine, we could talk for hours. I was open about my past, including the things I wasn't proud of, and all he said was, "Do you know what a remarkable woman you are?" Seeing myself through Lenny's soft uncritical eyes altered my impression of who I had been, and still it was nothing to what I would become with him.

I had never known anyone so knowledgeable about sex or so eager to discuss it. But then Lenny had been a sex therapist. He had stopped short of getting his license, but it didn't stop him from seeing patients referred by a psychiatrist he knew. When Lenny described the sessions, he said their problems were more about sharing feelings than anything to do with sex. Part of the treatment might be forbidding them to have sex until they were able to talk to each other and say what they felt. He whispered these stories to me in candlelight as he stroked my back and described how he had the couples lie down together fully dressed, holding each other and touching in a non-sexual way.

I wondered where he saw these clients. If they came to his place and lay on the indigo sheets like we were doing now, I didn't want to know. It was a sofa bed, but when I came over it was always a bed. I didn't want to think about anyone else there but us. Yet I had to because after he brought stories of his patients into the bed, he started bringing fantasy men into our sex life. I don't remember when the narrative began to diverge. It seemed one night I was listening to stories about his patients, and the next I was listening to a story about us with an imaginary third party. A fantasy man who would make love to me while Lenny watched. Lenny was creative, using his experience as a director to describe what I would be doing, how I would react, how I would feel. The scenes he described were graphic and specific, and I never asked him to stop because he touched me as he spoke, and all I felt was him.

Sexual fantasies were a revelation. I had never had any myself, or known anyone who shared theirs before. The only kind of fantasy I'd ever indulged in was being a different sort of person like the French actress I once saw in a movie. There was a scene where she flicked the hair back from her face and shouted at her lover while she dunked a baguette in her coffee and threw it at him in a hail of curses. I would have loved to be as free as that.

Then one night Lenny said, "We can do it for real you know."

"What?"

"Some people do it for real," he said.

"They do?" I didn't think he was serious. I thought fantasies were just for make-believe, an end in themselves. I didn't see the point in making them real.

"You're the kind of woman I could do it with," he said.

I wasn't sure. I wasn't sure it was even necessary. Then Lenny said it was about being more free. He talked a lot about being free. He thought being close to someone while remaining what he called 'free,' was the key to happiness. We both had a fear of being trapped, though his fear was almost pathological. He described how his grandmother put him in the clothes dryer when he was a baby, supposedly to keep him from rolling off the table. And how his father was so devastated by the death of his mother that he had to be restrained from jumping into her grave. Lenny said, "That's the kind of relationship I don't want to have." I could only wish my own parents had had a fraction of that kind of love, but I liked the idea of being free.

Then he said he found someone. A doctor, recently divorced, who came into Lenny's office looking for an apartment. Lenny was no longer working in the Village; his new office was uptown near Lenox Hill Hospital. "A nice guy," Lenny said, "but uptight. I had to work on him. He was worried you might fall for him. If you don't want to do it, just tell me. Or we could stop any time. Your call."

How did we get this far? I thought it was still on the idea plane. I could see it as an idea, even as Lenny's ideal. But Lenny must have worked on me too because my reservations began to fall away when I saw what my willingness would mean to him, and we went forward with what seemed like a play with Lenny as the director.

* * *

Scene 1: A candlelit room smelling of incense. A Bob Dylan tape playing on the stereo. A man and a woman sitting at a table sharing a joint. The guest arrives and takes a seat at the table. They talk quietly. Now and then one of them laughs as they pass around the joint. When the man moves his chair to the far end of the room it is understood that he is now the director telling the woman and the guest to go stand by the bed and look into each other's eyes. The next direction is to kiss, followed by undressing, followed by lying down, followed by making love.

Scene 2: The woman, fully dressed again, sits on the edge of the bed smoking a cigarette. The guest, also dressed, sits at the table sharing a joint with the man. Their conversation is as follows: 'Boy was that something!' 'I didn't think I could do it!' 'Do you believe this?' 'Aren't we something!'

Scene 3: The guest leaves. The man and the woman sit at the table. She watches him spoon Haagen-Dazs chocolate ice-cream from the container into his mouth. She says, 'Are you alright?' He swallows another bite and says, 'Oh boy, for a few minutes there I almost lost it. But I let go. I'm really getting through my jealousy now.' His eyes are shining. He leans across the table and gives her a cold wet chocolaty kiss. 'You were great!' he says before taking another bite of ice-cream.

* * *

In Scene 2, did I wish I could have been like that French actress in the movie? It's hard to say. Part of me couldn't believe Lenny had talked me into it. Another part was too disengaged to believe it was really happening. It wasn't until later that I realized the scenario wasn't all that different from *Au-Pair Girls*, the movie I did in London where the daughter of the family I worked for gave me to her boyfriend as a gift. Of course this was real life instead of pretend sex, but I was still acting, still doing what the director told me to do. Why was I still trying to please the director?

According to the book I picked up at Doubleday's, *Stop, Look and Write*, being the detached observer was good if you were a writer. This was already my natural tendency, like the night I was on my way to Lenny's, waiting for the light to change and a taxi pulled up with a young woman in the back, her face by the window, her expression sad and forlorn. The light changed, the taxi sped off and I continued on my way, but the look on her face stayed with me. I thought I might paint it someday. The sad face of a woman en route in a taxi.

I was 'en route' too. That night with the doctor was only the beginning. Yet I seemed willing to try new things, cross lines I had never thought of crossing before, not only because I could remain detached, but because the line itself had been smudged somewhere and I'd lost sight of the cutoff. Lenny could say, "It's your call," but I never felt I had any voice in the matter. Never mind I had spent years training my voice so that could I be heard in the last row of the balcony. That was for playing other people. It was different when I was myself. The night Lenny took me to a club called the Botany, I had no voice at all.

4

THE BOTANY

Need and struggle are what excite and inspire us.
It is only by risking our persons from
one hour to another that we live at all.

— WILLIAM JAMES

The Botany was a swingers club. It wasn't listed in the phonebook, but Lenny had been there once years ago and remembered it was on Madison Avenue somewhere in the Twenties. He assured me the Botany was just a meeting place where we could have a drink and maybe meet another couple. Though he made it sound harmless, we would be leaving the safety of his apartment and taking something private and whispered in candlelight, out into the world.

I met him at Peartrees on the corner of his block and we ordered appetizers, lingering over our plates because Lenny was too excited to eat and I was too nervous. Lenny said it was better to arrive late, but I think he wanted to prolong his hope the Botany was still there. I secretly hoped it wasn't, and that was why it wasn't listed in the phone book. Then

Lenny hailed a taxi, and when we came to Madison and Twentieth and the driver headed uptown, I looked out one side of the cab and Lenny looked out the other. Suddenly he shouted, "There it is—I see it!"

The Botany was open. Lenny paid the cover charge, twenty dollars a couple, only couples allowed. The lighting was dim, the music loud. Lenny said, "See? What did I tell you, it's just like a regular bar." I only had to appear open to the idea for him to be happy. There was hardly anyone there; maybe we wouldn't have to stay long. The cover charge came with a drink. A club soda for Lenny, a white wine spritzer for me. We sat at a table near the front. Lenny squeezed my hand. "I love you so much," he said. I said I loved him too. Marcy, the married woman, was history. At some point he had quietly given her up without my having to say anything.

Lenny said, "Let's take a walk. I'll show you the back." There wasn't much to see. Aside from the tables in front and a few in the rear, mostly unoccupied, there was a small disco area with a strobe light. No one was dancing. No one else was walking around either. I think Lenny just wanted to see who else was there, but it felt like he was parading me around. We went back to our table. As more couples began trickling in, Lenny kept his eye on the entrance. "I could fancy that one for the night," he said. I took another sip of wine. I didn't want to look at the women coming in any more than I wanted to look at the ones already there. But most of all I didn't want to look at the men they were with, let alone imagine having sex with them.

A heavily made-up woman came up to our table and gave Lenny a big smile. Her hair was dyed-blonde and she wore a gypsy blouse with layers of beads. "Want to have some breakfast with us?" she said.

Lenny looked startled. "Now? You want to have breakfast *now?*"

She giggled and held out her hand. "Hi. I'm Gail. Nice to meet y'all." Her high-pitched girlish voice grated on me. I guessed her to be about thirty-five, but it was hard to tell in that light. She said cheerfully, "Why don't y'all come sit with my husband and me at our table?"

Lenny glanced at me. He was grinning madly. I wouldn't have thought she was his type but I think he just liked being asked, because before I even nodded okay he was getting up.

Gail's husband Rick wore a red lumberjack shirt and looked as if he hadn't shaved for days. Maybe he was growing a beard. Either way he wasn't the sort I would have given the time of day to. He stood while Gail made the introductions and we sat down opposite them. They were both drinking beer. Gail leaned over the table. "I was attracted to you two because you were holding hands. I could tell you're in love. I liked that." She inched closer to Rick and nudged him with her shoulder. "We're in love too!"

I looked at Lenny. He was staring at Gail. The light was better at their table and now I could see she must have been at least forty. I couldn't believe he was attracted to this dyed-blonde, beer-drinking, overly made-up woman who said 'y-all' in what sounded like a fake southern accent. Rick said they were from California and they lived on Staten Island. He began telling us about a deal he was putting together for a club. He said, "I want to show scenes from *Oh, Calcutta* and *Hair*. Get families involved so that we can be all-around friends with other couples."

Families? I pictured couples barbecuing in the backyard, children running around. Then what—orgies in the den?

Rick said, "The scene is so much better in California. It's

more of a life-style there you know, having friends and all. Here it just seems to be about fucking."

I sucked in my breath and Lenny tried to change the subject. He said, "How long have you guys been swinging?"

Rick said proudly, "Twelve years for me, three-and-a-half for Gail here." He made everything sound like a boast.

When Lenny asked Gail what it was like for her in the beginning, I knew it was for my benefit. Gail seemed to know this too the way she looked at me and giggled again, saying in that high-pitched voice, "Oh, I was so jealous in the beginning! And so unsure of myself too."

"How did you feel about it?" Lenny prodded.

"It's been so long now it's hard to remember!" She looked at me again. "It's hard to put myself in your place, honey."

I thought it was hard to be in my place too. I didn't like being talked down to, having someone like Gail feeling sorry for me. Then Lenny mentioned our recent history, and said that I was okay with the idea of a three-some, but not a foursome. Or at least not yet.

Rick looked at me. "Isn't that selfish of you? I mean, you can let your man watch, but you won't allow him the same pleasure?"

I froze. My face felt hot and my ears were burning. My eyes filled with tears and I stared down at the table, then at the hands on my lap. I wanted to tell him I didn't want anyone to be watching anyone, but I couldn't speak. I heard Lenny saying my name, but his voice sounded far away, at the other end of a tunnel. He was calling and calling, but I didn't want to be found. I wanted to leave, but I couldn't move. Yet if I didn't say something this would never end. Without looking up I said dully, "Can we leave now?"

"No. We can't. I want you to look at Rick and answer him back."

I was shocked. I hadn't wanted to come to the Botany in the first place. I had only come to please Lenny, and now he was being cruel. I don't remember what I said to Rick, or if I said anything at all, but a minute later they were gone.

Lenny said, "I'll never take you swinging again."

He sounded annoyed. I thought at least we could go now, but Lenny said we had to calm down first so we went back to the bar. I didn't want another drink. I felt perfectly calm. Being frozen is the ultimate calm. I think he just wanted to savor another fifteen minutes at the Botany because he knew I'd never come back. Then it turned out we didn't have to go to a place like the Botany for me to become immobile; it could happen at the movies.

I Never Promised You A Rose Garden had just opened and Lenny wanted to see it. Though I'd heard of the book I didn't know what it was about. If I'd known it took place in a mental asylum I wouldn't have wanted to go. The soundtrack was unbearably loud, especially when there was screaming. It was grueling to watch. If we hadn't been sitting in the middle of the row in a packed theater I wouldn't have stayed. But getting up would only have created more disturbance, so I shut my eyes and waited for it to be over. I felt better once we were outside again. Crowded sidewalks in New York on a hot sticky Saturday night was better than bedlam on the screen in that cold dark theater.

Lenny steered me to a nearby restaurant which was thankfully quiet and peaceful. He was attentive over dinner and sounded in awe when he said, "Boy, you really went through something back there." It was things like that that made me think maybe I should stop trying to break up with him, at least for now.

I had been trying to lose him that summer, going out with other men who were better looking and closer to my age with more years ahead than behind. But now I was thinking maybe Lenny wasn't being mean at the Botany. Maybe he only wanted me to stand up for myself. Trying to break up with him hadn't worked anyway. When he called and I told him I was busy, I thought he'd get the message and move on, but he accused me of 'doing a number.' "I know you," he said. "I pick you up."

What I knew was that Lenny took me to the place of buried feelings so I'd feel their sting again.

5

THE PATH OF RETURN

In trying to leave the past behind,
people walk blindly into it again.

— MICHAEL MEADE

I did a play once called *Return Trip*. What we call a round-trip ticket, Brits call a return. They mean the same thing, going somewhere and coming back to your starting point, yet they suggest something entirely different. A round trip is only a figure of speech, but when I think of round I think of a circle, and I've never gone on a train journey and come back in a circle. When I think of trains I think of linear tracks. I go to my destination on one set of tracks and come back on another. The play wasn't about trains, it was about revisiting a place you'd been to before. That's what Lenny did, he took me to a place I'd been to before. But he didn't leave me there, he brought me back. It was completely different from that time I was seventeen and my mother left me at her boyfriend's and I had no way of knowing how I'd ever get back.

* * *

In 1967 a few weeks before I left for college, my mother said her boyfriend wanted to give me a farewell party. I was surprised. Oscar had been around for more than a year by then and we'd hardly ever spoken. She said it would only be the three of us, but I was still touched by the thought. The following evening my mother and I walked over to Oscar's studio apartment nearby. He'd not only bought a cake and a bottle of pink champagne, he'd hung crepe-paper streamers over the dining area to make it seem festive. My mother put candles on the cake and told me to make a wish. If I had known what was coming I would have wished I'd stayed home. After the cake my mother got up to leave. I stood up too and she said, "No, you stay here, honey. Oscar wants to talk to you."

There wasn't to be any talk. When I tried to leave he barred the door. When I threatened to tell my mother and he said, "She knows," it felt like a knife in my heart. I sat down then and tried to stay calm. When I asked him why, he said my mother thought I was still a virgin and he was going to introduce me to sex before I went to college. I was caught between horror and disbelief, but I held out hope he would listen to reason. Keeping my voice as steady as possible I explained I wasn't a virgin but I hadn't told my mother. Oscar said we had to do it anyway. "Can't we just tell her we did it?" I said, and he burst out laughing. I slapped him then, but it made him laugh even more.

The situation was too dire to take in. It would be useless to try and fight him. Fighting might even excite him. So I did the opposite and pretended to go into a dead faint. When he carried me to the bed anyway I slipped further away, picturing myself drowned at the bottom of a pool.

Rather than be conscious in a world where I was betrayed by my mother and held prisoner by her boyfriend, I went to a dead place inside where I could never be found and was safe from feeling anything.

I walked home afterwards and confronted my mother. "Why did you do it? *Why?*" She said she was sorry, she'd made a mistake. I could see her remorse, but I wanted to know *why* she did it, because I knew she loved me, and how could she not know it was wrong? I never saw Oscar again because by the time I came home for Thanksgiving they had broken up. I thought I could put it behind me when I went off to college in Pittsburgh and fell in love with a boy at school, but there were repercussions. Even in London I'd still walk into traps I'd think I couldn't get out of. Once it was a stranger who offered to lend me money that was in his hotel room. Another time it was a producer who took me to Paris for an audition but booked only one hotel room. Each time I thought I was stuck. I didn't have to ask myself why at those times. All I could think of was that it was happening again and I didn't think I'd be allowed to leave.

Now, ten years later it was still happening. Someone I loved that I knew loved me, wanted to take me to his friend's house for sex. A return trip to the place where I had been given away. The place where I pretended I was dead because something in me died. I didn't have to remember it consciously; the memory was in me, a reality I couldn't shake. The difference was this time Lenny prepared me beforehand so it wouldn't come as a surprise. And unlike before when my mother left me there, Lenny would stay, and then he would bring me back.

6

HADES CAVE

It's when you're accepting of the trauma
that you don't need it to go away.

— MATT KAHN

In the taxi downtown Lenny reminded me that I didn't have to do anything. "You're in charge. It's your call," he said. But was it really? I don't know that I'd ever felt I was in charge around Lenny. He would have a fantasy, then refer to it as a possibility, then say it was my call. Yet somehow it became a reality, as if he was just waiting for me to catch up. It never seemed to take long. I liked thinking I was unconventional, freer than most people. Lenny seemed to think I was, never mind that night at the Botany. I liked that he thought I was a free spirit, maybe because for five days a week I was chained to a desk. But despite him saying it was my call, simply getting into the taxi felt like I had already agreed. Not to mention I was wearing the black garter belt and stockings that Lenny said Hank would appreciate.

Hank was the one who introduced Lenny to the idea of swinging, and Lenny introduced the idea of Hank in our bed long before he took me downtown to meet him in person. 'Hank is going to do this to you, Hank is going to do that.' It made Lenny excited just talking about it, and when he was excited I got excited too. Alone with Lenny in his candlelit room, 'you're going to feel this, you're going to feel that' was all mixed in with the music and the way he was touching me. I didn't know who this Hank person was; I only knew I was with Lenny, letting myself go in ways I had never imagined. Lenny went on about how handsome Hank was and how rich, and how he could get us invited to yacht parties. I could care less about yachts, and parties weren't even on the table, but Lenny said Hank was the next stage. After our visit to the Botany he said, "You're not ready for Hank yet." Then not long afterwards, he said that I was. And for reasons I didn't care to look at too deeply, I agreed to go along.

The taxi dropped us off in Alphabet Town on the Lower East Side, which at that time was a gritty neighborhood of immigrants and the impoverished elderly. Lenny said Hank owned the building along with a few others, but I hadn't expected him to live in a slum. His apartment was on the ground floor off the lobby. When he opened the door, instead of the handsome stud Lenny had described, I saw an aging libertine in Bermuda shorts and a garish Hawaiian-print shirt.

We followed him into the living room. If Hank had money, he didn't spend it on his living quarters. The furniture looked old and shabby. The windows were streaked with dirt, and the noisy thrum of the air-conditioner neither cooled off the room nor muffled the sound of children playing in the street. After handing us apple juice in paper cups, he leaned back comfortably in the big easy chair and rolled a joint. Lenny and I sat on the thin-cushioned red sofa, drinking juice and taking turns with the joint. I would have preferred a glass of wine. I knew where I was with wine. The first glass was for relieving tension, the second for relaxing a bit more, and the third loosened my normal constraints. Pot on the other hand could land me anywhere.

Lenny was grinning at me. His face was flushed, his eyes were shining when he said, "Are you ready to do a strip for us?" I looked at him as if I'd never really seen him before, and all I felt was loathing. And yet I stood. As I took a few steps to the middle of the room, I wondered how could I have allowed myself to be in this place again. Hank was touching himself. Lenny was looking up at me adoringly, and all I could think of was how pathetic they were. But if they wanted a show in that ugly room with all the lights on, I'd give them one. Then, as I watched them watching me, waiting to see what I'd do next, a strange thing happened. I saw myself as the one with the power, not them. Why had I thought it was up to them? I didn't stop though. I was enjoying my power. When Hank got up and took my hand to lead me through the beaded curtain, I didn't give Lenny a backward glance.

Down the hall was a dark mirrored room with colored lights and a floor covered in mattresses. I saw myself in the mirror and watched us in the mirrored wall. I watched us on the mirrored ceiling too. I saw what Hank was doing with the woman in the mirror, and I said Yes to Hank, yes to pleasure. When Lenny came in I said yes to him too. In that dark padded cave I said Yes to the images in the mirror. Yes to Hades, Pluto's Horn of Plenty. And in a strange sort of way, saying yes to the present was like saying yes to the past. And allowing it to be.

I went back to Lenny's that night, and in the morning when he took me to our regular coffee shop for breakfast, I marveled how the world looked the same as it had the day before. We could sit at a table and study the menu as if nothing had changed. The waitress sloshed coffee into our cups and belted the order out to the cook behind the counter the same way she always did. The smell of bacon frying and the sound of dishes clattering was the same too. When the man at the next table rustled his newspaper I realized the night had come and gone and we were having breakfast like normal people. No one would know the difference. Not even me.

We went down to Hank's again when his girlfriend Janet was there. Lenny hadn't met her before and neither of us knew what to expect. Janet was naked when she opened the door. I looked at her pale, spongy-looking skin, the long stringy fair hair and the roll of fat below her pendulous breasts. Serves Lenny right, I thought. I couldn't imagine him doing it with her, but I misjudged things like unspoken codes between men, and not losing face. And Janet herself, a woman who may have been plain and washed-out looking, but she could sprawl naked on the living room rug without a shred of embarrassment. I envied the way she seemed so comfortable in her body, but why didn't she take better care of it? I knew I was being petty and judgmental, but her face could have used some color. What was the harm in a little mascara? A bit of humor wouldn't have gone amiss either. Janet was the opposite of giggly Gail at the Botany. Gail had been funny and sweet compared to this lumpish woman of Hank's. On the other hand, would I have wanted Janet to be girlish, playing the coquette?

Janet stretched lazily on the floor with her head propped on one arm and said she liked swinging because, "It got past the bullshit of relationships." Her voice was whiny and nasal and I wondered what Hank saw in her. Lenny said they had been together for years. But then she was a nurse, which might have explained her matter-of-fact, no-nonsense attitude. I couldn't tell what Lenny thought of her, but his face had a rosy glow from his two favorite pastimes, pot and swinging. He said being around swingers relaxed him. I felt more relaxed this time myself. I wanted to be able to let go of jealousy and possessiveness, and thought I would be okay watching him with Janet. Then I saw them. Before Hank took me through the beaded curtain, Lenny and Janet were on the living room rug, her pasty-white legs wrapped around his back while she moaned with pleasure.

I was quiet in the taxi home. Lenny kept shaking his head saying, "I don't know how I did it." Yet he seemed proud of himself, as though he'd passed some kind of test. He didn't hold back how proud he was proud of me either. He called me his Ideal Woman and was attentive and loving the rest of the night.

My private thoughts were something else. I wrote in my journal that it had been a disaster. I didn't say why or offer any details other than it was painful. The next paragraph was about the onion soup I'd made the other night. I had no end of things to say about the soup, describing how many onions I sliced and how many ounces of cheese I grated for the topping. I even gave a bit of history about how I acquired the oven-proof bowls I used in order to melt the cheese, and ended by saying how delicious it was. Onion soup I knew. This other thing I didn't. Not at all. Not why it was part of my life or how it had come about. It was all a muddle.

Years ago in London when I'd been in another muddle,

I'd gone to a psychic at Marble Arch. I wanted to know why my mother couldn't have married Milton. I imagined her happier then, and by association I would have been happier too. "Oh, no, my dear," the woman said. "You chose everything to be exactly the way that it was." The news had astonished me.

7

STAYING IN THE LIGHT

I cannot cause the light; the most I can do
is try and put myself in the path of its beam.

— ANNIE DILLARD

When Phyllis at work invited me to come bar-hopping with her on a Friday night, I said, "I don't think I'd like going to pick-up places."

"Why not?" she said. "It's fun. It's only a meat-market if you look at yourself that way."

I would have liked to be as breezy about life as Phyllis seemed to be. I also would have liked to meet someone I could have a more conventional relationship with. Someone with normal hobbies. Lenny called swinging his hobby. When he wasn't calling it his hobby he was calling it the next step in human evolution. I was more interested in my own evolution, which I hoped would involve a man who, if he had any fantasies, would keep them to himself.

Phyllis said we should eat first, so we stopped at a salad place before heading over to First Avenue in the Sixties where the singles bars were. I wasn't familiar with the area. New York is a city of enclaves. I worked in the East Forties, lived in the East Fifties, and wasn't aware of hangouts for singles further uptown. We passed on the over-crowded bars where music spilled onto the street, and kept walking until we found a quieter place where we could see a few empty tables inside.

I met Daniel that night. First I liked him because he was slender and dark, and with his beard and a black turtle-neck he made me think of D.H. Lawrence. Then I liked him because he was nothing like Lenny. But soon I stopped liking him because he was nothing like Lenny. Lenny never would have told me I should get a tan and lose ten pounds. The next time I went with Phyllis I met a tall fair-haired Virginian named Mike who sent me a dozen roses before our first date. I was prepared to like him a lot until he began dropping hints he was looking for the wife of his future self as a bank president and thought I might fit the bill.

Oddly enough, it was Alice Tully Hall at Lincoln Center which settled the matter with all three, Daniel, Mike and Lenny. Mike took me to a couple of Mostly Mozart concerts and suggested we go dutch for the next one. I said no thanks. I was saving up for a writing class in the fall. If I wanted to listen to Mozart I could play one of my records at home. Daniel's taste was Boz Scaggs, the flamboyant show-bizzy singer from Australia. We were at a Boz Scaggs concert during the blackout in July. Phyllis was on a dinner cruise around Manhattan and witnessed the astonishing moment around sunset when the city blinked off. At Tully Hall the concert had only just begun when it went dark and silent. We all assumed it was a technical problem and kept our seats until the singer came out with a bullhorn and announced there was a city-wide power failure and could we please go home.

Luckily Daniel had a car, though I might have gotten home faster if I'd walked. I had been at home during the Blackout of 1965 and was unaware how a power-outage slowed everything down. It took ages to get out of the underground garage at Lincoln Center, only to emerge into a strange, unfamiliar landscape where we crept along in slow motion through chaotic intersections lit with car headlights. Buses with their own interior lights rolled along like magic lanterns. As we inched across town Daniel complained about the twenty-eight flights of stairs he'd have to climb when he got home and how hot and stuffy his apartment was going to be without the air-conditioner. Then he thought of the food in the fridge that was going to spoil and how he wouldn't be able to shower or even flush the toilet. It was a relief when he finally dropped me off. I only had five flights to climb, the same five flights I had to climb every day. There was nothing much in the fridge, and I couldn't bemoan the loss of an air-conditioner I didn't have. What I did have was an oversize bathtub and plenty of water to fill it with. Maybe it was only the new buildings that used electricity to pump water. Mine was built when there were still gas lights. I lit a candle and took in the strange eerie silence without the ubiquitous whir and hum of the city I had taken for granted.

I don't know where Lenny was the night of the blackout but I can't imagine it put him in a bad mood. He was always even-tempered, never complaining about anything. His work was stressful, but afterwards he took time to unwind. I was with him once when he came home from work, and before he would speak to me he said he had to lie down for half an hour. He prayed every morning and thanked God for getting him into AA. He said, "First I love God, then I love myself. Then a few other people besides my kids." When he was hit with something unexpected he got down on his knees, raised his arms and said, "Okay, God, what do you want from me now?" It was inspiring.

When Lenny took me to Tully Hall it was for the Sunday morning service of Unity led by Eric Butterworth. I thought Butterworth's style was a little hokey, like having us sing about togetherness while we held hands with the stranger on our other side. The greeters were friendly though, smiling and saying, "Hello, how are you today? Good to see you," as if New York was no different than a small town. The crowd, and there was always a crowd and not enough seats, couldn't have been more diverse with different ages and races, everyone in their Sunday best. And at some point I started to take in what Butterworth was saying, like how our essential nature was Divine. I'd never heard that before. Or that changing your thoughts could change your life. These were novel ideas to me at the time.

After the service we always went to Fiorello's across the street for brunch, and it was there I got a lesson from Lenny on not being judgmental. I wasn't aware how critical I was of others until I made a disparaging remark about the old ladies at the next table who were talking with unbearably loud voices, and Lenny said quietly in an off-hand way, "I try not to judge people." It put me to shame.

I judged my own self harshly in those days, which was probably why I couldn't get enough of Lenny telling me I was remarkable, the most wonderful woman he had ever known. That these comments tended to revolve around our sexual exploits didn't seem to faze me. I thought Lenny was remarkable too. Apart from my shrink in London, who didn't count because he was being paid, no other man had ever encouraged me to talk. When Lenny sat back and asked questions, he seemed genuinely interested in my thoughts. So much so that I began to outdo myself with insights. How could I let that one thing, his sexual peccadillos, come between us. Maybe I had bargained for them. I knew there were shadows dogging my footsteps. I may not have voiced them to myself, or even noticed them consciously, but I knew they were there. I hadn't forgotten that when I got stuck at the Botany, Lenny fished for me. When he took me down to Hank's apartment, he didn't leave me there. But I think his biggest draw was how his idea of me matched my Ideal Self. I wanted emotional freedom too. I agreed that jealousy and possessiveness were destructive and I didn't want those feelings any more than he did. Lenny said a person was either worked-out or not worked-out. Not worked-out meant you were still listening to old tapes. He was gentle when he pointed mine out and reminded me that I was a free-spirit. When he talked about growing and overcoming and evolving as human beings, I felt myself becoming more expansive. I hadn't forgotten the day I walked out of the bookstore in Sheridan Square with Rimbaud's *Illuminations* and saw the sign that led me to Lenny.

Illuminate: *to brighten or light up. To make lucid or clear. To throw light on a subject. To enlighten, as with knowledge.*

Lenny's favorite saying, "Love and be free," felt like a calling.

8

THE WRITING COURSE

Wherever you don't want to go, whatever that risk is,
Wherever the unsafe place is, that is the gift you have to give.

— AMANDA PALMER

In late September when the sun's arc dipped lower and the breeze held a slight chill, I stood at the bus stop between the marble lions, Patience and Fortitude guarding the entrance to the 42nd Street library. How fitting that I would be catching the bus to my writing class in front of that great Beaux Arts repository of the written word. I was enthralled with the idea of being a writer. My new fall heels, brown with the suggestion of a gold buckle on the lip, reminded me of pilgrim shoes, and writing as a kind of pilgrimage.

The class for Beginning Fiction at the New School was taught by Gilbert Sorrentino, a poet and writer I'd never heard of, but others obviously had because that first night was standing room only. He came in wearing a black beret, black turtleneck and leather jacket over his jeans, and with his graying goatee I might have thought central casting had sent over the quintessential New York intellectual. He slung a scuffed briefcase onto the desk and surveyed the throng before saying dolefully, "So, you want to be writers." He told us not to worry about the over-crowding since at least a third of us would drop out. It was an intimidating start and his mood never really lightened. When he strolled in five or ten minutes late and tossed his briefcase onto the desk, he would sigh as if we had already disappointed him, those of us who were left. Then he paced before the blackboard and stroked his goatee while initiating us into the grim reality of what it takes to create a world. Or he'd rant about how few books were sold, how the number of readers was constantly dwindling. He took out a cigarette and struck a match as he told us to stop going to the movies. The match burned out and he struck another, lighting up while ordering us to spend our money on the books of living authors instead. He said writers were like insects with long antennae who sensed the *zeitgeist* before regular people did, but you had to write from your heart. He touched his forehead and said an idea begins in your mind. With a long slender finger he traced the path on his body, describing how an idea travels from the head down to the heart, then down through the arm, out through the fingers and onto the page.

I was entranced. Though whatever inspiration I came away with seemed to evaporate by the time I sat down at my typewriter. I thought I knew what I wanted to say but I'd stare at the keys with my mouth open and nothing came out. It was like the nightmare I used to have that I would forget my lines on stage. At least in those days I'd had lines to forget. What made me think I could write my own lines? I used to hope I'd meet a playwright who would tell my story. Now, writing a novel or even a single story seemed equally far-fetched. Did I think something magical would occur if I took a class? My practice of keeping a journal and writing down what I noticed or overheard, didn't seem to be helping. My recent entries had been longer and more detailed, proof that I was beginning to think my experiences, however small and insignificant, were worthwhile enough to record. Still it wasn't the same as creating a narrative. That I managed to hand something in the following week was due more to the fear of not handing in homework than anything else.

The story was about the time I joined a flower club in London because I had been wishing someone would send me flowers. The florist was nearby and I had the money in those days to buy a bucket of blooms, but it was the thought of having them delivered as if they were from some anonymous admirer. The first week I received a single stem of white freesias. The delicate bell-shaped petals were lovely to look at and smelled like citrus, but a single stem was a bit paltry when I had been expecting a bouquet. I didn't have a small enough vase and had to put the stem in a glass of water, which wasn't at all the effect I had in mind. The following week I received another single stem of white freesias. Why couldn't they send me daisies or carnations? I didn't expect roses, but why couldn't I have had chrysanthemums at least? When the freesias continued for a third week, I went down to the florist to complain. "Why am I only getting freesias?" I asked. The woman said they sent what was available, but that couldn't have been true because her shop was filled with all sorts of flowers in different shapes and colors. I cancelled the order. The purpose of the flower club had been to cheer me up, and instead it had become another dashed hope. If I were to write that story today, I would have looked up the meaning of freesias. I would have learned they symbolized friendship, and how the underlying message might have been one of being a friend to myself. But I wasn't capable of such nuances then.

Sorrentino chose my piece to read aloud as an example of how not to write. When I heard the muffled giggles I assumed they were laughing at my writing as much as at my pitiful attempt to feel loved, and I was desperate to light up a fag. We were allowed to smoke in those days and tiny aluminum pie-tin ashtrays were sprinkled around on the desks. But Lenny had been after me to quit and it was just my luck that I had chosen the day of class to give it up. Sorrentino summed up my story by calling it juvenile and full of clichés, but he didn't make it sound hopeless.

That night I dreamed Sorrentino outlined my lips with his finger as if to say, *This is where your words come from. They don't come from the air. They don't seep into your mind from somewhere outside yourself. Not the real ones. The real ones come from deep within. From back behind the dark cavern of your throat. Tell me those words.*

I wanted to more than anything, and for the next assignment, the first chapter of a novel, I sat at my typewriter with hands poised above the keys, only to have them fall back to my lap again. My mind was flooded with images yet I felt as silent as Lavinia in *Titus Andronicus*, the only Shakespeare I did the whole time I was in England. Mute, helpless Lavinia, tongue cut out and hands cut off. But I had hands. I had a tongue. Where was my voice? I was so angry with myself that I started banging on the keys about my time as a barmaid.

It was a slow night and I was polishing the mahogany bar with a rag when Maggie came up and set down her tray. 'I just heard of a club where we can make a pile of money for doing practically nothing—and you get to sit down the whole time!' she said.

'You mean they pay you for just sitting there?'

'Well, you have to ask the customers if they want to dance. But you get to drink all the champagne you want. And they buy you food. Chicken or steak sandwiches, strawberries with cream.'

My mouth started watering just thinking about those strawberries. I ate them with my fingers, dipping them into a bowl of freshly whipped cream and washing them down with champagne. French champagne in silver buckets with linen napkins draped over the side. I wrote about the swizzle sticks that looked like honey dippers, and how surprised I was when the other girls at my table twirled them in their champagne before taking a sip. I asked one of them later what the sticks were for. 'They're for getting the bubbles out,' she said. But bubbles were the reason I liked it.

I didn't finish the chapter. Sorrentino said we didn't have to as long as we wrote a brief synopsis of where the novel was heading. I wrote, 'The narrator is going to be destroyed.' The following week when Sorrentino returned our work, he commented in red ink, "Be very careful that you don't slide into melodrama or soap opera— (It is quite something to "destroy" people)." I was taken aback. Did he think I was going to destroy someone? What a mistake to have used that word. Where had it even come from? Something had been destroyed, but it wasn't me. My life was moving forward. I had a job, a relationship. At long last I had stability. Perhaps it was better not to dwell on sad things from the past anyway. I continued going to class and doing the reading assignments, but I couldn't bring myself to finish the chapter, let alone start a new one, or even admit how worrisome it was to have come up with a word like 'destroyed.' Better to live in the moment. Just be with whatever was happening and stop trying to put it into words. I put my journal aside too. If I wasn't going to be a writer there was no use practicing. I didn't have the right words for the past, and I didn't know where to begin describing the present. I never could have written about the night Lenny took me to Plato's. Even if I had, I wouldn't have been brave enough to hand it in to Sorrentino. Not while I was still making my way through the darkness of Hades Cave.

9

THE UNDERWORLD

Eros will have naked bodies;
friendship naked personalities.

— C. S. LEWIS

For months, ever since I stopped trying to break up with him, Lenny had been silent about all things pertaining to swinging and I thought he'd given it up until he began talking about a club called Plato's Retreat. Hank told him about it ages ago, but it was only for couples, and Lenny never had anyone to go with until he met me. "We can just watch," he said. "We don't have to do anything."

"I'm certainly not going to do anything," I said.

But already I felt guilty when Lenny gave the taxi-driver the address of the Ansonia on Broadway and 74th Street. I was sure the driver knew that rather than visiting a friend in one of the elegant apartments in the Ansonia, we were headed to the famous sex club in the basement. When the cab dropped us off at the corner Lenny said, "Let's take a walk around the block first." That was fine by me, only it was November and the night was bitterly cold. When we turned down towards the river the wind was so fierce it hurt to breathe. Lenny wasn't wearing a hat and his nose and ears were bright red. He laughed and said, "Are you sure you want to go through with this?"

I would rather not have come at all, but I knew if we didn't go through with it that night, we'd only end up coming another time. "I can't take this wind anymore. We might as well go in and get warm!" I said.

We went inside to get out of the cold, and it turned out the club was so warm it was like spending an evening in the tropics. The small lobby off the side entrance had an admission booth and a turnstile like at the movies. We checked our coats, and when we went down the narrow escalator I was relieved to see the couple coming up didn't look any different from couples we might see at a restaurant or the theater. The air became warmer the farther down we went, and by the time we reached the bottom it was positively balmy. And still there was a lower level down the grand staircase, a hot humid clime with soft lighting and palm fronds and a floor covered with artificial grass. It was hard to imagine that at the turn of the century, the basement of the Ansonia had been an arcade where they sold fresh eggs and produce to the tenants upstairs, which at various times had included people like Toscanini and Stravinsky.

Lenny and I held hands as we strolled past the waterfall and the garden chairs beside little bamboo tables. There was an Olympic-sized pool lit with turquoise water, but no one was in the water or sitting at the tables. I had dreaded seeing naked bodies cavorting around, but other than a few patrons at the bar in the distance, fully clothed I noted, the place seemed empty. "Where are the people?" I whispered.

"Hank said you never know what kind of night it'll be. Maybe we came too early."

I don't know why we were whispering since there was no one around to hear. I wondered aloud where the swinging room was and Lenny pointed to the red curtain on the other side of the pool. He said that was probably it so we made our way over. I could hear heavy pounding music as we came closer. A beefy young man in gray sweats and a tight tee-shirt sat perched on a stool in front of the curtain. He said, "You can't go in like that. You have to change in the locker rooms." Then he grinned and added, "Don't worry, there's plenty of towels."

I had been wondering where everyone put their clothes, and imagined a big heap somewhere, and losing mine, or only being able to find one shoe, so I'd worn one of my least favorite work outfits. Lenny was wearing a suit and tie, but then he always did. So far the place was more civilized than I expected. The Ladies Room was spotless. I don't remember any instruction signs such as showering first, or wearing disposable socks or donning a bathing cap for the pool. Though I didn't know why would we need a bathing cap if we didn't need a swimsuit.

Lenny and I met up outside the locker rooms and laughed to see each other wrapped in big fluffy white towels. As we walked back to the curtain wearing our towels and holding hands, I might have thought I was as much a thrill-seeker as he was. The guard smiled and nodded approval. The curtain was pulled aside and I felt a blast of heat. The room smelled of bodies but it was so dark I couldn't see anything at first. The floor was spongy plastic, the music was deafening, and as my eyes adjusted to the dim light I couldn't make sense of what I was seeing. I wasn't prepared for the shock of so many people packed together like on the subway. So many naked people. There could easily have been a hundred. Or maybe only fifty. I couldn't tell. There was so much going on I didn't know where to look. I could make out people standing and sitting, some wearing towels, some not. And then there were the people lying down, coupling in various positions. It wasn't like the subway at all unless you were having a nightmare.

We found a space on the mat and I lowered myself gingerly to the floor, making sure I was not only covered with the towel but sitting on it as well. It seemed rude to stare at the couple beside us engaged in the act, but as I shifted my gaze around I didn't see anywhere that was safe to look. What if I accidentally caught someone's eye and gave them the wrong signal? I wished I hadn't worn my contacts. Everything would have been blurry then, and I wouldn't have known what I was seeing. Not that I knew now. You couldn't tell who anybody was or what they did for a living without their clothes. Some were older, some younger. Some were fat, some thin. There were white people and black people and Hispanic people, everyone as ordinary looking as the people I saw walking down the street every day. But I didn't want to see them naked, or watch them having sex. I had prided myself in being better than Lenny's cousin's wife who said she'd rather die than set foot in Plato's. With her face and body she thought she'd be set upon as soon as she walked in.

But it wasn't like that at all. Everyone seemed to be minding their own business at the same time they minded others. There may have been moans and the slap of bare flesh but it was all very respectful, this primal world behind the curtain. It made me think of pagan fertility rites I'd read about. I couldn't make up my mind if what I was seeing was crude and distasteful, or beautiful and loving and human. Was I witnessing a regression to a more animal state, or a progression to a higher stage of human evolution like Lenny chose to think. I could see it as a reverence for our humanness that went beyond the individual, beyond personality likes and dislikes, and being open to what we had in common. And all this under the sidewalks of New York! I didn't think I'd be able to look at people on the street the same way anymore because I would be wondering what they got up to behind closed doors. However normal they might appear would be no guarantee they wouldn't be bringing their wives or girlfriends to Plato's. It didn't occur to me to think the woman might be behind it. I didn't know any women like that myself. Though if I did, who's to say she would have told me.

Lenny was sitting on his towel but it no longer covered him. I wondered if he wanted me to touch him, but we were too self-conscious and it made us giggle. I said, "Can we go now? I think I've seen enough."

"But we just got here."

"I want to go in the pool. Let's have a swim."

I hadn't been skinny-dipping since childhood, and I felt a child-like freedom stepping down the ladder with nothing on. There was no one in the pool but us. The water was warm and exhilarating. The pool alone was worth the price of admission. An older couple, fully dressed, stood watching us as if we were zoo animals on display. I wondered if the woman envied my free spirit or if she looked down on me as an exhibitionist. Lenny and I wore our towels back to the locker rooms to change. When we passed the curtain he stopped and said, "Let's go back in for a few minutes."

Nothing was going to get me in there again. "Not

tonight," I said. "We'll come back another time." Ten minutes later we stood on the corner looking for a taxi, shivering and laughing in the cold, telling each other how brave we were. We agreed we'd have to come back, but we never did.

10

ART WAS LEFT

Art enables us to find ourselves
and lose ourselves at the same time.

— THOMAS MERTON

Acting was finished, writing was out of reach, but there was still art. Pictures rather than words. I gave up art at fourteen because I didn't think I was good enough to make a career of it and had gone to Performing Arts High School instead. I didn't know if I would be any good at acting either, but the prospect of being with others on stage was more tempting than being alone drawing and painting. Yet Lenny seemed to think I was a born artist. He saw it in my hand on our first date, reading my palm on the Greyhound bus as we sped up the West Side Highway to Yonkers racetrack. He had already told me he was a writer, a director, an actor, an acting teacher and a therapist. This was aside from being a real estate agent, and now he was a palm reader too.

I almost didn't come. He said to meet him after work at Walgreens in the Port Authority, the bus station that like much of New York's public spaces in the Seventies was shabby and run down. Walgreens on the lower level had a worn, grungy look. Lenny wasn't there at the appointed time and I didn't like standing around so I took a seat on one of the wobbly red vinyl-covered stools at the lunch counter and ordered a coffee. I thought he had a nerve asking me to meet him at Walgreens. But when he finally came he was so apologetic and had such a pleading look in his eyes that I instantly forgave him and we hurried off to catch the bus.

He flexed my hand this way and that so it caught the light from different angles, then he ran his finger over the lines. "You're an artist!" he exclaimed. "You have to paint big!" He sounded in awe of the discovery. I was in awe too. As soon as he said I had to paint big, a vision flashed before me of an artist's studio filled with huge canvases.

"I'm psychic," Lenny said, still holding my hand. I could well believe it as I got to know him better and saw how insightful he was about people. When he got to know me better and said, "I know you. I pick you up," I wanted to believe that too, because at twenty-seven I was still wondering who I was.

* * *

My identity had been thrown into confusion ever since my mother told me Milton was my real father. My name would have been Rachel if she'd married him. I think she still hoped there was a chance and that's why she converted to Judaism after I moved to London. She wanted me to convert too, and sent me books like James Michener's *The Source*, and Martin Buber's *I and Thou*. I wasn't having any of it. Before I left for England I begged her not to tell Dad I wasn't really his. She did anyway, but as long as I stayed abroad I didn't have to deal with it.

I was aware that being with Lenny who was not only Jewish but decades older than me might have something to do with looking for this other father who was gone. Not as a replacement—Lenny wasn't fatherly, not even to his own children he only saw one evening a week—but as a connection to something that was missing. I think that was why I was so willing to take direction from him. But was playing the role of his ideal woman the real me? By the end of that first year in New York I was already sensing that England had been the place where I felt most myself. I had been saving up for a trip back and by the new year I had enough paid vacation days to make it feasible. Lenny wanted to take me to the airport, and when he came upstairs to help with my suitcase he said I looked different, more beautiful, and asked if I'd done something different with my hair.

It wasn't my hair, it was London, and I was so excited I could hardly stand it. We drove to the airport during rush hour when traffic was heavy and the streets were slushy after the snow turned to rain. I kept looking at my watch and checking my purse to make sure I hadn't forgotten my passport. I worried something unforeseen would occur at the last minute and I'd miss my rendezvous with a past I wasn't ready to let go of yet. We arrived with time to spare, only to find the plane had been delayed. We said our goodbyes and I settled into a chair by the gate until it was time to board.

This waiting by the gate was one of the few things I remembered about the trip, as if I'd slipped into another reality once I boarded the plane. As if I wasn't just flying across the ocean, but flying back in time, back into a dream I'd once lived. I have only the barest recollection of what I did during those ten days in London, mostly due to the photographs I brought back, maybe because I was revisiting a past where I'd had a different persona. Seeing friends I'd left behind, parking myself temporarily in their lives so that I could retrieve a bit of my own, was to remember what I'd been like before my reinvention in New York. Someone said, "You're a *sec-ra-tree?* But that's not you!" Of course it wasn't. How could I have thought that it was? Had my mirror grown so cloudy that I needed to be reminded I hadn't always been someone with such dogged perseverance to a job, no matter how regular the paycheck? My old self, which was perhaps my real self, wouldn't have been caught dead in a permanent job.

The trip to London was more than a reality check; it was like I connected to a different energy source. Reattached some vital part I'd left behind, because when I returned to New York with a new shaggy haircut I handed in my notice at work. Throwing caution to the wind made me feel like my old self again. I had proved I could be a *sec-ra-tree.* My new goal was to become an artist. I could work as an office temp while I took classes at the Art Students League. Then Lenny's cousin Mel said he knew a woman who made a lot of money at the Nassau Bar down near Wall Street. You had to wear a bikini, but according to Mel's friend, I could work part-time and earn twice as much as office work in half as many hours.

I didn't even last a week. It wasn't just the lousy tips and pouring drinks to unsavory types wiling away the afternoon on a bar stool. It was the cook in the basement. The locker room was in the basement, a badly lit warren of pipes and noisy machinery with walls painted an ominous dark green. I had come down to use the loo, which meant walking past the kitchen. Normally, the kitchen doors were open and you could smell the greasy fried food, but as I headed back towards the stairs the doors were closed and I was ambushed by the cook, a little man in a white hat and apron saying something in Spanish. I had no idea what he wanted, though it sounded urgent in a friendly sort of way. When he pulled out his wallet, I assumed he was going to show me pictures of his family. Lots of people liked showing off family photos they carried in their wallets, even if you had just met them. But when the cook opened his billfold, the only picture he wanted me to see was the one of Andrew Jackson on the wad of twenties.

I shook my head vigorously. "No-no-no!" I said, waving my arms for effect. I didn't like being alone with him in the basement while all I had on was a bikini. I slipped past him and hurried up the stairs. But even as I told myself he was harmless and nothing had happened, I felt like it had. I finished my shift but called in sick the next day and never went back. In the bars and clubs where I'd worked in London, it was an unspoken rule that none of the staff ever approached the girls. I was angry at Lenny for encouraging me to take the job, and angry at his cousin Mel for telling me about the Nassau Bar in the first place. But most of all I was angry with myself for thinking I could still do that type of work. Didn't I realize I had changed?

I recently googled the Nassau Bar to see if it was still in business, and learned that in 2008 the Feds accused it of being a sports betting operation controlled by a member of the Bonanno crime family. *The New York Times* called it "an unapologetic dive," and said it was a creepy place where "pathetic, gross old men ogle bartenders in bikinis." *The Times* went on to say, "the bartenders are surprisingly nice and friendly, despite their horrible surroundings," adding, "The liquor is cheap, the place is dirty and crowded with guys drooling over the bartenders and trying to get their attention."

But the cook actually did me a favor because Mel was sorry, and to make amends he gave me a job at his ice-cream parlor, then laid me off soon afterwards so that I could collect unemployment insurance. It covered my living expenses as well as classes at the Art Students League. Art school was an antidote to everything mean and lowly. As soon as I came through the grand entrance on 57th Street and walked up the marble steps, catching a drift of the pungent odor of turpentine, I knew I was home.

I signed up for the Life Drawing Class five mornings a week, and purchased the list of supplies from the small shop off the lobby. All I needed to start was a large pad of newsprint, a box of vine charcoal, a kneading eraser and a chamois cloth for blending. The drawing studio was large and airy with high ceilings and tall windows. Twenty-five or thirty of us sat in a wide oval on rickety wooden folding chairs. We propped our newsprint pads on a second folding chair placed in front of us. I looked around at the other students while we waited for the model to appear. They were a mix of young and old and in-between, some sharpening pencils with a razor blade, others working on a sketch or reading a book, and the rest were just gazing around like I was.

At nine o'clock the model came out from behind a screen at the back I hadn't even noticed was there. She walked slowly up to the gray wooden platform in the middle, slipped off her kimono and draped it over the side. When she stepped onto the platform and struck a pose, heads were suddenly bobbing up and down, glancing from model to paper and back again. This sudden flurry of activity was silent except for the soft scratching of charcoal. I was still looking at the model, not quite sure how to begin, when the monitor yelled *Change!* and amid the ruffling of newsprint being flipped to a fresh sheet, she struck a different pose. How did they work so quickly? I barely managed to orient myself to one pose before the order came to change it. In time I adjusted to the speed of those one-minute gesture drawings, but I was always relieved when they advanced to five and then ten-minute poses. The twenty-minute pose before the break felt like a luxury.

The models were different every day. They came in all shapes and sizes, but to us they were simply nudes. Most were young, though some were middle-aged, even old from time to time. I was amazed at their lack of embarrassment, their willingness to show themselves so freely. How different from being naked on a film set. I came out wearing a robe too, but I didn't take mine off until the lighting and sound were ready. Meanwhile, another woman stood in my place so I wouldn't be seen until the camera was about to roll, and only after the assistant director shouted for everyone to clear the set. I felt protected, but of course I wasn't, not when the film came out.

The strangeness of the class wore off quickly, and by the end of the week I saw how freeing it was to study bodies while being neither critical nor admiring, simply seeing them as examples of the human form. I started noticing shadows and light. At home I studied artist anatomy books so I would know where the bones were and where the muscles. If the model was an old woman with sagging breasts, so much the better. There was character in every line. Flabby, sagging skin was more interesting than the smooth, unblemished younger models. The more lines, the more character. I rejoiced when the model had folds of flesh. Unsightly bellies and double chins were a feast for the eyes.

With the young and slender, I prized a sad expression or stringy hair. Previous standards of beauty flew out the window. A kind of equality took over. An equality of seeing, where everyone was captivating in their own right.

I didn't quite realize the effect all this was having until the night Lenny hailed a taxi and one happened to stop in front of us to let a passenger out. She was a large woman and it took her a while to extricate herself from the backseat. Before the drawing class I might have been impatient. I might have judged her for letting herself go and been critical of the red dress that clung to her overblown form. But now I was thinking only of form and mass, the red fabric pulling and stretching with her movements and the strain on her face. I looked through her dress, then through her skin, imagining the bones and muscles beneath the flesh. Once I related to her this way and saw past her physical form, all I saw was her beauty. As if to pierce her flesh with my eyes was to glimpse the soul within. When she had freed herself from the taxi, I climbed in and scooted over to make room for Lenny. The door slammed shut, we drove off and it was just another night in the city. But I thought about it afterwards, how learning to draw was changing the way I looked at people. At everything really. As if it all became beautiful simply through the act of observation.

Another leap in awareness occurred during the second week of class when the model was in a half-sitting, half-lying position on the platform with her back to me. Her hair was pinned up and I could see how the line of her neck curved into the line of her back. From the first few strokes of charcoal I saw I had captured the feel of that line as if I was feeling *her*. I was amazed this could happen, and it occurred to me that getting the shadows and the bones and muscles right wasn't enough. It was capturing the feeling of the model that brought a picture to life. And I had done it. I had sensed how she felt by drawing her. And with only a flimsy stick of charcoal. Observation was vital, but without feeling the form, feeling what you were seeing, what good was it.

It struck me then that the reason I had loved Renoir and Modigliani as a child was because they had connected me to my feelings. At ten I was attracted to Renoir because he showed me how the world could be happy and beautiful and full of light. Modigliani showed me sadness and loneliness when I didn't have the words. The feelings came through the lines. I began to feel like a musician reading music the way I could read the notes of the model through the line of her back and capture something intangible. An aliveness that couldn't be taught, only discovered, because it came from an unknowable place within. A feeling place I couldn't connect to in my stories for Sorrentino, but I could draw it. It was just like Sorrentino had said. The idea starts in the head—that would be my eyes, my vision—then travels down through the heart and out through the hand. The feeling of the model had traveled through my heart so that I had been able to feel her from across the room. What Sorrentino said about connecting an idea to a feeling, I could do in a drawing that bypassed the analytical mind where words come from.

During the break I walked around to see what the others were doing. Some were obviously beginners like me, but some of the work looked professional, and indeed I found out that professional artists often came to hone their skills. But that day, now that I was looking with fresh eyes, I noticed that even the most accomplished and academically correct drawings didn't actually look like the model. She could have been any female nude. Who she was as a person didn't enter into it. They didn't feel her, so they couldn't make me feel anything. None of the instructors mentioned connecting to the model in an emotional, feeling way. The models existed as just another object to portray in lights and darks and degrees of color. Renoir and Modigliani might not have painted their women and girls as they really looked either, but their work spoke to me. It was a kind of magic when a picture spoke to you, reached you on a level nothing else did. And now it was like I was reaching myself.

Not long after this discovery and still feeling the rush, I happened to bump into an actor I'd gone to college with at Carnegie-Mellon. We brought each other up to date on what we were doing, and I told him I was in art school. Then, unable to hold back my excitement, I burst out, "I'm going to be a great artist!"

He looked at me incredulously and said, "You can't just decide that."

11

"ARE YOU AN ARTIST?"

Art is meant to disturb,
science reassures.

— GEORGE BRAQUE

In the movie *New York Stories*, Nick Nolte plays a successful artist with Rosanna Arquette as his student assistant. In the scene where she asks him if her work was any good, he says he can't tell her that because it's something she has to know for herself. Nolte's character was an oafish bore, but I had to like him for that.

I never had to ask. When my work wasn't good I knew it was because I hadn't learned enough and I would improve. But I didn't really think in terms of good or bad because I knew my work was a reflection of how I saw things. If someone didn't care for it, it only meant they saw differently. I don't know where this overweening confidence came from. I didn't have it when it came to writing, and I couldn't say I had it as an actor. Everything I did as a performer was because of the script and the other actors and the director, whereas painting and drawing came only from me, and it was only an expression of my ability at that particular time. I knew I would improve, but even in those early days I never thought anything I did was bad except once. The scene I did from my imagination was so bad I threw it away. I wasn't interested in painting from my imagination and never would have tried it in the first place if Lenny hadn't suggested it. I preferred drawing and painting from life and what I saw in the outer world.

Lenny liked those too. After we were married, when anyone came over he showed off my portraits and paintings of models as if I was a budding genius. Whenever I came home with a new picture from the League, he would gasp and clap his hand over his mouth in amazement. I knew he was biased, but I drank in his praise anyway. Then one day out of nowhere he said, "I like abstract paintings. Why don't you paint something abstract?"

"I don't think so."

"If I had your talent I would paint something abstract."

"I wouldn't be any good at it." I didn't relate to abstracts. I thought them purely decorative, a free play of form and color that told me little about the world and nothing about myself. My idol at the time was Rembrandt because he could see through a face into the soul of a person.

Lenny kept on at me. On another day he said, "I'd love to see what you could do with your imagination. That's where your power is."

He had me then. But I couldn't think of anything I wanted to imagine. I had forgotten the Dream of '76 and waking up with the sense I had knowledge inside. Some kind of information I would only learn through art or writing. I had written down the dream, how I was shot and fell into the sea and a door opened underwater, but it was filed away in my desk somewhere along with other papers from the past I no longer thought about. Now Lenny had me wondering about making something up. I did it all the time as a child, surely it wouldn't be difficult to try it again. A picture of above and below came to mind, a cross-section of the city with buildings above ground and the subway underneath. I couldn't help being aware of the subway underneath since our new apartment was directly above the station at 86th and Lexington. We couldn't hear anything from the third floor, but if I put my ear to the wall I could feel the vibrations.

I placed a rectangular canvas on the aluminum easel I had for painting at home, and after I covered the surface with a warm ochre wash I drew a line across the middle. The above area was a hodge-podge of tall buildings while below suggested the pillars and archways of a subway platform. When I stood back to look I found the subterranean half dark and unsettling. I showed it to Lenny that night to see what he thought, and assured him it wasn't finished yet. He was reading the newspaper and barely glanced at the canvas. "You're off to an interesting start," he said before disappearing behind the paper again. I had been hoping for more. Didn't he know I was only doing it to please him?

The next day when I took a fresh look at the picture, the top half remained promising, but the shadowy forms below seemed more murky and sinister in comparison. It wasn't a place I wanted to explore further, and I was angry with myself for even this minor attempt. What did I want with the below anyway. The whole idea had been a mistake. All I wanted to do now was get rid of it. The only question was how. If I put it in a bag and took it down to the garbage in the basement, someone might get curious and open the bag. I didn't want anyone to see it. Better to remove the canvas from the stretchers and dispose of them separately. This was easier said than done. I bought canvases ready-made in those days and had never tried to take one apart before. Staples inserted by machine were tough to dislodge and I had to wedge a dinner knife under each one to raise it slightly before I could wrench it out with a staple remover. And still the canvas didn't come off because it was glued to the frame. After much tugging and ripping I folded it up and stuffed it into the kitchen garbage, pushing it down until it was covered in coffee grounds and chicken bones and wilted lettuce leaves. I realized later it would have been simpler to just whitewash the whole thing and paint something over it, but I would have known what was underneath. No matter what I painted over it there would still be that other 'beneath' which had been painful to look at and too disturbing to carry on with. I wished I had never tried it in the first place.

The problem was it was in me already. Ever since my shrink in London introduced me to the bridge over an abyss, I had pictured something horrible below that would be dangerous to fall into. Then I'd see myself falling in and never being able to climb out. I didn't connect how I'd destroyed the painting to how I predicted the narrator in my story would be destroyed. I'd given up writing after Sorrentino's reaction, and now I gave up painting from my imagination. Lenny might think that was where my power was, but that day it felt more like my power was in cancelling it out, refusing to look. Folding up the canvas felt like folding up shop. I didn't want to think about the below and what might lie deeper. The shadows were best left to themselves. It was enough to be in the moment. Stick to painting things that were in front of me that I could see and touch in the visible world. I wasn't ready to deal with anything more.

Yet I don't know that I would have gotten that far if I hadn't thrown my lot in with Lenny. I almost didn't. That winter when I came back from the trip to London and was still in my own apartment, my doubts about him were stronger than ever. In the spring when I started classes at the League and a whole new world opened up I withdrew from him further. And on one of those days when the weather turned fine and it felt good just to be alive, I met someone else.

I was riding uptown on the Third Avenue bus. It wasn't crowded and there were plenty of seats, yet he deliberately chose the one next to mine. From the corner of my eye I saw he was wearing a suit and tie, and when he leaned over to put his briefcase on the floor I saw he was young with dark hair. When he began speaking to me I considered changing my seat until I glanced at his face and saw he was handsome in a breathless kind of way. He was funny too. I don't remember what we talked about, only that we laughed, and my stop came much too quickly. I stood and said good-bye only to find he'd followed me off the bus. We stood on the sidewalk, squinting at one another in the bright sun as the bus pulled away. "Is this your stop too?" I said.

"No, but I'll walk the rest of the way. It's not far." Then he nodded at the portfolio under my arm and said, "Are you an artist?"

"I'm trying to be."

He held up his briefcase. "Then I guess you could say I'm trying to be a lawyer."

I laughed, and when he complemented me on my striped knee-socks, I laughed some more. He wanted to go for coffee and I said I couldn't, but he had charmed me and I gave him my number when he asked for that. We said goodbye again and I walked away with a smile that lasted the rest of the day. He called, maybe later that day or the next, and maybe there was more than one call. All I remember is the night he came up to my apartment sometime that week. We were supposed to go out for a drink or maybe for dinner, but when he rang the buzzer I let him in, and we never made it outside. First he asked if he could take off his jacket. It was a warm evening, and after climbing five flights it was no wonder he wanted a glass of water too. Then he joked about the heights he had to climb to see me, as if I was a princess in the tower, and when he cast his eyes around the kitchen and living room he said, "I love what you've done with your place. It's enchanting."

We were in the realm of enchantment now, and when we spent the night in my tiny bedroom on the single bed, he never stopped holding me. The night was warm, we were bathed in sweat, and still he didn't let go. I fell asleep from time to time, and whenever I opened my eyes he was looking at me. He said, "I haven't felt this way about anyone in a long time. I thought I never would again." I didn't know what to say so I said nothing. As the night wore on I was already thinking I should have gotten to know him better first. Then daylight came and we untangled ourselves from the bed. I put on a robe and felt shy asking how he liked his coffee. While he was getting dressed I said, "Where are you from?"

"Valley Stream."

Long Island then. I'd never been to Valley Stream, but I knew a girl in high school from there and maybe he was upper-middle-class-Jewish like she was. His parents wouldn't approve of me, and what would he think of my crazy family? Now he was putting his briefcase on the table, taking out a dark blue cashmere sweater still in plastic. The tag was from Bloomingdales. He said he wasn't sure whether or not he should keep it or take it back, and asked what I thought. I mumbled something about how it looked alright to me, and wondered if this was the sort of thing he discussed with his previous girlfriend. Maybe he was still seeing her. I couldn't imagine someone like him ever being without a girlfriend. Then he said he didn't want to be late for work and gave me a brief kiss goodbye. "I'll call you," he said.

And he did call. The handsome young lawyer from Valley Stream who thought my place was enchanting, said he would call and he did. But Lenny called first. I had broken a date with him and was vague about making another. Lenny said, "You're doing a number." He'd said that the last time I tried to break up with him. It was my fault for being vague. Lenny, on the other hand, was very clear. He said he was coming over that night "to have it out."

We stood across from each other in the kitchen that was no longer enchanting under the harsh overhead light. I had never seen him so upset. He was wearing a black leather motorcycle jacket like Marlon Brando in "The Wild One," but there were tears in his eyes when I told him there was someone else. "It's him or me," he said. "You have to choose. Because I'm not going to see you again. I love you. I've never felt like this with anyone else, but I'll get over it. I'll be alright." I couldn't stand seeing him in pain. The thought it could end that night in my kitchen was too much to contemplate. I wasn't in love with him anymore, but I loved him and I couldn't imagine letting him go for someone I had just met.

We got engaged on a rainy Saturday morning a few days later, and after he left for work I called my mother to tell her the news. She wanted to meet for lunch at the Bagel Nosh to celebrate. "Are you sure?" she said. She was teary-eyed and said she was happy for me, then said again, "Are you sure you want to do this?" After lunch the rain had stopped and neither of us felt like going home yet. Perhaps I was already feeling at sea when I suggested a ride on the ferry. We took the ferry to Staten Island where the sky seemed brighter and strolled around aimlessly in the residential area near the terminal. The air was cold and damp, and when we came to a coffee shop we went inside to warm up before taking the ferry back across the bay.

When the lawyer from Valley Stream called, I told him I was engaged. He said, "Isn't that a bit sudden? How can you get engaged so quickly after spending the night with me? Don't you think you should wait a while?"

I knew he was right just as I knew the die had already been cast. He said he wanted to see me again, and to call him if I changed my mind, but I knew I wouldn't. When I put the phone down it flashed through my mind that with Lenny I was going to become a real artist. I had only been taking classes a little over a month and hadn't even started painting yet, but I knew if I stayed with Lenny I'd stay with art. I'd have to, because with him there would always be that edge to keep me in the frame.

12

ART AND MARRIAGE

Let there be spaces in your togetherness

— KHALIL GIBRAN

When Lenny and I moved in together a few months before the wedding, I took a break from art school to fix up the new apartment. Being that he was in real estate I thought he would have found us something better than a third-floor walk-up above Leo's Coffee Shop near the corner of Lexington and 86th Street. Aside from a busy commercial area it was a transportation hub too. A stop for both local and express trains as well as the crosstown bus. But it was cheap and Lenny would be paying the rent.

The first room you walked into, supposedly the living room, looked onto an airshaft, whereas the room at the back, supposedly the bedroom, had a view of the street and was flooded with light. In between was the dining room and tiny kitchen and bath which made sense, but these other two had to be switched. I didn't like the idea of company coming into our bedroom first thing, but it was better than sitting in a living room that looked onto a brick wall. I hid the airshaft with gauze curtains and brightened it up with a light carpet and a yellow bedspread. I had no end of ideas to brighten things up, like laying down shiny new kitchen floor tiles and putting a coat of white paint over Lenny's dark wooden dining table and chairs. Leafy green plants hung in the front windows to partially block out the view of Gimbels department store across the street. My brother wasn't around this time to drill holes for the brackets, and Lenny said he was no good with tools, so I rented a drill from the hardware store and did it myself. It was easier than laying down floor tiles, and less time consuming than staining and shellacking the bookcases and coffee table I bought from the unfinished wood store, and by the time I finished I was starting to think there was nothing I couldn't do to make our house a home. When I heard Lenny come in after work I dropped whatever I was doing and ran to give him a hug. After a few weeks he asked me to stop. "I need some time to cool out," he said.

Cooling out meant being alone to lie on the bed for half-an-hour reading *The Daily News* or *The Post* before acknowledging my presence. My feelings were hurt, but I remembered before we lived together he always needed to rest after work. It was a small thing and I adjusted. When his newspaper left a gray smudge on the new yellow bedspread, I adjusted to that too. Then he asked me not to make dinner every night. Two or three times a week was okay, but he couldn't handle more than that. I swallowed my disappointment. Lenny hadn't lived with a woman for a long time, and it was only natural he would want to preserve his old habits. Some nights he only came home to change his clothes before going to the race track. Or he might go straight to an AA meeting after work, and then to the track. Or come home to "grab a bite" as he called it, before heading out again. Those were the nights he bought himself a barbequed chicken from the take-out place and ate it with his hands while he read the newspaper on the bed. Once or twice a week he took me out for dinner. I knew lots of women in New York who didn't like to cook or had no time for it would have loved this arrangement. In a few months when I went back to work and resumed classes at the League, I would appreciate it too. But just then I did not, and it surprised me to realize I was a homebody at heart.

September came and we were married in the spacious garden behind his cousin Mel's house in Connecticut. Lenny wore a morning suit and I wore a long white silk Indian dress with a pink Indian print scarf for a veil that streamed down my back and was crowned with a wreath of artificial pink flowers I'd sewn together. The day was overcast, threatening rain, but as we stood with the Justice of the Peace inside a circle of white carnations, the sun broke through. Everyone said it was a good omen. The circle of flowers was my idea. It was also my idea to ask the Justice of the Peace to read a verse from Khalil Gibran's *The Prophet.*

Let there be spaces in your togetherness,
And let the winds of the heavens dance between you.
Love one another but make not a bond of love:
Let it rather be a moving sea between the shores of your souls.

The day after the wedding we flew to Mexico and I was sick with Montezuma's Revenge the whole time. When we came back I found a temporary office job and enrolled in a painting class five nights a week. A few months later Lenny mentioned he was thinking of taking a trip by himself.

"You want to go on vacation without me?"

"It's only for a week. To Guadeloupe."

"By yourself?"

"With Club Med. It's a terrific deal."

"But isn't that a singles thing?"

"I need a break. The job is getting to me." Lenny was working at Gardner Realty on the corner, the same office where I'd gone two years ago when I arrived back from England. He was making good money, but he said his boss was a slave-driver.

I had never heard of Guadeloupe. We were in bed, I think it was morning, but it could have been night. It was hard to tell in a room that was mostly dark either way. He was lying on his back, looking up at the ceiling as he explained in a calm measured voice how the trip was going to strengthen our relationship. And then, possibly because I said nothing, he added, "You knew what I was like before you married me." Still looking up at the ceiling, he explained his absence would be good for both of us. Give us some space. Then he turned to face me. "I'll only be gone for ten days. Are you going to be okay with that?"

It wasn't just an idea then; the trip was already booked. He'd probably prepared his speech in advance to counter any objections I might have. I wasn't a beach person, I didn't feel the need to get away and I wouldn't have wanted to go. It was that he wanted to go without me. Before we moved in together Lenny had said that for most couples, the sheen wore off after two years and one or the other might stray. He didn't want that to happen to us. Neither did I, but we had only been living together for six months and married for three of them. I thought he would be as happy as I was until he began with the instructions. Don't hug me when I come in the door. Don't make me dinner every night. He didn't know what it did to me. I said, "Sure. You go. I'll be okay." He leaned over and kissed me, then slid on top of me and pulled up my nightgown.

Lenny took off in early December. I dreaded telling my mother Lenny was going on holiday by himself. She had been so happy at our wedding and I didn't want her to feel sorry for me. I tried to make light of it when I said, "It'll be nice having some time to myself."

"But you've only been married three months!" she cried. "You're still a bride!"

I assured her it was okay and I was going to be fine. I believed in the poet's line about having space in your togetherness, I just didn't think it would be so soon. The first week he was away wasn't so bad. I worked until five answering phones and updating listings at a real estate office in midtown, and afterwards went to my painting class at the League. I didn't get home until after nine, and by then I was ready for bed. Then the weekend came. I got up early Saturday morning and set up my new aluminum easel in the dining room. I was going to paint a still-life with fruit and my Japanese teapot with blue flowers. Lenny's dark-patterned tablecloth was bunched up around them since I needed to practice painting folds. I wanted yellow fruit, preferably bananas, but I was afraid they'd turn brown before I finished the painting so I used lemons instead. The composition was sketched in and the colors were laid out on the palette before I started thinking about Lenny. He hadn't called. He said he wasn't going to call, something about Club Med not having phones, but I still ran to the phone every time it rang, hoping it was him. Once I started thinking about him I couldn't stop. Outwardly, I was dipping my brush into the colors, mixing them on the palette, daubing and blending them on the canvas. Outwardly, I was painting lemons and a blue-flowered teapot, while in my mind I was picturing Lenny sunbathing beside a turquoise sea, wondering if he was looking at other women. Maybe doing more than just looking.

I have always been slow to react. My physical reflexes are almost too quick, while it might take days, even weeks for an emotional reaction to surface. I was good at rationalizing, eager to be the understanding, non-possessive ideal self. I had kept it up all week while I was working and going to class, but it was different now that I was alone, painting no less. To paint, however calm and passive it might appear to an onlooker, required intense concentration. If it didn't involve my whole nervous system then I wasn't paying attention. By the end of the morning I had worked myself into a heightened state of awareness that might have been good for art but not necessarily the artist. For I had opened myself up to feeling, and once that door was ajar I couldn't lie to myself anymore. When the tears finally came I stopped pretending I wasn't angry and hurt that Lenny had gone off by himself. My sobs were all the more virulent for having been held back so long. And still I kept working, only putting my brushes down to blow my nose. I couldn't stop the tears, but I wasn't going to let the tears stop me.

And then, as can happen with the senses on high alert, I started noticing things I hadn't seen before, like how the warm yellow lemons jumped forward when the background became darker and cooler. How the darks and lights played off one another as I played off them. There was a giving and a receiving. Whatever I gave to the painting, it gave back to me. If I added more blue to the tablecloth, it receded. A spot of white on the teapot made it shine and come forward. It was the science of color, the law of cause and effect. But it was also about control, and feeling myself in control of a picture. This had always been the case, but I hadn't experienced it on a such a visceral level before. Until now I had only been painting in class, aware of the people around me. This was the first time I was painting alone when I was free to be myself. It meant allowing myself to feel whatever I was feeling, and feel it during the act of painting.

Something else occurred to me then. The idea of devotion. I had never really thought about my need to give, or how happy I was when I dedicated myself to something. It could be learning typing and shorthand or fixing up an apartment. I had given my all when I studied acting, and now I was doing the same with drawing and painting. I was already devoted to art, but that morning I decided to make it my life. Put Art above everything else. Above Lenny. Above our marriage. Art would never let me down. Whatever I gave to painting, it would give back to me. I would devote myself to Art. Let art be my true love. I felt defiant, but humble too, like a supplicant to the God of Art. I couldn't allow myself to be emotionally dependent on Lenny. I always knew there would be that edge he'd take me to. 'You knew what I was like before you married me,' he said. I had allowed myself to get carried away with homemaking, forgetting what I already knew. That with Lenny I would have the kind of life where it would be impossible not to paint. That Saturday while I worked on a still-life with lemons and a teapot against a dark patterned cloth, I went from anger to calm, but it was a new kind of calmness. A sense that I had something indestructible inside me. As if all along I'd wanted to find the power in my own two hands.

When Lenny returned from Guadeloupe looking younger with a deep tan, he was more loving and attentive than he'd been in months. I felt shy with him at first, and kept my distance, but it wasn't long before I got used to him again. Then Christmas came, and with the new year both Lenny's tan and Guadeloupe faded into the annals of marital history.

13

MY PRIVATE GUADELOUPE

You are the instrument of your own illumination.

—VIVIAN GORNICK

My easel became a permanent fixture in the living room. Paintings of models at the League and still-lifes at home began covering the walls like a vibrant colorful mold. After the teapot and lemons I saw the potential of still-lifes everywhere. There was the mirror with various paraphernalia on my dressing table, or the crumpled napkin by a plate with a half-eaten sandwich on the dining room table. A ready-made tableau whenever objects were grouped together. They had been there all along but I hadn't seen them before. *Learning to write is learning to see...that they which see not, might see.* I didn't learn to write, but I was learning to see, learning to speak through pictures, as if painting was a kind of voice. I learned that colors had value, more for the ones in the foreground, less for those in the back. Shadows made objects look three-dimensional. When I studied the houseplant my eye jumped from wholes to parts. First I took in its mass for a general idea of placement, then I focused on individual leaves, their shapes and the lines of their veins, and where they caught the light. After a while I was noticing patterns of light and dark before anything else.

But I was more interested in people than still-lifes, and every subway ride was becoming an opportunity for study. If I was standing and holding onto the rail above, I looked down at a seated passenger and mentally calculated the distance between nose and ear, eyebrow and eyelid. Or if I was on the platform waiting for the train, I took out my sketchbook and drew people standing still for a few minutes. I filled a whole sketchbook with quick drawings of coats, pant-legs and footwear, hands clasping shopping bags or briefcases. After I took an anatomy class I was aware that beneath the coats and skirts and jeans were femurs and fibula, patellas and tibias. Under deltoideus and trapezium were clavicles and scapulae. Skulls behind faces, black holes rather than eyes. I saw death in life, life pared down to the bone, an ever-present mortality, a deeper design permeating ordinary life I had never thought about before.

Drawing or painting a model, studying them for hours, was something else again. For to really look at a face was to ingest it. Connect to its livingness as if there was no separation between us. No sense of 'otherness.' Nothing was ever alone in a picture. Everything had to be seen in relation to what was beside it. It might be a neck meeting a collar bone, or a strand of hair tucked behind an ear. Hair and ears were two different things, but in a painting they became part of a unified field of color and form. Even air had a color. Empty space had form.

I went to the Metropolitan Museum as often as I could.

Many of the pictures were familiar to me since childhood, but it was different seeing them as a painter. I got as close as I dared without alarming the guard, and studied Monet's Haystack. How did he find so many different shades of color in a single square inch of paint? When I moved back a few feet all I saw was light blue, but up close, the 'light blue' contained not only different shades of blue, but tiny bits of green, even yellow and orange. Colors that seemed to vibrate in a dazzling play of light, shifting me into a realm where everything was more than I thought it was. Monet obviously saw more than I did because his vision was more developed. But it also struck me that he was more aware, more conscious of what he was seeing. It gave me hope to think a beautiful painting was the result of a state of consciousness as much as talent or genius. Or maybe genius itself was a state of consciousness.

I painted the nude at school and portraits at home of any friend or relative who would agree to sit still for a few hours at a time. Sometimes I took my portable French easel to Central Park, but I had more of a feel for the model than the Great Outdoors. Two of the female nudes I had done at the League hung on opposite walls in the bedroom. They were hanging there for months before it occurred to me that they looked no different from nudes I had seen painted by men. Did I look at a woman the same way a man did? Did I have a view of my own, or had men taught me how to look at women. At myself too.

The canvas over the bed was a side view of a woman with long black hair and creamy white skin. She lounged against a pile of cushions. Her stillness looked as if she was waiting for someone or something. The nude on the opposite wall was a frontal view of a woman sitting behind a table. She had small round breasts and a hard, unforgiving stare. I hadn't thought what kind of message I was sending, or what I wanted the viewer to feel when they looked at these models. And because it seemed important, I began a dialogue with myself not only about what I was seeing, but how I was seeing it, and why. Then one day it ceased to matter. Objects, as I was drawing them, lost their names. Models at the League were already nameless. They were either male or female, young or old, fat or thin. And none of it mattered. A human form in space, that's what they were. The more of them I drew, the more they lost a sense of their own individuality and became part of me. Visual art is about seeing, noticing what you see, and possibly what you have failed or neglected to see. For me it was all of that, but it was also about feeling the world. Becoming more attuned to what I was seeing, trying to grasp it visually. To draw a thing is to study it, deeply. To know it on another level simply by attempting to recreate its shape, its form. The unspoken question before I began a drawing was always, what am I seeing? What is that? And that?

I was seeing myself differently too. Perhaps the greatest difference between acting and art was how it changed my way of being. When I was an actress I drew attention to myself. On stage you want people to notice you. I was overly concerned with my appearance, my voice, how I was coming across, what others thought of me. Projecting my physical presence on stage or in film brought with it the curse of self-consciousness. With art I tried to make myself invisible. Make myself disappear. Be nothing. No one. Or no one in particular. Drawing attention to myself was the last thing I wanted. I didn't want people to look at me, I wanted to look at them. They were the subject, not me. I was only a recorder. I had to keep my ego out of it. I told myself I was just practicing a trade I had a knack for, like a plumber with a knack for drains. I began sewing my own clothes and shopped for a new handbag at Woolworths over on Third Avenue rather than the department store across the street. I rummaged for bargains in thrift shops. I was too old for the scruffy art-student look, but I wanted to see how little I needed to spend on myself. I never dreamed I would become a person who would rather splurge on art supplies rather than a new pair of shoes.

As the world became more alive, the world began to tell me a different story about itself. Where once I might have seen my building, my street, my teapot, my coat, I now saw verticals and horizontals, curved lines or straight. Nothing belonged to me personally anymore. Things were subjects, objects to divine with pencil or paintbrush. What connected these objects to one another was not only a floor or a shelf, a sidewalk or a stretch of green. It was a shadow where the light was blocked. To show the darkness I had to show the light. Where the light hit and where it faded, and where it disappeared. This object or that street, whatever I focused on, existed on its own level, in its own right, regardless of me or anything about me. Objects I owned, like the reddish-brown ceramic candleholder I brought back from England, took on another dimension when it became a subject of study. When it was a series of cross-hatchings in pen and ink against a white background, it didn't matter where it was from or what it was made of. It was timeless, as old as candle-making itself.

The night I sat at the dining room table sketching the candleholder, Lenny was in the living room on the other side of the French doors watching television with his cousin Mel. When Mel was leaving they came through the dining room and stopped to watch me put the finishing touches on the candleholder. "Can you draw buildings too?" Mel asked. Mel bought and sold buildings. The ice-cream parlor was only a sideline. That night he gave me my first commission. Twenty-five dollars for a pen and ink drawing of a three-story building he owned on First Avenue.

The next day I walked over to First with my supplies and a little folding sketch stool. Mel said the building was on the southwest corner, so I went in the afternoon when it would catch the sun, and placed my stool out of the way of pedestrian traffic. It was an older building replete with intricate moldings and delicate carvings, the kind of detail I relished. The paint was peeling and the moldings were chipped, yet its run-down appearance added to its overall charm. I began the sketch in pencil and used my ruler for a straight edge while I got the proportions right and tried to ignore the traffic and noise and the sheer number of people traipsing past. I didn't notice the time or the bus stop on the corner, or the sudden appearance of children getting off the bus. I didn't notice the little boy coming towards me until he was standing beside me, saying innocently, "What are you drawing?"

I didn't sense danger from a curious young schoolboy. Without looking up I replied, "That building across the street." I should have looked up. That was my mistake, not looking at his eyes. He said, "Can I help?" and before I knew what was happening he put his hand over mine and pressed with all his might, forcing my pencil to zigzag all over the drawing. Then he let go and ran away laughing. I stared at the paper in shock. The lines were dark and heavy and made ridges in the paper that couldn't be erased. The picture was ruined. Such mindless destruction astonished me. It upset me more than the thought of having to throw away hours of work.

I returned the following day with Lenny's Polaroid and left my drawing paper at home. Sketching on the street was too risky. I never tried it again. The work went faster indoors anyway. Mel was happy with the drawing and gave me another commission. He had a lot of buildings he was in the process of buying or selling, and every other week he seemed to have a new job for me. I bought a T-square and a triangle and experimented with different kinds of paper. I strained my eyes peering at those small Polaroids for hours on end, but working on a solid table was better than my lap any day. My skills improved quickly, though not my speed. In fact, the better I got, the more time I spent on each rendering. When I told Mel I needed to raise my price he increased my fee to thirty-five dollars. I was happy with that until a repairman came to fix the refrigerator.

I was working in the dining room when the repairman came over to look at my drawing and said, "How much do you get for one of those?"

"Thirty-five dollars," I said proudly.

"Really? You should get a hundred for that kind of work."

I don't know how he knew that, or even if it was true, but from then on I began to feel cheated. All the joy went out of my work. Lately Mel had been sending me to properties downtown which were a great deal more than three stories high. When I tallied in subway fares and the cost of film for the camera, I was hardly making any profit at all. I told Mel I wanted fifty dollars. He readily agreed, saying my work merited the increase, but then he stopped commissioning as many, and I was actually earning less than before.

Portraits came with a different set of challenges. One of my early attempts was a woman friend who said, "Why did you make me look angry?" I was a guest at her house at the time, and the portrait was meant to be a gift for her hospitality. I hadn't intended to make her look angry, and the last thing I wanted was to cause her distress, but now that she mentioned it, I saw that she did look angry. And in fact she was angry that day. Not at me, but angry in general, and I had picked it up. I told her I was sorry and reminded her that I was still a beginner with much to learn.

One thing I didn't think I would ever be able to learn was how not to pick up other people's energies. Lenny used to say, "I know you. I pick you up." I didn't know I could do it too until I started drawing people. But unlike Lenny I had to draw them before I could really see them, and then I saw there were feelings in every line. I realized I had felt the energy transfer in my earliest days at the League when I felt the model through a piece of vine charcoal. No matter how crude my drawings were in those days, I could still see the feeling in them. And now I was seeing myself as someone who could transform feelings into lines that breathed. Maybe because I had touched something alive in myself I hadn't known existed before. A silent awareness that hadn't had a means of expression until I held a piece of charcoal in my hand.

I didn't have much faith in my ability for landscapes, but I kept on with them, and the first painting I sold happened to be an outdoor scene. Lenny and I had gone to the country for the weekend and I had taken my French easel and box of paints. He knew a couple who were staying nearby, and Sunday morning when they invited us to go into town for brunch, I begged off saying I wanted to paint the view of trees down the road. What did I want with food and conversation when I had the sky and the trees and a box full of colors. A few hours later when they drove Lenny back, the painting was propped on the mantle. They asked how much

I wanted for it, and the picture was sold before it was dry. I had been planning to work on it again later that day, but no, they wanted it just as it was. Lenny couldn't have been more proud. After that, whenever we went to the country or to the seaside he said, "Don't forget to bring your paints!"

14

MARRIAGE AND SWINGING

The cure for pain is in the pain.

— RUMI

It was wishful thinking that Lenny's desire for swinging would disappear once we were married. We hadn't discussed it. The only hint that Lenny might have had other ideas was the book he gave me after we were engaged called *Open Marriage.* The authors were pictured on the cover, a middle-aged couple who looked like grandparents. Lenny was fifty but I never thought of him as middle-aged, and I didn't see what the book had to do with us, especially after I skimmed a few chapters and saw it was about having affairs. I was planning our wedding, not some future infidelity.

Now, less than a year after our marriage, Lenny started mentioning "the power of swinging." He wanted to try a club down near Wall Street that Hank recommended. He talked about it as if it was understood that swinging was going to be part of our lives. He said it would improve our sex life, meaning his. I thought we were fine the way we were, but he brought up our age difference, reminding me how much younger I was. He said he might not be able to keep up with my future needs. What future needs? I was happy with him, happy to be finally settled with one person. I loved being married. I didn't want anyone else. As far as I could tell, Lenny didn't either. But then he didn't think of swinging as wanting to be with someone else. It was more the freedom to know that he could, and I would acquiesce. I didn't delve into the psychology of it. It didn't occur to me to analyze his behavior, or mine for that matter. I took things as they came. Now it was this club down near Wall Street Hank told him about. Apparently during the week it was a regular restaurant, but Saturday nights for the price of a drink and the buffet, it was the place to go if you wanted to be invited to private parties.

Lenny still dreamed of being invited to private parties. He said, "It's only a meeting place, no different than going out for dinner, except we'll have the chance to meet people. We'll have a drink and a bite to eat, and just look."

I knew I wouldn't like it. Neither did I think I would be casing a bar after I was married. But like the Botany and Plato's, I knew I wouldn't hear the end of it until we went. If I wanted to keep my title as the most wonderful woman he had ever known, having a drink and a bite to eat and possibly a conversation didn't seem a big deal. I had never been able to resist Lenny's power of persuasion anyway.

The restaurant was a large nondescript space with cozy-looking booths, some that could sit as many as six or eight, but instead of waitstaff patrolling the aisles there were customers—closer to Lenny's age than mine—walking around in pairs. Lenny might whisper as we passed a table, "What do you think, could you go for him?" I'd say, "Maybe," meaning never, and I'd look at the woman and wonder what Lenny saw in her. I knew it didn't have to be anything particular. The possibility that she was available was the only thing that mattered.

Though we didn't meet anyone that night, Lenny considered the evening a success. He said he just liked being in the company of other swingers. When he called it his hobby, as if it was a special interest he could take up or leave off, I believed him. I didn't want to see it as anything more serious. If I saw how swinging released him from the bonds of marriage, the very restrictions I was grateful for, I didn't mention it because whatever he called it, he was always more loving when I agreed to go along. So we went again another Saturday night. Since neither of us was the type who made the first move, it might not have been until our third visit that Steve and Amy introduced themselves and invited us to a party at their house in New Jersey the following weekend. Or rather Steve did. He was the outgoing one, tall and fit with bushy brows and thick salt and pepper hair. Amy, blonde and petite, was mostly silent. They were older than me but younger than Lenny, and they were nice. A nice suburban couple from New Jersey.

Lenny had a car at the time, an old banger he bought from his cousin, and we had no trouble finding their house in the suburbs. The staid, solid brick colonials on a tree-lined street all looked alike, but only one had a driveway filled with cars. Shiny, late-model cars, unlike ours with dull peeling paint. Lenny parked down the block and lit a joint. We smoked with the windows rolled up and giggled like teenagers, then walked up to the house holding hands. This prelude, imagining what carefree wildness might be going on behind the door of the brick colonial, was the high point of the evening.

Inside the front door were the toys and little boots left

behind when the children were packed off to grandma's, and we came into what seemed an indoor garden room where a small group of guests, all fully dressed, were sitting comfortably on the couch or the floor, drinking wine or soda from paper cups and munching on pretzels and potato chips. The normality of it all was disconcerting. I wondered why there were so few guests compared to the number of cars spilling onto the street. But it was a large house, so maybe they had spread out. Then Steve's tall frame appeared in the doorway, and without a word he took my hand and led me off to a room upstairs and closed the door. Later, when I returned to the garden room, Lenny was still sitting on the couch where I'd left him. I thought it strange he wanted to go to these things, yet seemed ambivalent about participating. My own ambivalence hardly bears thinking about. If I said swinging went against the grain, that would be true, yet I'd come to accept Lenny's 'hobby' because I put it in a box that was only opened a few times a month and had nothing to do with our real life.

We began seeing Steve and Amy on a regular basis, meeting them for dinner in the city and inviting them back to our place, or driving down to the Jersey shore, spending the day on the beach and going back to theirs. On one of those beach days when I was in the water with Steve, he said that if things had been different he would want to see more of me. You weren't supposed to say things like that. I knew Lenny would never say it to Amy. They were up on the sand, sitting on a blanket. I had no resentment towards her. Even when I saw her on the floor with Lenny, her small white hands clutching his back, I took it in stride. I did wonder though if Lenny could tell the difference between her touch and mine. I knew a boy once who used to study the shape of my fingers and talk about the specialness of my touch. We were eighteen, keenly aware of love's specialness. But then swinging was no more about being special than 'Love and be Free' was about love. Swinging, as far as Lenny was concerned, seemed more about being loved even though you wanted to have sex with other women. I asked myself why I continued to play along. When the fear went away, so did the sense of excitement. I became blasé about it, looking at sex as just another bodily sensation.

There were others after Steve and Amy. On several of those Saturday nights I now took for granted, we went to the home of an older couple who lived in a high rise in Fort Lee overlooking the Hudson River. The wife wore a flowered muumuu and served Entenmann's donuts. Though she was Lenny's age he said she was too old for him. Then there was Bob and Sara with a penthouse overlooking Third Avenue. After the bedroom antics there was ordering Chinese and watching tv in the living room. We probably would have been friends with Bob and Sara even without the swinging. They were the ones who invited us to the party in Manhattan.

We heard the music as soon as we got off the elevator. The door was unlocked and there was a naked couple on the floor just inside. We stepped around them and joined the crush of people standing around fully dressed, drinking and smoking like guests at a regular party. I had already lost sight of Lenny when a muscular young man wearing nothing but a thick mustache came up and said hello. All I could think of to say was, "And what do you do?" He said, "I'm a fireman." And with that we were somehow on the floor and my clothes were gone. Then the fireman was gone too and I was walking around naked, drifting through the bottleneck in the hallway where people both clothed and unclothed were standing around talking as if it made no difference one way or the other. At the end of the dark hallway I stepped into a large dimly-lit living room and what looked like a sea of bodies rising and falling like random waves. It was hard to make out anything specific until I recognized Bob coming towards me as if he had risen from the sea. When he pulled me in with him, I became a body with other bodies, with no more need to guard or protect than a wave in the sea. There was no sense of starting or stopping. No end or beginning, just this joining, this forgetting of self, and being no one. Or no one in particular. How far I'd come in those few years since coming back to New York!

I knew something had shifted when Lenny and I came home that night. I hadn't seen him since we'd arrived at the party and I think he said he didn't do anything or even undress. It was all the same to me, but the night wasn't over for him until it was just us again. He always wanted me when we got home after swinging, but that night it didn't feel like 'us' anymore. I was still me, but I was more than just me. I could have been any woman. Or Everywoman. I was Her, the feminine element, as if I had expanded, found my place as the nameless, voiceless eternal She. It was freeing, like being cut loose from my moorings. Lenny was He. We were a he and a she. An aspect of elementary forces joining together to create something as natural and necessary as the sun rising on a new day. I was compelled to take him in and accept him as much as he was driven to take me. It was the natural order of things. It was personal and impersonal, not belonging to us, yet we belonged to it. An aspect of the universal desire for two ends meeting, drawn inexorably towards one another like a magnet. The union of all things dissolving into one. The many in the one he and the one she. Love and the longing for connection on an elemental level like air and water, fire and earth.

I didn't share these thoughts with Lenny. I wouldn't have known how. I didn't think he would understand. I didn't think he would appreciate hearing me say that I was the embodiment of all women, and he didn't need anyone other than me. He was rolling another joint. He wanted to stay high, and I was high in a different place. In order to process the night I had come up with something transcendent. But it made me wonder how Lenny could treat sex so casually, calling it a life-style, thinking of it as his hobby. He didn't know what we were dealing with. I was only beginning to see it myself. One day I would learn about energy fields and compare it to the feeling I had that night of the party. Forgetfulness of self in a wave of humanity. Wave upon wave, a sea of bodies rising and falling. No different from those pagan fertility rites I'd read about when you'd give yourself away, give yourself to the god.

We never went to another party. There was no need. Something in my field had changed. As if light had been shed on a dark patch, and I could give myself away without guilt. It was only my physical body. It wasn't Lenny giving me away anymore, it was me. The darkness around it had broken up and dissolved. And the light had come through. I never thanked Lenny for it. Never told him it was Rimbaud's *Illuminations* that had led me to his office on Sheridan Square. The journey had been more painful than poetic.

I was ready to move on, have it be only us now. When Lenny would bring up plans for the weekend on a Wednesday or Thursday, suggesting we call one of the couples we knew, or go downtown and meet someone else, I started dreading Saturday nights. When I said I didn't feel like it, he didn't stay home or take me to a movie, he went to the track. As more Saturday nights piled up without swinging, he started to mope. The more he sulked the more I felt guilty, as if I had gone back on a promise. What he was fond of calling "our love," and "the greatest love he had ever known," seemed to depend on swinging. When I said, "Maybe you should think about getting some therapy," he claimed it would take at least ten years of therapy to get through it. Ten years sounded like an eternity, and what if it didn't produce a clear result. What if I didn't like the new Lenny. So I gave in, and we went a few more times but it felt meaningless. I finally came out and said, "I'd like it to be just us now."

Lenny sighed and got up from the bed. "I knew this was coming."

"You're not too disappointed?"

"We had a good run. What am I going to do?"

"Maybe we could get some help," I said, meaning him.

He rolled his eyes. "No, that wouldn't do any good. It would take ten years to get to the bottom of it." Lenny, the former sex therapist, didn't want therapy for himself. "Let's just forget about it," he said. "I told you in the beginning that swinging isn't for everyone. Very few people are free enough."

I hated when he said that. It made me feel lacking in some way because I wanted to be monogamous. I *was* free. Probably more free than I'd ever wanted or needed to be. He once told me I was freer than he was. There was no point in reminding him. He went to the kitchen and took a pint of Haagen-Dazs from the freezer and a spoon from the drawer and disappeared into the living room. I heard the tv come on, and pictured him hunched over the container, mindlessly spooning ice-cream into his mouth. He was probably hoping I would change my mind like last time, but I was done. Sexual encounters with strangers had been demystified. The fear was gone. There was nothing more to gain from those recreational pot-driven couplings that were the opposite of real intimacy.

It hadn't yet occurred to me that our own intimacy was purely physical. If I hadn't saved the letters I wrote to him I might have forgotten how much in love with him I was in those days. During the rare times we had been apart I wrote to him every other day, addressing him as My Darling Love. When I found the letters in his drawer mixed in with a jumble of envelopes and receipts and bits of crumpled paper, I took them back. He would never know they were gone.

Lenny was the type that called instead of wrote, which was fine, but he didn't read books either. He said he'd read everything he'd wanted to by then and there was nothing more he could learn from books. I couldn't imagine such a fate for myself, and at some point I realized I didn't want to have a child with him. It had been my one condition of marriage, not necessarily that we would have a baby, but that he would be open to the idea. He said he was, but he already had two children and he didn't seem keen to have another. I wasn't ready myself, but I was about to turn thirty, and I was wondering what the future would look like.

Then I learned my father was dying. My father who loved to read books and plays and write them too. Now that life was taking a more serious turn, the window to swinging slammed shut for good.

15

THE AGE OF RECKONING

My belief is that in life people
will take you at your own reckoning.

— ISAAC ASIMOV

I must have had a premonition of my father's death when I picked up a biography of Karl Marx in Foyles. I had grown up with my father's passion for Marxism, my eyes glazing over whenever he mentioned 'dialectics,' or worse, 'dialectical materialism.' I never managed to grasp the concept no matter how he explained it. Yet now in Foyles on Charing Cross Road the well-known face of Karl Marx leapt up at me from the display table. I opened the book at random. "When Marx was asked what his idea of happiness was, he answered, 'to fight.'" It reminded me how much I enjoyed battling a canvas. Maybe there was something about Marx I could relate to after all.

Lenny had taken me to London to celebrate our first anniversary and I went to Foyles for something to read on the plane home. I knew my father would be pleased I was taking an interest in Marx after all these years, and when I told him I was reading his biography he said, "Why don't you come to my study group?"

This was the first I'd heard of a study group. They met on Sunday afternoons, rotating between apartments and taking turns presenting the reading assignments. Along with my father, there were five other members, two men and three women all in their twenties and thirties. When I joined they were in the middle of *The German Idealists* and had started on *Monopoly Capital.* I struggled with both. Just staying focused during the meetings was as much a challenge as the homework assignments. I couldn't help being more interested in studying the other members than in trying to understand theories of the ruling class. The men were bookish types who slumped in their chairs, and none of the women wore makeup or did anything with their hair. One had a man's haircut, another had a mass of dark blonde curls. I wondered if they were natural curls or the result of a perm, and decided they had to be natural since a perm would have been too bourgeois. None of the members looked as if they would enjoy a good fight like Marx, but it warmed my heart to see them looking to my father as a fount of wisdom, deferring to his comments and asking for his take on the readings. As far as I knew, not since my sisters and brothers and I had been small had he experienced that kind of respectful, almost worshipful attention.

When we met in Cobble Hill in Brooklyn, the woman with curly hair made coffee in an old-fashioned percolator. As we sat around the kitchen table by the stove, she kept reaching over to adjust the flame—higher to bring it to the boil—lower when the water bubbled into the little glass knob on the lid. I forgave myself for finding this lesson on tending the flame more interesting than the class struggle or the history of capitalism. And I forgave myself for tuning out my father's voice when I became captivated by the way the light hit his tan corduroy trousers, turning the ridges into stripes. And how his old suede shoes with the laces had molded themselves to the shape of his feet, because I was spending time with him, giving him a show of faith. Later, when he became ill, I was glad that I did.

His illness was unexpected. Though he was seventy-two and hobbled on arthritic feet, he still went to work every day. His parents had lived into their nineties and I took it for granted that he would too. Then one Sunday while we were waiting for the express train to Brooklyn, he mentioned he hadn't been feeling well and was going to see a doctor. A few weeks later he rang me at work to tell me he had cancer and the doctor gave him six months. I put the phone down and wept.

I used to think sudden death was the worst shock to cope with, but that fall when his breath seemed to get shorter with the days, I found waiting for someone to die was a new kind of agony. It was only a year ago that I had done his portrait in charcoal. He was delighted when I asked him to pose, and when he sat across from me on the sofa and I studied his face, I realized I had never really looked at him, never really seen him before. He was just Dad, the father I had known all my life. I could have easily described the high forehead, the warm brown eyes and prominent nose. A strong face, I would have said, surrounded by a head of thick, neatly combed white hair. Yet it was different studying his face as an artist, taking each feature one by one and fitting them all together. Not only peering at the bone structure underneath, but noticing how the light hit his face. And still that was nothing compared to the way he was beaming at me, as if his face was lit from within. As I rubbed and smudged the charcoal and tried to capture his expression, it was all I could do not to cry, because all I saw was love.

My father said, “I’m going to lick this.” By the time they operated it was already too late, but he remained undaunted. When I came to see him in the hospital and asked the nurse how he was, she clicked her tongue and said, “As soon as he came out of the anesthetic he said, “The workers of the world will unite!” She smiled and shook her head as if to say, isn’t that unbelievable? But of course it wasn’t to me.

When they sent him home I prepared meals for him and carried them over on the crosstown bus. I stirred my hopes of his recovery into the rice and vegetable dishes and the chicken pot pie, and baked prayers into the oat bran muffins and chocolate-chip cookies. For Christmas I sewed him an ankle-length belted robe in plush royal-blue velour. Though his skin and the whites of his eyes were already turning yellow by then, his hair was snow-white, and when he put on the robe he looked like an ancient priest. When I came over, he would invariably be sitting in the recliner, freshly shaved and dressed and reading a pamphlet by Friedrich Engels. Along with the food I brought my tape recorder to tape his lectures so that I could play them at the next study group. When his voice began to falter and he was too sick to continue, I could no longer face going to the group. And still he kept reading Engels. What use was Engels to him now?

* * *

In the winter of 1980 when the Iran hostage crisis dominated the news and my father fought a battle he was never going to win, Lenny went to Cancun and I got my first portrait commission. A friend was raising money for the anti-Communist rebels fighting the Soviets in Afghanistan and the portraits would be auctioned at a benefit gala in the spring. There were to be three paintings. Amānullāh Khan, the king who ruled Afghanistan in the 1920s, his middle-aged son and heir-presumptive, aka the prince, and the prince with Muhammad Ali praying in a mosque. Only the prince would be painted from life and the others from 8x10 glossies, but it was a heady proposition for someone who had taken up painting hardly more than a year ago. I tried not to think of the irony of lending my painterly skills to the anti-Communists while my father was dying, though the idea of them restoring the monarchy probably would have amused him.

I was used to copying buildings from photos but never a portrait before, and after this I hoped never to do it again. Not that painting the prince in the flesh was any easier. Known officially as His Royal Highness Prince Hassan Durani, at present he was selling neckties at Bergdorf's. He arrived for our first session on a cold rainy night and complained about having to stand for a portrait after standing all day behind the counter selling ties. I addressed him as Mr. Durani as he had yet to be crowned, and along with a cup of chamomile tea with honey, I gave him a pillow to stand on after he removed his wet shoes. But he was a peevish man who didn't want to be pleased.

The portraits weren't finished until various epaulettes, ribbons and medals from additional black and white photos were draped on the royals. Then they were sent to be framed, and I didn't see them again until the benefit at the end of April which happened to fall on the day my father died. The last thing I felt like was going to a party that night, but I was in a daze, unable to think. All I could do was keep my focus on what was next. After the doctor called early that morning, the next thing was a trip to the hospital to collect my father's things and sign the papers. I automatically went to his room, but of course he was no longer there. The empty bed stripped down to the mattress was the first painful reminder of his absence. I had thought it admirable of him to donate his body to medicine, "To save you children the trouble and expense of a funeral," he'd said. Now there was nothing to take away but a blue plastic hospital bag with the clothes he'd walked in with.

After I came home with the plastic bag, the next thing to do was iron my dress for the party that night. I slid open the door of the storage unit of raw pine, reached for the ironing board at the back and felt a sharp stab of pain. A splinter had lodged under my nail and was too deep to remove the way I normally would, lighting a match and sterilizing a needle before digging it out with tweezers. I cried with frustration and it felt good to cry about a finger when I was too numb to cry for my father. Then I called Lenny to tell him about the splinter and he asked around the office if anyone knew a doctor nearby. Fifteen minutes later I was sitting on the examining table while a doctor held my hand. He had no more luck prying out the splinter than I did, so he sent me to a specialist also conveniently nearby. I have no idea what he specialized in, but the second doctor had the splinter out in no time and I was home again within the hour. It seems unbelievable compared to what I might have had to go through today with the healthcare system, especially since Lenny's insurance went to his ex-wife and children and I had none of my own. Yet I don't remember the cost being much at all.

Lenny didn't want to come to the party so I went alone. I didn't think I would mind until I arrived at the town house and found it was a society-do replete with photographers, men in black-tie and women dressed to the nines. I made my way through the crush, past the cash bars and banquet tables piled high with delicacies. It felt wrong to be surrounded by such decadence when my father's body was barely cold, but I wanted to see the portraits. I couldn't find them anywhere, and it was a while before I could even find someone to ask. I was told they were downstairs which meant searching for the stairs next, and when I finally found the pictures hanging on makeshift screens I was horrified to see how the spotlights glanced off the paint in uneven patches, making the pictures unreadable except at certain angles. Had I mixed the paints with too much linseed oil? Was there some kind of matte finish I might have used to avoid this disaster?

I was so absorbed in bemoaning my mistake I didn't notice Mohammed Ali was sitting inches away on one of the folding chairs. I might not have seen him at all if one of his party hadn't asked if I was the artist. Then he then introduced us. The boxer held out his hand and said, "You painted those? You're great!" I shook his hand and said, "Well, you're pretty great yourself!"

As it turned out, the cost of the gala was far beyond whatever the auction brought in, and the percentage I was promised in lieu of a fee never came about. But those kind words from a man who was truly great was compensation enough.

When the Soviets withdrew from Afghanistan at the end of the 1980s, the so-called 'prince' was found to be an imposter. The necktie salesman at Bergdorf's I had painted as royalty and given him a pillow to stand on, was an Afghani hairdresser who conned the society crowd of Palm Beach along with his various supporters among the American military, including the general who purchased all three of my paintings at auction.

* * *

That I would lose my father was expected, but adjusting to the reality was something else, and I spent long periods lying on the couch. Lenny was disappointed I'd taken up smoking again but I didn't care. I no longer felt bound to him, as if my father's death had released me. Not that I married Lenny to please my father, but I knew it would please him if I did. His office was a block away from the League and every time I went up to see him he asked about Lenny.

Lenny had charmed my parents the first Christmas I was back in New York. They had been divorced for years by then and had mellowed enough to prepare a turkey dinner together. Lenny talked about plays with my father who loved the theater, and all he had to do with my mother was let her know she was still an attractive woman for her laughter to ring through the apartment the rest of the evening. But it was what he did for my sister Ellen that put him permanently in their good graces.

Both Ellen and my brother Frank had been diagnosed with paranoid-schizophrenia. Frank took his meds on and off, and was taking them at the time, but Ellen refused. She had been in a bad state for years and my parents were at their wits end when Lenny said he knew a doctor who was a genius at figuring out the right cocktail of pills. The problem of getting Ellen to see him was solved when she asked me to lend her the money for a new blouse and Lenny said to do it on the condition she saw this doctor. It worked, and in less than a year Ellen had a job working in statistics at Citibank and was back in school finishing her master's in social work.

I happened to drop by my father's office a few days after spending the night with the lawyer from Valley Stream, and when he said, "How's Lenny?" I said I was thinking of breaking it off with him. My father seemed genuinely disappointed. "I'm sorry to hear that," he said. "I really liked Lenny." I did too of course. I felt bad disappointing my father. I thought I had disappointed him enough already by not being his biological daughter. It was all water under the bridge, but now that my father was no longer around and there was no danger of disappointing him, I was thinking how Lenny had disappointed me. What bothered me even more were the times I'd disappointed myself.

The last straw had been my birthday last fall. He was going to take me to dinner at a new restaurant in the neighborhood, and when I came home from work that evening I learned he had invited his friend Greg to come with us. Greg was an actor from L.A. who had dropped by unannounced. Greg said, "Is that okay with you?"

"Why not," I said good naturedly, because I was always happy on my birthday. Then Lenny handed me my present, a flat oblong box, obviously something to wear. I was planning to open it later, but Lenny wanted me to open it now. I took off the wrapping, and after removing yards of white tissue paper I pulled out a long slinky raspberry-colored nightgown that was more a present for him than for me.

Lenny grinned and said slyly, "Why don't you try it on for us?"

"What—now?"

"Why not? I bet it's going to look beautiful on you."

I knew that look of his. He was showing off in front of Greg. But I went along and changed into the nightgown with a lacy bodice and spaghetti straps to show him I didn't care. When I came back into the living room Lenny said,

"Oh my god!" and clapped his hand over his mouth. "You have *got* to wear that when we go out tonight."

"To the restaurant? No. Absolutely not!"

"Why? It looks like an evening gown. I bet no one would be able to tell the difference." He turned to Greg to back him up.

Greg shook his head and said, "Oh, no you don't. This is between you two."

Lenny kept on. "What do you say honey? Will you do it? If anyone could carry it off you could. Come on, I dare you!"

It was the dare. Lenny had always been daring me to do things, but long before I met him I had been daring myself too. Why not celebrate my thirtieth birthday with some chutzpah? I had taken off my bra but I was still wearing pantyhose and heels, and nothing showed but some cleavage. All I needed was my coat. We left and went outside, and after a few minutes in the freezing night air I knew I'd been an idiot. I felt naked under my coat without a bra and wished I had thought to put on a sweater. By the time we reached the next corner I knew the whole thing had been a mistake. The nightgown was full of static and clung to my legs. My coat was knee-length; everyone could probably tell the thin raspberry-colored shiny fabric that went down to my ankles was a nightgown not a dress. What a fool to let him talk me into it. Lenny wasn't even walking beside me. The sidewalk was narrow and crowded. We wouldn't have been able to walk three abreast anyway, but he was behind me, chatting with Greg. It was my birthday and I felt left out.

The restaurant was practically empty. Normally this would have been a sign the food was bad, but it had only just opened, and that night I was relieved we had it almost to ourselves. Unfortunately, the room was brightly lit with tables out in the open and no place to feel unnoticed. The waiter led us to a table in the middle. I sat down with my coat on. Lenny said, "Aren't you going to take your coat off?"

"I'm cold. I'll wait till I warm up."

Lenny had said no one would be able to tell it was a nightgown, but the young waiter who took our order seemed to know right away. My coat was draped over the back of the chair by then, and he was staring down at my breasts, trying to stifle his laughter. I was mortified, and felt my ears turning red. I was angry at Lenny. He wasn't even sitting next to me. The table was round, big enough for six, and Lenny was on the other side, sitting closer to Greg than to me. On any other night I wouldn't have minded him talking to his friend, catching up on old times and people they knew. But this was supposed to be my night. I'd let him talk me into wearing a nightgown to dinner and he was ignoring me. My so-called bravery was pathetic. Not chutzpah at all, but the act of a woman so insecure she'd do anything to please her husband. I was disgusted at myself. This wasn't who I wanted to be. When I heard the waitstaff laughing in the service area at the back I assumed they were laughing at me, the silly woman in a nightgown. At the end they all sang Happy Birthday and gave me a cupcake with a lighted candle, but nothing could make up for the feeling that I had demeaned myself.

Not long afterwards when I was in the kitchen preparing a brown rice and vegetable dish to take over to my father's, I burst into tears. At first I was crying because my father was getting worse and I hated the thought of losing him. Then I started hating myself. Self-loathing was an old fallback when things seemed hopeless. I hadn't been to that place in years. Then, as I stood sobbing over the bowl of rice, I noticed how tiny each grain was. There must have been thousands of grains in the bowl and every single one contained nutrients. They all looked the same, one not more valuable than another, and they didn't even have to do anything to prove their worth; they just had to be rice. Was I any less valuable than a grain of rice? If God created rice, how could He have created me as anything less?

16

WHO ARE YOU

In April 1882 my father died; and I was at once whirled out of my land of dreams into a very different sphere.

— EDWARD CARPENTER

April 1980 came with a couple of wake-up calls at dawn, both of which caused me to spring out of bed. One was the news my father had passed, which was not unexpected. The other was from my subconscious, and maybe it shouldn't have surprised me either but it did. In the dream I was standing before a panel of judges sitting behind a table like the judges at auditions I used to go to, and I was just as nervous now as I'd been then. When one of them said, "Who are you?" I stood there dumbly, unable to speak. The judge repeated it louder and it sounded like an accusation. "Who ARE You?" My mouth was dry with fear. I didn't know what answer to give, but since some response had to be made I reached magically into my stomach and pulled out what looked like a piece of umbilical cord. It was about the size of my little finger but it looked dried out as if it had been mummified. I held it out wordlessly to the judge as if to say this is who I am, hoping they'd be able tell simply by looking at the cord. The judge was not impressed. He demanded a third time, "WHO ARE YOU?" By now my mouth was so dry I couldn't swallow. I whispered, "Renoir," and woke up.

But I couldn't be. It was true that sometimes when I was painting I caught myself stroking my chin as if I was stroking an imaginary beard or goatee, but it was absurd to think I had been Renoir in a past life. I scrambled out of bed to look at myself in the mirror. There was one in the bedroom but I didn't want to turn on the light and risk waking Lenny, so I hurried into the living room where there was a big mirror above the couch. I was half-afraid I might see the face of an old bearded Frenchman in a straw hat—Renoir's final self-portrait—but even in the early morning light I could see I looked the same as always.

The dream remained a mysterious oddity until a few years later when I stopped seeing Renoir as a name and saw it as a combination of 're' and 'noir.' Noir means black. The prefix re could mean again or back. When I said Renoir I could have been saying, I'm back to the black, or I'm looking at the black again, the black being the dark, the unknown, the subconscious, to learn what I knew inside. If that was the case, then the dream was a warning to get busy on what I was supposed to be doing, finding out what I knew inside. I knew I had to do it after the Dream of '76 when I realized I had information within. That had been four years ago. But if I'd forgotten it, my subconscious hadn't. It knew about the mummified umbilical cord preserved within. I could see it too, but the only answer I could give was re-noir, as if to say I'm regarding the black, the dark. But I couldn't see anything yet.

My use of the name Renoir became even more interesting later when I realized it sounded like *renoit*, French for reborn. Meanwhile, that April when I was thirty and my father died, I wasn't ready to peer into the dark. I'd thrown away that first painting from my imagination because the lower half, the murky subway part, was too disturbing to carry on with. For the present, all I could do was look in the mirror for a self-portrait.

I did the first one for Lenny, painting myself wearing the black felt wide-brimmed hat he liked seeing me in. But it was a picture of a woman with eyes veiled in sadness. A woman in hiding, lost somewhere inside herself. I did the second self-portrait in Illinois when I went out to visit Gramps and stayed in the house in Decatur I'd known all my life. The only mirror was the one on the medicine cabinet above the bathroom sink, where I remembered having to stand on a stool to reach the faucets. And the day when I could finally see the top of my forehead in the mirror without standing on a stool. This time I wore my beret instead of a hat, and glasses instead of contacts, and not only did I look like the art student I was, but I looked younger than I was, probably because my child-self was still very much alive in Decatur. Both portraits were just the head and shoulders, nothing in the background to show where I was, yet both paintings seemed to reflect my location.

Seeing myself was one thing, but I was looking at Lenny too, wondering why he wanted to go to the track rather than spend Saturday nights with me. And why he always had to smoke pot before sex, or bring porn magazines into bed with us now swinging was out of the question. I thought we should talk about it, but it never seemed the right time. It certainly wasn't the right time to say, "I'd like to talk about us," when he was at the front door putting on his coat, but I didn't mean that particular moment. He probably would have said the same thing though. "Take it to an Al-Anon meeting." I was beginning to think Lenny was using his alcoholism as an excuse not to deal with me. I used to like going to the meetings for friends and relatives of alcoholics, and for a while I thought I had found my niche. Lenny had A.A. and I had Al-Anon with my own Little Blue Book and its daily page of advice which was mostly about 'letting-go-with-love' and working on yourself rather than trying to fix the other person. Perhaps if I had known him before he was sober I would been more grateful for A.A. instead of thinking of it as a shield he used to keep me at a distance.

I said nothing when he flew off to Cancun with Club Med that winter. He needed the sun and I needed to be near my father and cook wholesome food that might help him get well. When Lenny came home it seemed natural to share the new insights on diet and nutrition I had been reading about for my father. Lenny always said he got two colds every winter and sure enough he did. One night when we were on the sofa, Lenny complained of a headache and said he felt a cold coming on. He was lying with his head in my lap, which he had never done before, and I was delighted. I sat there stroking his hair as if to stroke away the headache, thinking how nice it was to be cozy like this, and suggested maybe he could choose not to get a cold this time. When I said changing his diet might be one way, or exercising, since he often complained about his back or his knee, he pulled away and said irritably, "I don't want to be mothered." Then he got up and went into the other room.

I thought I was just passing along information, not mothering him, and it struck me that from the beginning Lenny saw his role as the teacher. I used to love it, but that ground had been picked clean. That he didn't want to learn anything from me in return felt like he didn't see me as an equal.

Maybe it wasn't just a coincidence that around that same time I was starting to feel I had outgrown my instructors at the League too. It wasn't that I didn't have anything more to learn, it was that I didn't know what more I could learn from them. My painting class at the time was taught by an elderly man who hobbled around with a cane. When he saw me struggling with the model's face, he picked up one of my brushes and painted it out with white. "Don't be afraid to start over again," he said. He was right of course, but seeing him paint over my work reminded me of the little monster who scribbled all over the drawing I was doing of Mel's building on First Avenue. Then he helped himself to another brush and began repainting the model's face himself, making it look effortless. His work was far better than mine, but it wasn't my picture anymore and I couldn't get on with it. He'd spoiled it for me.

The following month I switched to a pastel class with a different instructor. I had been experimenting with pastels on my own, and found the cleanup quick and easy compared to the time it took to scrape a palette and wash a load of brushes. I thought I had a good likeness of the model that night, but when the instructor came over he found all sorts of faults with it and didn't seem to think I was doing anything right. At the end of the session he singled out the work of another student and heaped it with praise. I don't remember the picture, only that I didn't think much of it, and I lost faith in his judgment.

This was all happening the winter my father was dying, Lenny was sunning himself in Mexico, and I was turning thirty. I was in no mood to please someone else and do it their way. Rather than spend money on a class at the League,

I bought a custom-made model platform that fit into a corner of the living room. From now on I would find my own models and paint them how I wanted. I also painted a third self-portrait, dressing up for it in an orange cotton-print Indian dress with long earrings to match. The canvas was large enough to show me holding my palette of colors out like a tray, as if saying to the viewer—or to my image in the mirror, or perhaps even to God, 'Here are my colors, what shall I paint next?'

Renoir, re-noir. I'd already given myself the answer, had I known. Look into the black, the subconscious. Remember what you know inside. But I'd forgotten the Dream of '76. Forgotten the No Exit dream of my childhood when I drowned in a steel box, then drew a girl being carried up a path to the house set back among the trees. I didn't know who's house it was or who the man carrying her was. All I knew was that she was being taken up the path towards the dream of home.

17

MORE LIGHT

The more light you allow within
The brighter your world will be.

— SHAKTI GAWAIN

It seemed an act of providence when the apartment next door became available at the same time Lenny's cousin was looking to invest in a rental. The plan was for Mel to sign the lease and Lenny to sublet the two front rooms for me to use as a studio. The room in the back with kitchen and bath would be sublet to someone we knew. The problem was that while the front rooms had the light, the back had the entrance. To get around it we would have to knock out the wall between the two closets in the front rooms. Lenny and I wouldn't miss the closet on our side. It was small and the tenant before us had built a wall-to-wall storage unit in the dining room, the one that gave me a splinter under my nail. My brother Howard did carpentry so he was given the job of knocking down the wall. I fled the house when he started hacking at it with an axe and the plaster crashed down.

When I returned late in the afternoon Howard was scooping a pile of rubble into industrial strength garbage bags. "Door's open," he said, "go ahead inside!"

With the hanging rail gone it no longer even looked like a closet. I stepped into the narrow space and Howard called out, "Don't trip over the molding. I had to leave it—it's structural support!" I swiveled to the left, stepped over the molding, swiveled to the right, and I was in the closet next door. One more step and I was in the apartment next door. My footsteps echoed on the bare wooden floorboards. Northern light streamed in through uncovered windows. I never thought I would be grateful for the big-box Gimbels department store across the street, but its black and white striped façade facing south acted like a giant reflector, bumping up the wattage of this perfect northern light for painters. We had the same view in our apartment, but Gimbels wasn't what you wanted to see out your living room window, which was why I kept the lower halves shuttered and the upper halves covered with hanging plants. The studio windows would remain bare.

I quickly adjusted to the magic of going into the closet, leaving one reality behind and entering another. One was married life, the other was the studio life, and in between was a secret passage. The model platform was brought in, and with my small share of Dad's insurance I was able to buy a proper wooden easel, a taboret and a drafting table, as well as a couple of chairs for models from the secondhand store. Now that I had ample floor space to stretch my own canvases, I experimented priming them with the centuries-old tradition of rabbit skin glue. I'd heard about it at the League, how you mixed the powder with water and heated it over the stove until it became thick and gelatinous. But it was a slimy concoction and stank to high heaven, and it was simpler to take the subway down to Pearl Paint on Canal Street and buy a roll of canvas already primed.

I remember that summer as a never-ending continuum of bright sunny days with friends and acquaintances coming by to pose. At night I was too busy sketching or practicing anatomy to notice or care whether Lenny had gone to an A.A. meeting or the track. I needn't have worried about having enough models; people liked being asked to pose and told their friends to come too. I was touched by their willingness, and studied them with something akin to reverence. Most people had no idea how much they revealed about their inner self during those silent poses. Lenny came out looking younger than his years, I think because his spirit had always been youthful. My brother Howard had a mustache at the time, and with his hair parted in the middle he looked like an Edwardian poet or man of letters, which I could well believe. I had no idea why my pictures came out the way they did, and no one seemed to mind until a seventy-year-old woman chided me for making her look too young. "You don't have to flatter me," she said. I assured her that flattery had been the last thing on my mind. But it made me wonder if the younger self remains like an indestructible essence that never completely goes away. The younger person inhabits the old. Perhaps the other way around too, and it's only time that separates them. When I took LSD years ago and looked in the mirror, I saw myself morph into an old woman, then back again to nineteen. Time seemed no more than a loop that went round and round, old-young, young-old, neither one permanent, both arbitrary and constantly changing.

With our friend Jimmy it wasn't the mask of age I pulled back, it was the mask itself. Jimmy was always clowning around and telling jokes, and with his large expressive eyes and receding chin, he could look comical. But when he sat for me he relaxed. He didn't have to be entertaining so he became still, and I saw the sadness and disappointment of a lonely man. Jimmy said, "You saw that?" My paintbrush did. I wielded the brush, but I had no control over what I picked up. I may have thought I was only trying to get the features right, but the feelings behind them always came through. It felt like a kind of magic until I learned about energy fields and picking up people's energies through their features and expressions.

My first model was Howard's girlfriend, a twenty-year-old black-haired beauty Goya might have painted. When I had her in one of my kimonos from Toshi, then the green silk I wore to go punting on the River Cam, it was like reliving my London days through someone else. I was glad I'd kept the cobalt-blue gown with ostrich feathers, because even though I never wore it again it was a perfect match for my friend Colleen with auburn hair. She was sitting down in the pose, one foot in a satin slipper and the other foot bare, and for added color I gave her a yellow rose to hold. But holding the rose made her look like a forsaken Cinderella. She must have felt it too because after a while she started to cry and we had to stop for the day.

Another model that looked sad was the gray-eyed girl from the muffin shop down on 86th Street. I went there several times a week for their carob-banana muffins with crusty tops, and when we got to talking she told me she was studying dance and her dream was to be a dancer. I thought posing for me in her leotard and tights might give her a boost, but somehow the picture came out like a frontal view of Christina, the crippled girl in Wyeth's *Christina's World.* The next time I went back to the muffin shop it had closed, so I don't know what became of her dream of dancing.

My dream was to become a professional portrait painter. I had the studio, the right location and the northern light, and when Lenny talked one of his colleagues into having his portrait done I thought I was on my way. But it didn't lead to anything else and I was at a loss how to find clients. They seemed even farther out of reach when I was introduced to a successful portrait artist and his advice was to hang out around wealthy people and mention I did portraits. "The rest will take care of itself," he assured me. Maybe for him. I didn't think much of his gauzy, sentimental portraits, but he was an older man, a European with Old World charm and the accent to go with it, which probably went a long way. But I needn't have worried. Those invisible threads of fate were already weaving a path to my front door.

18

THREADS OF FATE

Serving others uplifts you.
Serving yourself transforms all.

— MATT KAHN

Lenny's friend Greg and the girl he brought with him were hardly in the door and hadn't even taken off their coats yet when the girl burst out, "Do you know you're unlimited? I'm going to take this course called Direct Centering next weekend—want to come? I've already learned how to change the molecules around my body—and I've only been to the introductory meeting!"

This was Liz, the irrepressible twenty-three-year-old Greg found at the Actor's Studio. She had tight blonde curls that bounced when she spoke, and such an intense way about her that she got me to promise I'd come to the next meeting. It was held in a loft downtown where six or seven clean-cut 'graduates' as they called themselves, sat on a raised platform to tell us how the course had changed their lives. But rather than saying how, they said it was something you had to experience for yourself, which meant shelling out two-hundred and fifty dollars for the weekend course. I got up to leave during the break and was set upon by a couple of assistants.

"Are you ready to register?" said one.

"No."

"What's holding you back?" said the other.

"I don't have that kind of money." I thought my tone would have ended it there, but they were just getting started. They alternated with, "It's not about the money, it's about being powerful, having things go your way." And, "Just do it. You're unlimited!"

I returned to my seat but did not change my mind, and went home thinking that was the end of it. I forgot that before the meeting we filled out forms stating our goals, and soon friendly voices were calling and asking how my goal was progressing, saying, "You *can* be a portrait artist! You can, you can!" I thought I could too, but I didn't see how taking their course was going to bring it about.

We saw a lot of Liz that winter. Her goal was to be an actress, and after posing for me she rehearsed her monologues with Lenny. Regardless of how her acting career was going, her high spirits continued unabated. That summer when I moved my studio into the apartment next door, we invited Liz to move into the other half. I rarely heard her in the back, and by then we were all too busy to see one another unless we happened to meet in the hallway. Whenever I met Liz she would invariably say, "Are you ready to take the course yet?" I'd laugh and say "No!" Then one evening we ran into each other when I was coming home from another boring day as a temp, and after being squashed in the subway and walking up from the station and then three flights of stairs to the apartment I was in no mood for her shenanigans. I was fishing for the keys in my bag when she said cheerfully, "Are you ready to take the course yet?"

I dropped what remained of my polite English accent. "Look honey, I'll let you know when I'm ready, okay?"

Liz nodded, her curls bounced, and she said gleefully, "That's good! It's good to see you're not hiding your anger for a change!"

She was impossible. Yet unaccountably, a few days later I handed her a check for the deposit. It was only fifty dollars, but she squealed and jumped up and down as if I'd handed her the lead in a Broadway show.

The deposit entitled me to a detailed written questionnaire where not only did I have to be specific about my goals and intentions and the steps I planned to take, but I had to report on my progress in follow-up calls from interminably friendly voices cheering me on. They also wanted to know when I would send in the balance. My vagueness prompted the next question. "What's holding you back?" I finally gave up and asked Lenny for the money.

As the weekend approached I was excited in spite of myself. Then I was told that instead of the course being held at the center downtown, it had been moved to Philadelphia. I could either come down to Philly or wait a month for the next course in New York. I was psyched for the current weekend and asked where I would stay.

"Manifest a place to stay. Let go of the fear and a place will turn up."

I had never been to Philadelphia and I wasn't sure about traveling alone for a mysterious course billed as life-altering. If Lenny had signed up with me we could have taken the car, stayed in a motel. But Lenny wanted to wait and see how I liked it first. I packed a small case and went down on the train. The taxi dropped me off at an elegant townhouse in a quiet, well-kept residential area. Once I signed in I was directed to the large attic room filled with cots and cushions for the out-of-towners. Why couldn't they have told me about this provision beforehand and put my mind at rest? Liz hadn't mentioned it either. I looked around for her since she promised she would assist at my course, and when I asked where she was I was told she wasn't coming.

There were twenty-five or so participants, and for the next two days we were all going to have the chance to stand on the platform and be grilled by Gavin, the engaging, disarming, charismatic teacher-guru-leader. This short slender boyish man with light-brown hair and light-blue eyes who was so ordinary looking you wouldn't notice him on the street, lorded it over us from a high canvas director's chair in the large parlor room. While one female assistant stood behind massaging his neck and shoulders, another kept his water glass filled and supplied him with freshly squeezed juice as one after another we went up to the platform. Gavin's first question was always why were we there and what did we want, and before you knew what was happening, Gavin would be nailing the issue, telling you to let it go. He called it "discharging," which meant breathing out whatever it was you were wanting. Then he said, "Do you feel lighter now?"

During the breaks we were allowed to stretch and have a glass of water or use the restroom, but it was hardly a break when the cadre of assistants moved in with, "How's it going for you?" "What's coming up?" "What are you attached to?" "Let-go." "Breathe." "Discharge." "Do you feel lighter now?"

I was one of the last to go up, and by that time I was in awe of Gavin and nervous what he might say. I felt so shy about standing on the platform in front of everyone it was hard to believe I once reveled in being the center of attention on stage. Though Gavin was a good twenty feet away I could feel him looking straight through me. He began with, "Why don't you wear contacts? What are you hiding behind those glasses?"

From watching the others, I knew I wouldn't be doing myself any favors if I explained that I left my contacts at home because I didn't know where I would be staying and it was a bother to travel with the disinfecting kit. Gavin wasn't looking for explanations. He was looking for a weakness in the façade. Next he took aim at the choker of large plastic beads around my neck. "Take it off," he said. "It's cutting your head off from your body." As with the glasses, he accused me of hiding myself under the loose-fitting top, calling it a deliberate attempt not to look sexy. This got him started on a rant about the value of looking sexy, and he switched his attention from me to the rest of the room, telling us that showing yourself as a sexual being was a way of serving others because it was an acknowledgement of their sexuality too. Which was nothing less than the life-force, the energy that keeps us all going. I immediately thought of Marilyn Monroe, and for the first time I thought I understood why she was so loved. When Gavin turned his attention back to me and asked why I was taking the course, I said, "I want to be a full-time painter."

"What? I can't hear you. Say it louder!"

My hands started tingling. Everyone was staring at me and it was like that dream when the judge yelled *Who ARE You?* The tingling moved up through my arms and I shouted, "I WANT TO EARN MY LIVING AS A PAINTER!"

"Now breathe and let go of wanting it."

This was his answer to everything. It made no sense until you realized that the act of wanting something presumes you don't have it. To let go is to allow the space for it to come to you. It was all about breathing through the fear.

Dinner that night was a heaping plate of noodles with tofu and vegetables lathered with sesame sauce, the best I had ever tasted. We were all famished since there had been no lunch and breakfast had only been a cup of fresh cantaloupe juice because Gavin thought hunger would keep us awake. On Sunday before we dispersed he gave a lecture on the importance of serving others. Service was the only thing that mattered. If we liked what we learned over the weekend, the only way to keep it was to give it away. Staying centered in your truth by centering others, either by enrolling them in the course or becoming an assistant, preferably both. About half the group, myself included, signed up to assist at the loft downtown.

The center was a hive of activity with assistants coming and going, talking on the phone, talking to one another. There were artists and students, musicians and actors, as well as people in business or the health-care professions. That first week I cleaned the bathroom and vacuumed the main room. The second week I was put to work in the kitchen preparing a meal for thirty people. I thought it must be like joining an ashram, all of us running around, taking orders, doing whatever was needed. I learned that making a space 'flat' meant putting everything away so you could feel the energy of a room rather than be distracted by all the stuff it contained. Cupboards and closets had to be 'flat' too because it was all about vibrations. Even if the door was shut and you couldn't see inside, what was inside affected the energy outside.

Gavin called the exercises where we mirrored each other, intuiting what the other was feeling, a form of 'duplicating.' And since we were always clearing one another, reminding each other to breathe and let go, discharge the limiting thought, I was reminding myself too. When we did distance healing, mentally projecting a beam of white light, I started seeing auras. And when Gavin told us to look at an object until it disappeared, I took him at his word and stared at a lump of quartz crystal for so long without blinking that my eyes watered and the thing did disappear, at least for a moment. Maybe it was only the power of suggestion, but it felt like a new world was opening up. One night I arrived late for a meeting when everyone was already seated in some kind of meditation, and I saw the room bathed in a mist of other-worldly blue light that made me feel I was seeing into another dimension.

Then Gavin commissioned a portrait of himself and I decided to do it big. When Lenny read my palm on our first date he said, 'You've got to paint big!' Now seemed the time. I stretched a canvas five-feet tall. Gavin came up for the sitting and took my picture while I was painting him. He said he'd never seen me so focused and I saw what he meant when he gave me a print. I looked fierce. I may have just been concentrating on the job at hand, but as I stood before the canvas, body taught and at attention, I might have been a warrior going into battle.

After Gavin hung his portrait in the loft I was inundated with offers to pose, and several were commissions. Gratifying as it was, I wondered if my real work might not be at Direct Centering, or *cennering* as they pronounced it, changing people's lives rather than observing them with a paintbrush. There was talk of moving to a larger space and expanding the courses. Gavin was training new teachers, looking for more full-timers. I was spending more and more time at the loft and it would mean being paid. Gavin said in the future everyone would be an artist. One of the assistants said, "Do you want to be in an art history book, or do you want to make a difference *now?*" I wasn't ready to give up art just yet, but it was becoming difficult to fit painting into a schedule that included temping during the day, assisting at night and spending entire weekends downtown when there was a course or an event going on. Lenny and I rarely had time for each other anymore. He had taken the course too and became an assistant for a while, though at different times from me. His goal was to get out of real estate and have his own theater company with Mel. At home he was always with Mel discussing their plans.

It caught up with me on a Friday when I was already exhausted and had a seven a.m. breakfast meeting with my squad. I was up before six that morning knowing I wouldn't be home again until midnight since there was a course on and I'd have to stay for cleanup and another meeting afterwards. Then I'd have to be up before six again on Saturday and spend the whole day there. I used to enjoy strategizing and sharing notes for the upcoming course over breakfast at the coffee shop, but just then I didn't have the energy or the desire for analyzing other people's issues. I arrived late and the group was already deep in conversation. They had a booth by the entrance and I was distracted by the door opening and closing, then by the waiters darting this way and that and the busboys clattering dishes into carts. I thought I'd perk up once we left the crowded restaurant, but outside was just as bad. As we made our way back to the center and the others were still discussing our assignments, I was aware of the cars and people rushing by on their way to work, and felt hemmed in by the tall buildings on either side of the street. Was there no escape from the noise and the crowds? And just as I was thinking how I wanted it all to stop, my knees gave way and I would have fallen if one of the assistants hadn't grabbed me. I limped the rest of the way back to the center with one of them holding me up on either side. They wanted me to come upstairs and lie down but I felt like I'd blown a fuse and all I wanted to do was go home.

I stayed in bed for a week, and for once I was glad the bedroom was always dark. Colleen said, "You forgot your floating-time." Floating time. That was it. I pictured myself drifting freely in a timeless realm. While Lenny went to work and the rest of the world went about its business, I floated towards the horizon, maybe to slip through that sliver of space between sea and sky. The gap between here and there I once pictured on my ocean voyage five years ago. A world where space seemed unlimited and time uncertain when you had to keep changing the time on your wristwatch every day. You could be here or there or somewhere in between and there was no way to tell when the fog rolled in. I thought of the Direct Centering logo, a thick black coil spiraling inwards. I had been caught in its spin, and all I wanted to do now was unwind. Float in a timeless, boundless world.

When I did go back to the center it wasn't for long. I knew I was finished the night I stood before the group and pointed to the far corner of the ceiling as if it was a star-filled sky. "I want to go back there," I said. I had never told anyone this before and I don't know where I got the courage that night. It was one of the regular meetings Gavin held for assistants when he talked about plans for the future and we could ask questions or share whatever we felt like. I raised my hand because I thought if anyone understood the place I was talking about it would be Gavin. "Oh, you just want to go back to the womb," he said, and called on the next person.

The womb? I was stunned he would think that. It was an

appalling idea, starting life all over again. I didn't want to come back *here*, I want to go back *there*. I didn't know where it was exactly, just that it wasn't here. The longing began when I reached my teens and would look up at the moon or the stars and plead with them to take me back. I'd drawn a picture of it once on black scratchboard, scratching away the black to reveal a girl sitting in the window, bathed in moonlight, staring up at the moon. Scratching away the dark to reveal the light underneath. The light *back there*.

Now that I knew Gavin didn't really see me, I began noticing the other assistants didn't really see me either. I knew we weren't there to make each other feel comfortable, but it was getting tiresome hearing the newer recruits accuse me of not being real. What did they even mean by 'real'? I was good natured about it at first, smiling and saying, "I *am* being real." But it seemed pointless after a while. I knew the game too well. In the name of support you poked around for someone's weakness until they became defensive. Then you'd say, "Why can't you take support? What are you hiding?" A girl no more than twenty thought she could get a rise out of me by calling me old. If she was looking for a chink in my armor, she wouldn't find it there. I was thirty-one, and I had decided my thirties were going to be wonderful. If there was a chink anywhere, it was the gap in the horizon. I wouldn't have known where to look for it, but I knew how to float now, and I was already headed there whether I knew it or not.

19

THE DREAMER

Dreams pass through into the reality of action.
From the actions stems the dream again.

— ANAÏS NIN

I had no reason to think painting Martha would be different from painting any other model. She was a friend of Marcy, the married woman Lenny was having an affair with when we first dated. Marcy was divorced now and gave massages. I was used to Lenny staying in touch with former girlfriends, especially if they were in A.A. He hadn't managed to get Marcy into the program, but he liked a deep massage and went to her regularly. I didn't care for them myself, neither the giving nor the receiving, and preferred studying the shape and color of flesh rather than digging my fingers into it. When Lenny told her I was looking for models, he might have been hoping Marcy herself would pose, but she sent her friend Martha over instead.

When Martha called to set up an appointment I told her to wear whatever she'd like to see herself painted in. I said this to everyone now. It was more interesting to see people in their own clothes now that I'd grown tired of looking at them in mine. She arrived in jeans and sneakers but brought something to change into. I left her alone to dress, and when I came back she had on a bright green gown that set off her pale freckled skin and the lush strawberry-blonde hair cascading past her shoulders. A pendent necklace with a green stone lay on her chest. I didn't ask if it was a real emerald because I was going to paint it as if it was. I complemented her on the dress and wished I could have painted her standing, but the canvas I prepared wasn't the right shape so she had to be seated. I put the wicker chair on the platform and then felt like moving the platform from its usual place by the window and placing it in front of the French doors for a change. I had never used the doors as a background before, and I could see how the panes of glass would break up the space behind her and add something extra.

Martha stepped onto the platform and sat with her hands resting on her thighs. I said, "Would you mind taking off your sneakers?"

"Oh, sorry! If I knew you were doing a full-length I would have brought dress shoes." Her high thin voice didn't match the majestic persona on the makeshift throne.

"Bare feet will be a nice touch," I assured her. But her posture looked stiff so I looked around for something to raise one of her knees and break up the static of her pose. The milkcrate worked, and I went about setting up my palette. This was usually the time I chatted to models to help them relax and be more natural. Yet with Martha there seemed no need as she already appeared calm and serene, gazing into the distance as if she'd already floated there in her thoughts.

And there my recollection of the session ended. I have no memory of what it was like painting her, whether we finished it that day or if she came back a second time. This wasn't unusual. I often remembered nothing once I started a picture and entered that non-verbal zone only paint could describe. Yet for a picture that would come to mean as much to me as this one did, it seemed odd not to recall a single thing, almost as if I hadn't been there.

I couldn't help studying the canvas afterwards though. I always studied my finished work to see what I had done right or what I could have done better. Part of my morning ritual was coming into the studio with a mug of coffee and curling up in the green armchair to take an unhurried look at whatever happened to be on the easel or hanging on the walls. One after another, people had come to share themselves for a few hours and leave their presence behind. As new ones arrived I hung their pictures up to dry and put the older ones in the stack against the wall. Yet somehow Martha never made it to the stack. I found myself endlessly drawn to her likeness. She wasn't doing anything more than just sitting there with her foot on the milkcrate while she stared into the distance, yet she seemed to be directing my gaze there too. *Where, Martha? What do you want me to see?*

I called the painting the *Dreamer*, but she wasn't a passive dreamer, an asleep person. This dreamer was awake, focusing her eyes on something. Yet she didn't seem entirely in the waking world either. She was here, but not here. Or half-here, poised on the threshold to somewhere else. The dream world perhaps? She sat so still and attentive, her back to the open French door, gazing into the distance with a knowing look while I gazed at her. What did she see? She wasn't looking through the doorway. The door was behind her and she was already beyond it. What was beyond the doorway? What did she see beyond the door that was both here and not here?

It didn't occur to me to think it had anything to do with the doors to the closets that separated the studio from the apartment I shared with Lenny. They were two different worlds, art and regular life, yet they existed side by side, parallel universes at the same address on 86th Street. Maybe I was thinking of my Dream of '76 when a door appeared at the bottom of the sea and opened into more sea. Maybe I hadn't forgotten it after all. Maybe I was telling myself that the *Dreamer*, me, had come through the door. And I was beyond it now, on my way to the inner world, the inner-see.

Maybe it wasn't just by chance that a friend of a friend of Lenny's showed up one day and gave me pause. Maybe certain people showed up in our lives to move us along. Maybe I knew what I was doing when I moved the platform over to the French doors. Maybe I remained engaged with the picture long after the paint was dry because Martha's image was a reminder to keep looking for something I couldn't yet see. Her green dress like a green light was giving me the go-ahead to keep looking for the gap that led to another place. I couldn't see what she saw, but I could see *her* seeing it. And I called her the *Dreamer*, I think because part of me remembered my dream, even though I wasn't conscious of it. Whatever it was, the door was open. I'd found a way in through paint. All I had to do was keep going into that dreamlike space, that subtler world which was here and not here.

20

THE KEY

To invent your own life's meaning is not easy, but it's still allowed, and I think you'll be happier for the trouble.

— BILL WATERSON

Marcy of the wavy yellow locks came to pose next. Lenny said she was beautiful, but he'd been in love with her once. She was shiny, I'll give her that, but her lips were thin and there was a tightness around her mouth that gave her an unforgiving look. She changed into the long white terry robe she'd brought with her, the kind you'd wear at a spa, and covered her feet with thick white socks. When I invited her to take whatever pose she liked in the green armchair, she brought a knee up to her chest and clasped her arms around it protectively. With every inch of herself covered but her hands and face, she sat glaring at me with narrow cat-like eyes as if we were going head-to-head in the silence.

During the break when she shook out her mane, languidly combing her hair with her fingers, she told me about Roy. "I don't really want to see him anymore," she said. "He's twenty-five, a little young for me, but he's got an interesting face. You'd probably enjoy painting him. It would be good for him too."

I sensed the unspoken suggestion that if Roy posed for me, he could be eased out of her own life more smoothly. "Tell him to call me," I said.

A few weeks later Roy showed up to pose. Marcy said he was a Jewish Buddhist who taught fencing, but when I opened the door I saw a character from Dostoyevsky. His face was thin with high cheekbones and a closely trimmed beard, but it was the gravity of his expression as much as the intensity of his eyes. Then he came in, and when I saw the large cloth bag slung over his shoulder and heard the clump of his boots on the floorboards as I led him through the apartment to the studio next door, I thought of a woodsman in a fairy tale. There was another clump when he dropped the bag on the floor and said in a soft deep voice, "Where can I put this?"

"By the wall there is fine. What have you got in there, bricks?"

"Fencing equipment," he said, taking off his glasses along with his jacket. He was tall and wiry, all muscle and bone in the white tee-shirt tucked neatly into black sweat pants. His movements were slow and deliberate, and when he arched his back and did a few neck rolls, I thought of a panther. Then I thought of placing him on the cot with a throw blanket that had a black and brown design suggestive of tiger skin. I'd rented the cot for my mother's visit. She didn't live in New York anymore and had moved back to Illinois to look after Gramps. She stayed with us for a week, but the cot was rented by the month so I still had it. I said, "Would you like to try lying on the bed? You'll have to take your boots off."

He sat on the cot to untie the laces, then got into a sort of half-sitting, half-lying position against the pillow with one knee up on the bed and the other leg draped over the side with his foot on the floor. His white socks were glaringly out of place. I said, "Would you mind taking off your socks?"

Now it was the white tee-shirt that was jarring. When he took that off too, I saw how well it all came together. Dark hair and beard, dark curly chest-hair with the black sweat pants and tiger skin blanket. I was doing a side view, but I wanted to see more of his face. I held up a finger and said, "Could you look here so I can see more of your face?"

"I don't like my face. Can't you paint my foot instead?"

I was squeezing out a tube of paint and said absently, "You have a nice face."

"No one's ever said that to me before."

I looked up. He was looking away. My response had been automatic. I didn't know what to say in return so I got on with the sketch. We didn't speak for the rest of the session. I was engrossed in studying the beard that squared off his jaw, adding austerity to an expression that was already bleak. He looked open but so absorbed in his thoughts I wondered if he was meditating. We made an appointment for the following week, and after I showed him out I came back to clean up. Now that he was no longer in the room, I could see his expression was serious rather than bleak. The canvas needed some color though. It was all blacks and browns and beige. I had to think of something to brighten it up.

A few days later when I went grocery shopping, the red label on a coke bottle caught my eye. I bought the jumbo-size so it wouldn't get lost in the rest of the picture and poured half down the sink so it wouldn't look full. I doubted

Roy ever touched the stuff; he looked more the green tea, macrobiotic type. At our next session I placed the coke bottle beside his foot on the floor and said, "For a bit of color." Roy made no response. He was already in his still and silent place. I wondered if Marcy had broken up with him yet.

Being alone with him felt strange this time, almost intimate the way he was allowing me to look at him while he looked away. He was near me, almost too near, so that painting the hair on his chest was like touching his chest with my brush. I had painted other men alone in my studio before, one of whom lay completely naked on the platform. He was gay, but even the ones who were straight hadn't affected me. Maybe it was because I could read them, and I couldn't get a handle on Roy. Between this second session and the third I decided to call the painting, *Young Man With Coke Bottle,* and found myself staring at it for the sheer pleasure of looking at him in private. I wondered if I had a crush on him. I couldn't remember the last time I'd had a crush on someone, and it was surprisingly pleasurable to contemplate.

When he came for the third session I was all too aware it would be the last and I would never see him again unless I asked him to pose for another. If we did do another I would have him looking directly at me so that I could see into his eyes, maybe find out who he was. And then the painting was finished, and Roy, who had expressed no interest in seeing the picture in progress, came around to the other side of the easel to have a look.

"You've made me better looking than in real life," he said.

I was wiping my brushes on a paper towel and mumbled something about how that wasn't true, but of course I knew I had romanticized him. Softened the lines of his face and found a harmony in his features that wasn't exactly a lie, but neither was it the whole truth. I hadn't done it on purpose, yet neither had I made anything up. It just came out that way. After that remark about not liking his face, I assumed he was in the habit of looking at himself critically, but it didn't mean I had to.

He was sitting on the cot, lacing up his boots. I was going to miss seeing him lace up his boots. I felt shy about asking him for another pose, but it was now or never since in another moment he would be putting on his jacket and I'd be seeing him to the door for the last time. I tried to sound nonchalant, as if it was nothing to me one way or the other, but the words came out in a rush. "How would you feel about doing another painting with me?"

"I'd be flattered."

That didn't sound right. I didn't want him to think I was trying to flatter him. I said, "Maybe you could wear your fencing outfit and I could paint you as a fencer."

He showed up the following week dressed as a samurai. His whole persona changed when he put on the dark blue kimono, the heavy fabric down to his ankles disguising his slight frame, giving him an air of authority. I asked him to sit on the stool I'd placed on the platform so we'd be at eye-level, but it made him too high and now I had to look up at him. Instead of a foil, a curved sword lay across his knees. I got my wish of being able to look into his eyes, but it was like looking into the eyes of an executioner. His face was expressionless. The session was more like an encounter, which wasn't at all what I had in mind. It wasn't that his eyes were cold, more that they were devoid of sentiment, as if he had scraped away every last spec of his personality. And then, because he was looking at me, I felt him watching my every move. I could feel his eyes on me even when I wasn't looking at him. I squirmed inside, and if I hadn't been the one wielding the brush, I would have thought he held all the power with that unblinking stare that seemed to look right through me. It went against everything I found safe about painting. Being the one behind the easel, calling the shots, saying where to move, where to look, when to take a break. I thought I'd gotten over the fear of being looked at. Yet now, even when I was hidden behind the easel I felt exposed, and wished I'd had the foresight to wear a smock over my tee-shirt and jeans. I thought of putting it on during the break, but I didn't want him to think I was trying to cover myself up because of him. Of course there was also the possibility he wasn't thinking about me at all.

With so many extraneous thoughts running through my head, it's a wonder I stayed focused as well as I did. The canvas was larger than the first one, and though there was more space to fill, there was less detail. The background was formless swirls of orange and pink, violet and yellow. Warm bright colors to offset the severity of his expression and contrast the dark blue kimono that absorbed the light. The painting was finished in two sessions instead of three, and as I watched him fold the kimono and put it away, I wasn't going to ask him to sit for me again. I had come up with a better idea. I would ask to join his fencing class. That way I could see him on a regular basis and it would be in a group setting. I pictured us going for coffee after class. I said lightly, as if the thought had just occurred to me, "I used to take fencing at drama school and I'm thinking of taking it up again. Is that the kind you teach?"

He laughed. I'd made him laugh. Then he said, "I think you'd find my teaching methods quite different from those you had in the past."

"Oh?" This was actually good news since I hadn't liked

fencing at school. Then, from hardly saying a word to me before, he was almost loquacious as he spoke about the class and where I could purchase a foil. I wrote it down, including the address of the studio he rented by the hour in Chelsea. After he left I congratulated myself on this brilliant move.

That night I mentioned to Lenny I was thinking of joining Roy's fencing class. He looked up from the tv and said, "Fencing lessons? That's a great idea for you!" Then he shook his head and clicked his tongue as if to say what will she come up with next?

After I bought a foil I went to Woolworth's for some fabric to make a carrying case for it. I didn't need anything else. Roy said he supplied the helmets, breast plates and gloves. That explained the lumps in the bag always hanging from his shoulder when he came by.

The class met on Sunday afternoons after a belly-dancing session. When we began trickling into the large mirrored room with a shiny hardwood floor, the belly-dancing instructor would invariably be in harem pants, stuffing colorful chiffon scarves and tinkling bells into assorted tote bags. There were ten or twelve of us in the class, and never more than one or two other women. Roy said to wear exercise clothes and bare feet, so I wore the black leotard and tights I'd kept from dance classes years ago. He began with floor exercises for limbering up. I was stiff, and wished I hadn't given up jogging around the reservoir in Central Park. After the stretches we practiced the moves I remembered from school. *En garde* was for getting into position. The others, Advance, Retreat, Lunge, Deflect, Parry and Deflect, were self-explanatory, but they had a different meaning when Roy paired me with one of the men. At Rada I'd only fenced with other girls. Behind the vests and screened helmets I could hardly tell who was who anyway, but Roy didn't take our differences in height and weight into account either. He said, "It's not strength that matters but intelligence."

The gloves were large and bulky, soiled on the outside and uncomfortably damp on the inside. We were a faceless breed with muffled voices, menacing each other with metal sticks. Roy said, "Don't worry if your opponent hits you. A hit shows where you are vulnerable. Try to experience it as a kiss." It didn't feel like a kiss when I got poked in the chest. The breast plate softened the blow but it still hurt. After a few weeks I started wondering what I was doing there. I didn't like fighting. Not verbally, and certainly not physically, and aside from the nod he gave me at the first class, Roy paid no attention to me at all.

Then he paired me with Sam who was six-foot-four. One of Roy's instructions was, "Think of his next move before he does, like playing chess." But with Sam it was all I could do not to panic when I saw a faceless hulk honing in on me with a long stick. My brain said, *Retreat! Retreat!* but Roy might be watching. I reminded myself this was only pretend fighting, and Sam, despite his long limbs, wasn't particularly quick. Maybe he was slower than usual that day, or maybe along with dodging his foil, I thought of his next move, because I caught him off guard and lunged, and got him in the chest. There was a gleeful smile behind my mask as I mouthed to myself, *I won! I won!*

I was starting to like fencing. I looked forward to Sundays even though I was losing hope I would ever have that coffee with Roy. After class the other students crowded around him, wanting his attention. The self-contained presence he had shown in my studio, combined with his unquestioned authority as a teacher, brought out a worshipful adoration in his students. They knew he cared about them; I felt it too, but I could never get him alone. I tried lingering by the door with my coat on, and when he failed to notice, I timed it so we would arrive downstairs together. But when he saw me outside, he gave me a wave and headed west to his train. My train was east.

Since Lenny and I were practically leading separate lives by then, it didn't occur to me that Roy would think me off limits because I was married. Yet indeed this was the case, because one Sunday when I didn't expect it, we made it to the coffee shop and I mentioned I was in an open marriage. This wasn't actually true, but it felt true, and when the time was right I was going to suggest it to Lenny. I still had the book, *Open Marriage* he gave me when we got engaged, and I would tell him I had finally come round.

This much anticipated coffee shop event led to kissing on the street. How it came to that, and the order of things afterwards, remains a blur. The memories are piecemeal. A few hours here, a few there, made it all seem unreal. Except for the kissing. The kisses at the bus stop or in doorways when it rained always felt real. It was real when we sat on the grass in the park or on the sand at the beach when I packed a lunch and took the day off. I don't remember where I told Lenny I was going with the car. Lenny had nothing to do with it. This was about me and Roy.

Roy took me up to his sparse little room at the top of a brownstone that faced a dark courtyard. A room so small he had to keep the futon rolled up so there would be room to walk. Being up there with him was like being tucked away in a cubbyhole off to the side of the world. Time with him was time stolen from a day I could have been temping, an evening I could have gone to a sketch class or seen a movie with Colleen. But there was never enough time to be with him, so all of it was precious and secret, and stolen from somewhere else I could have been.

Lenny was wrong about 'love and be free.' If you loved someone, why would you want to be free? Love wasn't free. The cost might not come until later, but there was a price. And you'd willingly pay if love made you feel whole again, even for a little while. I had that feeling of wholeness with Roy. I didn't ask myself why or feel the need to verbalize it to myself, but now that I think about it, it had to do with his sadness. I saw it in his face that first time he came to my door and I thought I was looking at a character from Dostoevsky. Sadness was really too tame. It was more like he sensed the tragedy of life, even with his wry sense of humor. My tendency was to breeze past my own sadness. I didn't want to look at the darkness below the surface, and being with Roy seemed to balance me out. If he never seemed happy, he never seemed unhappy either. Maybe it was because he was a Buddhist. I couldn't forget that when the alter with a statue of the Buddha was always on his chest of drawers. And yet when I lay with him on the futon in that dark narrow room, I found something I hadn't known I was missing. And I cherished it, the more so as I knew it wouldn't last between us.

Roy talked of buying a boat and sailing around the world. Why shouldn't he? He was younger than I was and had a young man's dreams. I bought him a book on navigation to show him I understood. I liked giving him presents. I had nothing more to give Lenny, and Roy had so little, just that room hardly bigger than a utility closet.

Then I found something better to give him. I was in the Hallmark Store buying him a card, standing on line for the cashier and gazing at the rack of trinkets on the counter. One of them was a tiny gold heart the size of a thumbnail and came with a tiny toy key. And suddenly I knew that Roy was the key. I put it together, my attraction to the young man with dreams that didn't include me, and the summer I was seventeen when the first boy I loved left town without saying goodbye. I waited for the call that never came, and after a few weeks I vowed never to give myself away again. By the time a letter arrived saying he was sorry, explaining his sudden departure to the west coast, it was too late. My mother had left me at her boyfriend's. And still love found me, but he left for England. And though his dreams did include me—You'll come too, he said, it could never be the same. I saw it so clearly it was like the clouds had parted. Maybe it was Roy's stoicism, his lack of showing emotion, the way he never put anything on me, that allowed me to see myself.

I taped the key inside the card and wrote, "The key to my heart." It was my 'young girl's heart.' I got the phrase from Colleen who got it from Yeats, and spoke of her 'young girl's heart' as if it was the best, most indestructible part of her. I understood that now. It had to be that because I had been feeling like a teenager again. I was even craving french fries, ordering a side of fries to go with my salad when Colleen and I met at the coffee shop. Then I started going to coffee shops alone just for a salad and fries. It was the confusion all mixed up with being excited about life and wondering what would happen next.

The heart was mine but the key was for Roy. Through him I'd been able to unlock the place where it felt broken and bruised and see it for what it was. When I gave Roy the card with the key inside I didn't tell him the story behind it. He didn't need to know all that. "Thank you," he said in that rather formal way of his. But I felt him pull back slightly. I hoped he didn't think I was placing a burden on him. It was just a symbol that's all.

Then Lenny found out about us. I don't remember how. Maybe I'd gotten careless because I didn't care anymore. When Lenny said, "What do you see in that skinny guy," there were so many things I could have said, like how Roy let me nurture him.

It was while he was posing for me a third time after I quit the fencing class. He arrived looking more pale than usual and complained of a migraine. Lenny was at work and I told Roy to lie down on the couch in the living room. "Go on," I said, "take off your boots. Put your head on the cushion." I filled a bowl with ice-water and made a cold compress for his forehead, dampening the cloth when it became warm from his skin. He didn't accuse me of mothering him; he said it made his headache go away.

Roy was nude in this third painting, standing on the platform at ease in his body, holding onto a wooden pole that went up to his shoulder, using it like a walking stick, as though he was embarking on a journey. I was okay with that. He was leaving me, but I could put him on the platform and capture it, watch him in the act of leaving and see that he had to go. With his dark hair and beard and the air of solemnity that seemed ingrained, the word Biblical came to mind. Then the name Adam. I painted a landscape around him of grass and sky with hills beyond, and thought of him as Adam, the first man. And Roy, the first man to affect me through painting him. The first lover I painted nude. The first man I could open my heart to even though I knew he wasn't going to stay because he made me feel whole again. The first man, and maybe the only one, who showed me that despite everything, my young girl's heart was still intact.

21

AFTERMATH

New beginnings are often described as painful endings.

— LAO TZU

Then I saw there had to be an Eve. There couldn't be an Adam without an Eve. Until now each model had been in a narrative of their own. I'd never thought of paintings that went together as a pair, but Eve had to be here too. I started looking for her at the Open Sketch Class at the League from five to six which was free for members. There was a different model every day. I had no idea what she would look like or what I was looking for because she wasn't for me, she was for Roy's Adam. And then I saw Mindy, an exotic beauty of mixed race with a long slender body and short wavy hair. I waited for her in the hallway after class and said, "Do you ever pose privately?"

"No. I don't do that sort of thing."

I quickly added, "It would only be for me, no one else. My studio is at 86th and Lexington. It's really easy to get to. I'll pay you double what you get here."

"I can only do evenings," she said.

"Perfect."

Mindy was perfect. I didn't have a preconceived idea of how Eve would pose, and told her to take any position she felt comfortable with. My only request was that she look to her left as Adam was looking to the right because I wanted them to be looking towards each other when I placed the canvases side by side. Mindy shifted her weight to one leg and folded her hands in front of her crotch. Her large brown eyes had a wary look. But however shy and defensive the pose, Mindy herself couldn't have been more open and sure of herself when we started chatting. "I'm tired of being pushed around," she said. "If my boyfriend takes me to the movies and asks what I'd like to see, I always say whatever he likes is fine. Why do I do that? I just want to be myself. Who *I* am. I'm tired of trying to get their approval. I'm turning over a new leaf."

Mindy was from the Bronx. I didn't know anyone from the Bronx and I wanted to hear about her life, but I think she ended up hearing more about mine. It was like meeting a stranger on a train or a plane, opening up to them because you'll never see them again. First I brought up Roy to explain the Adam painting. I hadn't meant to tell her about our affair which had ended when Lenny found out. Then I felt the need to justify the affair by filling her in on Lenny's trips to Club Med and the swinging. She said, "No!" about the first, "Disgusting!" about the second.

My stand-in for Eve not only made all the right noises, she was more supportive than the female therapist Lenny and I were seeing after he put his foot down about Roy and said, "It's him or me." In the therapy sessions he played the wronged husband and cast me as the wife who strayed. Couples therapy wasn't going to fix us. I didn't see the point in rehashing the past and defending myself. I arrived wearing a black beret with a sparkling crescent moon pinned to the front and kept it on during the sessions because it symbolized my connection to Diana, goddess of the moon. Of all the gods and goddesses she was the one I related to, the free and independent huntress.

If the therapy sessions left me with a sense of failure, our marriage as a lost cause, painting Mindy left me energized and excited. Her Eve had feet firmly planted on the ground. If Adam was going off somewhere, leaving her behind, she may have looked sad staring after him warily as she watched him go, but she stood her ground as if to say, *It stops here.* She may have looked stricken, but she would be fine. No matter what Adam did she would be fine because she had herself. I would be fine too. There had never been any future with Roy and I'd had to let him go, but he would be fine, whether or not he ever went sailing around the world.

In the midst of all this I felt the need to try another painting from my imagination. Something in me had shifted and I wanted to express it somehow. I mentioned the idea to Mindy, telling her how I'd thrown away my first attempt a few years ago and wasn't sure I'd be any more successful this time.

"You have to!" she cried. "It doesn't matter how it turns out. Don't think of it like that. It's for you. That's the only thing that counts. *You.*"

I felt obliged to make the effort now. I hadn't asked 'what about me' in a long time, not consciously anyway. But yes. What *about* me. It wasn't Lenny encouraging me this time, it was Mindy, almost as if I had to do it for her as much as for myself. And I didn't want to let her down. I had to get on with it too if I wanted her to see it before we finished with Eve. Maybe I also had to do it for Eve. Like the key I gave to Roy that was more for me than for him, the Eve I painted for Adam seemed to be more for me too.

The whole thing was fraught from the start. I knew I was going to paint what I hadn't been able to say in words, and none of it was easy. From choosing the size of the stretchers to stapling the canvas to setting it on the easel and locking it in place, each step seemed to require another level of courage. Yet once I began I couldn't stop. I hadn't made any preliminary drawings and I can't say how clear the picture was in my mind before I began, but I went at it without second-guessing myself, so maybe I had the whole thing planned out in my mind beforehand. I had worried that I wouldn't be able to draw figures without a model in front of me, but I was so engrossed in the subject matter that I hardly noticed how easy it was. Neither did I stop to wonder whether the picture was good or not, or had any merit because it seemed as if it was painting itself. And even though I cried through most of it I didn't stop. I kept going because I had to. It was now or never. I had to be honest. I had to keep painting the feelings I couldn't tell Lenny and certainly not the therapist. Mindy knew without my having to spell it out. But it was a picture of sadness, not vindication, and it saddened me more to know that despite everything I had done to free myself, I was still carrying around not only the feeling of loss, but the sense that something had gone terribly wrong and I didn't know how to fix it.

It was a picture of a melancholy room with sad purple walls. The yellow paper lantern hanging from the ceiling didn't brighten the mood. A window in the background overlooked the city, and on the table was a vase of yellow chrysanthemums that signified happier days. The bed in the foreground with a brass headboard like the one I had growing up was half-covered with a green sheet, and on the sheet lay a woman facing the viewer. She lay on her side, her back to the man sitting on the other side of the bed. She was naked, he was clothed. She faced her nakedness, he faced the door, and she looked desolate. It was hard to look at. Whenever I left the studio I covered the canvas with a sheet. I'd never done such a thing before, but then I'd never shown myself so nakedly before. Not even in *Au-Pair Girls*. Lenny would know the truth now. So would everyone else who saw it. I hadn't thought of that, how there would be no more pretending.

Lenny never came into the studio without knocking, and if I didn't have a model I'd shout, 'Come in!' But not this time. Not with this picture that made me feel so exposed. Now when he knocked and called through the door, "Can I see what you're working on?" I yelled back it wasn't finished, even though it was. But after a few days I had to let him in because putting him off was only adding to his curiosity.

I'd been afraid to show it to him, afraid he'd see the real me, how I felt inside, but he saw nothing. He said, "Oh my god!" and clapped his hand over his mouth like he did in the old days when I showed him my new work and he wanted me to think it was wonderful. Lenny thought this picture was wonderful too. This possibility had not occurred to me. Didn't he know it was us? The woman didn't look like me and you couldn't see the man's face, but couldn't he tell? I may not have been able to speak the words, but the woman's face, their backs to one another, said it all. Even if he thought it was wonderful that I could paint from my imagination, the picture was the opposite of wonderful.

I decided to call it *Aftermath*. After all was said and done, this was where we were. And this was where I was, still feeling unseen. At least it was clear to me now. This four-foot tall, four-and-a-half-foot-wide canvas was a confession of what I knew inside. Maybe I was still in the place where I'd always been, but I could see it now. I wasn't afraid to look anymore. Five years after the Dream of '76, waking up at dawn after being given a light, knowing that I would only find out what I knew inside by painting or writing, I had painted my first picture. Painted what I felt inside. In my young girl's heart.

But I couldn't leave it like that. It couldn't be the end. Lenny once told me that if I felt rejected it didn't mean I had to reject myself. What would be next? What would happen now? Now that I knew I could paint without models, a follow-up image began taking shape in my mind. I began making sketches of a woman outdoors. She was out of the house, away from that melancholy room, having a picnic by herself. I was anxious to start the painting until I realized I couldn't do it while I was still under Lenny's roof. If she was alone, she had to really be alone. No more pretending. I was done with that. I had given voice to a silent place inside, and if I was going to be true to myself, there couldn't be any more lies.

Roy and Mindy's *Adam* and *Eve* had become characters in my inner play. If he went off to do his own thing, she could make a new life for herself, have a picnic on her own on the green-green grass, not that green sheet anymore. If Martha's *Dreamer* in a green gown, seeing through the doorway, had green-lighted the path to *Aftermath*, I would go to the green grass where Eve stood her ground, and claim it for myself.

PART II

JOURNEY TO THE DEEP
1982-1986

It isn't possible to love and part. You will wish that it was. You can transmute it, ignore it, muddle it, but you can never pull it out of you. I know by experience that the poets are right: love is eternal.

— E. M. FORSTER
A ROOM WITH A VIEW

22

FIRST CONNECTIONS

Brooklyn was a dream. All the things that happened there just couldn't happen. It was all dream stuff. Or was it all real and true and was it that she, Francie, was the dreamer?

— BETTY SMITH
A TREE GROWS IN BROOKLYN

When the train left Bowling Green, the last stop in Manhattan and rumbled under the East River, I left behind the only New York I had ever known. Brooklyn subway stations had names I'd never heard of. They looked dingier too, and not as well-lit as those in Manhattan. I stayed on the train until Utica Avenue, the end of the line, 27 stops from 86th Street, and by then I was usually the only white person left on the train. Coming up the stairs to Eastern Parkway, nothing towering over me but the blue sky above, added to the sense of being somewhere different. It was one of the first things I noticed about Brooklyn, the single-family homes and low buildings which didn't block out the sky and gave you the feeling of more air, more freedom, more possibilities. On my way down Utica Avenue when I passed the Arab-owned grocery store, the Haitian bakery displaying cakes and buns flavored with coconut, and the Korean produce stand with strange-looking fruits and vegetables I had never seen before, I might have thought I had landed in another country rather than another borough. But I had wanted somewhere different, and Crown Heights in 1982 was like being thrust into a host of new of streams all at once.

When I told Lenny I was moving to Crown Heights he said, "You can't move there. That's crazy!" His cousin Mel chimed in with, "It's dangerous! What about the race riots?"

There hadn't been any riots in years. I didn't care what Lenny and his cousin thought. I couldn't afford to stay in Manhattan. In the five years since moving back to New York the rents had skyrocketed. I wanted someplace new and unfamiliar, away from everything connected with Lenny and whatever else felt false about my life. I had only been to Brooklyn a couple of times, and not since high school. In those days I had no interest in the outer boroughs, but times had changed. I had a good feeling when I signed up at the real estate office on Kingston with the kindly old man with a long white beard and the black hat and coat worn by Hasidim. Then an equally kind younger man in a yarmulke took me for a walk down quiet tree-lined streets with houses that charmed me. The apartment I found on the second floor of a semi-detached, two-story house near the border of East New York had windows overlooking a grassy front lawn. The agent said the house number added up to fifteen. "A six in numerology. The number of Venus, goddess of love," he said. I didn't need a reminder who Venus was, but numerology sounded interesting.

The Hasidim were interesting too. My new neighbors with their uniform way of dressing and practice of ancient customs were a never-ending source of fascination. From my second-floor window I watched mothers in wigs and long skirts pushing strollers while a gaggle of small children trailed alongside. When the warm weather came I noticed that even young girls never went outside without long sleeves and tights, leaving only their face and hands exposed. Hasidic women wore dark or subdued colors, whereas the Haitian women on the other side of my house and up the block who also had lots of children, paraded down the street in brightly colored hats and shoes on their way to church on Sunday. Friday and Saturday nights, Hasidic men walked in groups with white prayer shawls draped across their shoulders as they sang on their way back from Shul. Friday nights if I looked out my side windows, I could see into the neighbor's dining room next door and have a partial view of them sitting around the table with their guests as they celebrated the Sabbath with songs in Hebrew. If walking down Utica was like being in another country, watching my Hasidic neighbors on President Street was like being in another century. Perhaps somewhere in Eastern Europe like the paintings displayed at the gallery on Kingston that celebrated village life in a shtetl.

The thought that my ancestors on Milton's side might have worn those same clothes and sung those same songs made me feel closer to them. I had grown up thinking I was a WASP with a dash of Irish Catholic until my mother broke the news I had a different father, which meant I had a different background and was a different me. When I left the country to be an actress in England, she sent me books trying to interest me in Judaism but all I cared about in those days was acting. I wasn't at the age when I wanted to think about my roots or be more involved with family. It was different now. And different here, in this strange and unfamiliar setting I had somehow gravitated to. My mother hadn't stopped sending me books either. When I told her about the neighborhood I'd landed in, she sent me *The Romance of Hasidism*. Colleen already thought my living in Crown Heights was romantic. When she braved the long subway ride from the Upper East Side she said, "You're adventurous. I think it's romantic, your living here." Dear Colleen. And I hadn't even had to tell her about my house being the number of Venus.

I thought of other things that made it special, like living on a street called President, the highest office in the land. The phrase 'Crown Heights' suggested more high places. My house was located between Utica and Schenectady, which were the names of cities in upstate New York, but Utica was also the name of an ancient Phoenician city, while Schenectady was a Mohawk word. Sss-connectedy. A place of connecting. Which was exactly what it turned out to be. For it was in Brooklyn that I realized calling myself 'Renoir' in a dream, meant Re-noir, regarding the black, the dark, the shadow self. The other side of the world of appearances. It was the second time a dream let me know I had knowledge inside, but it wouldn't be until I moved to Brooklyn that I started connecting to a hidden part of myself.

One morning soon after the move the landlord sent a man up to fix the leak in the kitchen faucet. Though he was Hasidic and wore a beard, he also wore jeans and an army-green jacket. And instead of a hat, he wore a cap to cover his head. I sat at the kitchen table with my coffee and watched him work. I missed having company, and when he finished with the faucet I asked if he'd like a coffee.

"Do you have a paper cup or an empty glass jar I could drink it from?" he asked. I did not. Nor did I know what it meant to be kosher. He sat down anyway, and I studied his face with high cheek bones and deep-set eyes while he reached for the thermos in his bag. He took a drink and said, "What's a woman like you doing out here?"

A shiksa, he meant. I had been so busy noticing the strangeness of my neighbors, I hadn't given a thought to how I must have appeared to them. A single woman without any obvious ties to the neighborhood, walking around in the jaunty men's fedora I found in a thrift shop. A woman alone in a neighborhood of families not singles, occupying the whole second floor of a house. I told him I wanted a change from the Upper East Side and all it represented, meaning my husband and his friends, but also the restaurants and shops and movie theaters. Any and all distractions from life in the studio so that I could paint what was next. And I had to be alone in order to do it. When he got up to leave I said, "Do you think you could pose for me sometime? A charcoal portrait, something like that?"

He said he would, and gave me his card. "Sender the Handy Hasid." His name was Sender. He said to call if I ever needed anything fixed around the apartment, but it was always the landlord who called him for the various little repair jobs. Sender always stayed to talk afterwards. I reminded him of his promise to pose, and he told me about his days as a deep-sea diver, or his time as a marine, or his side job selling Amway. I wasn't interested in household cleaning products, and would rather have heard about Hasidic customs than over-priced soap and kitchen cleansers from Amway, but whenever I brought it up he said he'd better get a move on. Sender always shook my hand as he was leaving, and it was only later I learned that shaking hands with a woman was forbidden.

Once we actually made an appointment for him to pose, but he called at the last minute to say he was tied up with a job. I was surprised when he told me he was married, and even more surprised when I happened to meet his wife, a matronly woman in an unbecoming wig and dowdy clothes. I was leaving the house one day when she was standing outside the front door with an Amway bag. Maybe she rang the bell for the landlord's wife, and now thought to interest me in buying the Amway starter kit. She held up the bag and explained what was inside, ending with, "It's only eighty dollars!"

I said, "I'm sorry, I don't have eighty dollars," but she continued her sales pitch as though she hadn't heard. When she complemented me on my outfit, the black skirt and matching jacket splashed with pink and white flowers from my London days, she seemed to be implying that if I could afford nice clothes I could surely afford an Amway kit. "It's ten years old," I said with a laugh.

"Well, that's fortune enough if you've kept your figure for ten years!"

I said I had to go then, and hurried up the block towards the subway, marveling to think of Sender with such a wife.

* * *

I used the living room with six windows along the wall as my studio, but they faced south and the light was always changing. After a while I gave up trying to keep the light steady by raising and lowering the window shades, and bought a special day-light bulb for the studio lamp. Then I gave that up too because I realized consistency of light only mattered with portraits and there were precious few of those. Except for Colleen, hardly anyone was willing to travel an hour or more on the subway to this dicey area of Brooklyn, no matter how romantic it seemed to Colleen and me.

One of those who did venture out was the oboe player I started seeing before I moved. He was Roy's age, twenty-five or six, and even if he hadn't been auditioning for orchestras, I knew it wouldn't last. I just didn't think it would end so soon. I was caught off guard the night he called and said he had landed a job in Seattle. I congratulated him, and when we hung up I went looking for the bottle of port I'd stashed away in one of the kitchen cupboards. It was sickly sweet and I must have bought it for cooking, but it was the only alcohol I had in the house and I was desperate not to cry. When Colleen called ten minutes later I was already feeling queasy. There was only time to tell her the oboe player was leaving before I said, "Hold on a minute, I have to go throw up."

When I came back to the phone Colleen said, "Ask if you can do his portrait before he leaves."

"I can't! It'll be too painful staring at him for hours on end."

"You've got to! It'll be something to remember him by."

He sat perched on the window ledge. The oboe laying across his knees played a mournful tune. But if my heart was heavy, my brush strokes were light as they played over his face, his wavy chestnut hair and the blue-gray eyes I was gazing at for the last time. Yet as I got more into the picture it became less personal. He became more an object of study. Without my having to think about it I was transferring my feelings for him onto the canvas. Colleen was right. After he left I still had the painting. And I'd have it for always. This new side-effect of portrait painting surprised me. If I could transmute my feelings onto a canvas, then no matter who I was painting, no matter if they stayed with me or not, I wouldn't lose them. It made me feel like I had something extra in my arsenal to guard against loss.

Now that I was alone it was time to memorialize the woman having a picnic by herself. The idea of her was what had spurred me to move to Brooklyn in the first place. Being truly alone if I was going to paint a woman alone. The idea being that I was going to look to myself rather than someone else for fulfillment. Painting her, inaugurating the new studio with a picture of the new me, or at least how I wanted to be, had always been the plan. I'd waited for months while I got all the moving sorted out, but now that I was here, another idea felt even more pressing. Two selves, inner and outer, side by side. One would be how I felt and the other would be how I looked. Because they didn't match. Or it didn't feel like they did. Oh, I could see photographs of myself where I was obviously happy or sad inside and out, but I was thinking about something deeper, like two sides of the self. Something the mirror or a camera wouldn't be able to show. I drew two figures side by side, one dark, the other light, standing before a large green circle that looked something like an apple. If it had fallen from the Tree of Knowledge it wasn't the sort of information that made me feel good, for the figures came out looking like Hope and Despair. The hope that I'd somehow find my way, and the fear that I never would. The light-haired girl had a window with a sky of blue and a smiling crescent moon. She didn't look real though. Her body was stiff and doll-like. Whereas the dark-haired girl looked all too real. She leaned against the window frame, arms crossed over her chest. Closed off, closed out, unable to see out the window, she looked down instead of out. She wallowed in her own despair and was as unhappy and dejected looking as the woman in *Aftermath*. That was it then. The light and the dark self together, yet each in their own world. And only the dark-self looked real. The other was there, and though she hadn't come to life yet, there was hope.

I put the picture aside and went ahead with the woman having a picnic on the grass. I'd waited a long time to paint her. She was supposed to be the new me, alone but okay with that, and instead, her new independence came out looking more like a lament. She sat on a clean white sheet to symbolize a fresh start and had fruit to eat, representing the fruits of change. It should have made her happy, not sad. Worse, for some reason I'd painted an arm curling over her head as if to shield herself from what might befall her next.

Moving to Brooklyn wasn't supposed to have been like this. I had to change the mood, see something to look forward to. The third painting was a joyful nymph with a colorful scarf snaking around her body as she stood poised on a path leading up towards a mountain, up towards the sun high in the distance. She glanced back at me with an impish look, her arm beckoning as if to say, *Come, follow!*

But I couldn't. I had been swept out to Brooklyn in a rush of enthusiasm and now the tide had gone out, leaving me in a dry and lonely place. I thought I would be glad to be away from Lenny and all the distractions of 86th Street, and now I didn't even have a tv. Lenny asked if he could keep it, though it had been a wedding present from my friend Toshi in Japan. Lenny called in the beginning, wanting to know when I was coming back, but it wasn't long before he found someone else. An aspiring actress even younger than I was when he met me, who moved into the apartment I had so lovingly decorated. And when they were married, it was a conventional, monogamous marriage where the prospect of swinging was never brought up. Or so Lenny told me later.

In March, two months after the move when a commission I had been counting on fell through at the same time my money ran out, I thought my luck had run out too. Luck had made the whole thing possible. It was sheer luck that Toshi happened to come to New York when I wanted to leave Lenny but didn't have the means. I hadn't seen Toshi in five years, not since our break-up in London, but we had stayed in touch. He was staying at the Waldorf and when I met him for dinner I showed him pictures of my work. I especially wanted him to see the one of Roy as a samurai, since Toshi's ancestors were samurai. I told him my marriage was over and asked for his help getting my own place. The money went quickly, and when there was nothing left in the fridge but an apple and a bottle of ketchup, I had to stop waiting around for commissions and thinking I could earn my living as an artist.

Temp jobs were easy to come by, and once I told the agency I was available, I had a job the following day. But working in an office again had not been part of the plan. Coming at a time when I was at a loss what to paint next made me feel that I had failed at everything, including marriage. When my sister called and asked how I was, I admitted to feeling a little down, but she could tell from my voice it was much worse. How the tables had turned! I had always been the one calling Ellen to ask how she was and cheer her up. But Ellen was a changed person since taking meds from the doctor Lenny recommended. She said, "You should see my therapist. You'd like her. She's nice!"

"Call me Chris," said the very pregnant, annoyingly

perky therapist. How could this radiant mother-to-be who smiled like she dwelled in perpetual sunshine, possibly relate to me? She said to list all the positive things I had done as if that would make a difference, when it only made me feel worse to see how far I had fallen. I stopped going after a few sessions, but they had been worthwhile if for no other reason than I saw I couldn't talk myself out of the shadows. I had to keep painting. I had to go back to the canvas. Maybe not that day or the next, but soon. Even if I didn't know what to paint, or how, and even if I didn't know what I was seeing, or if there was anything *to* see, I had to paint. That was key. And there was nothing to do but keep picking at locks until one of them opened.

I never got used to those breaks in the flow. I never learned how to take them in stride. My rational mind could appreciate the necessity for ground to lie fallow. I knew how the moon waxed and waned and how my body went through cycles. Yet I seemed to forget this whenever I encountered a dry spell and it all seemed for naught.

When I complained to Colleen she said, "Keep digging." So I did, at least pictorially. I drew a woman down on her knees, digging up the ground with a trowel, physically breaking through the surface of the earth as I would have liked to break through whatever was holding me back. But the layer I was looking for wasn't in the physical realm. I didn't know where it was and I had run out of ideas. Losing the thread of my pictures felt like I had lost the thread of my being. The place where I could speak my truth. I no longer knew what I wanted to say. What comes after acknowledging the two selves, the light and the dark? What comes after a woman makes a fresh start and finds herself lonelier than ever.

What came was a temp job at an economic forecasting

company. And it was there, at that most unlikely of places, that I would find what to paint next. For all I know, the nymph-like creature in her colorful scarf saying, *Come! Follow!* was leading me toward a symbolic mountain, a skyscraper called One New York Plaza, located down at the tip of Manhattan at Bowling Green.

23

BOWLING GREEN

I must be a mermaid, Rango.
I have no fear of depths and
a great fear of shallow living.

—ANAÏS NIN

When I arrived at Townsend-Greenspan in early March 1982 I was expecting another boring office job. But the Greenspan in the title was Alan Greenspan, and my first day of work happened to be the Monday after Ayn Rand died on his birthday. I'd never heard of Alan Greenspan since I'd been out of the country for most of the 1970s and didn't pay attention to politics back home. I'd read *The Fountainhead* like everyone else, but I was unaware of their relationship. He was nowhere to be seen that day, and if the office was abuzz, phones ringing more than usual and people chatting in the aisles, I wouldn't have known the difference.

Colleen knew who Greenspan was though. "He's a water

sign. Pisces the fish." Then she sent me a postcard of fish. She often sent me art cards from the gift shop at the Met, and this one had two beautifully painted fish facing in opposite directions like the symbol for Pisces, their scales embedded with jewels and outlined in gold. The effect was striking and to keep them in sight I glued the card onto the cover of my sketchbook. A few months later, water and fish began migrating into my drawings.

I was only booked for two weeks at Townsend-Greenspan, but they kept me on as a part-timer from one-to-five. I couldn't have asked for a more conducive arrangement as it meant I could paint half the night and catch up on my sleep in the morning. The commute was a single train, and when I got off at Bowling Green I only had to cross the street. My desk was in a cluster of gray cubicles by the door, but I had a window in my wall, so that along with answering the phone and typing an occasional letter or memo, I could sign for deliveries. The work was hardly taxing, and I had time to read a book or chat to the office manager or the bookkeeper. They thought it was exciting I was an artist and asked me to bring in photos of my work. I had recently put together a black zippered portfolio to show off my portraits, among them the former King of Afghanistan and the one with Muhammad Ali praying in a mosque. "Oh, you've got to show these to Alan!" they said. I hadn't seen Greenspan yet. He was away, either in D.C. or off on a speaking engagement, but I left my portfolio in the office as he was due back in a few days.

"Alan, you've got to see these!" they called to the tall man in shirtsleeves and tie hurrying past our cubicles. He stopped, and the office manager handed him my book and introduced me. He leafed through the plastic-covered sheets and said in a soft deep voice, "Where are you from?"

I got this question a lot as I still had traces of an English accent. "From here," I said, "but I lived in England for seven years."

"Ah, the Prodigal Daughter has returned," he said.

And just like that he enlarged my scope. And at a temp job no less. But one where calls from the White House were a normal occurrence. They usually went straight through to Greenspan's private secretary, but now and then one came through to my desk, giving me the sense that I was part of something larger having to do with national affairs.

My frame became wider still when the office manager asked me to do her portrait in charcoal. The canvas shoulder bag I made for carrying my foil to fencing class came in handy for transporting a portable easel on the subway. I parked it in one of the empty offices after work, and then other people started asking if they could have their portrait done too. I took pictures of the drawings and pinned them to the wall of my cubicle. By summer there were half-a-dozen, and when Greenspan saw my wall he called it a rogue's gallery. Then he asked me to do one of him.

He looked tired after work and his eyes had an unfocused, faraway look. When his lids kept wanting to close I started asking him questions to keep him awake. And so I learned he'd played the saxophone in the heyday of big bands. When he said that he had given up music because he didn't have perfect pitch, I thought of the sea and the pitch and roll of the waves that were so mesmerizing on my ocean voyage. Of course sound was a wave too. The deep resonance of his voice, combined with thoughts of the sea and the fact he was a Pisces, made me think of him as an old soul. Maybe as old and as deep as Atlantis.

Thoughts of fish and souls and a lost continent at the bottom of the sea might have ended there if I hadn't been asked to create some artwork for the office. The request came from VP Kathryn Eickhoff. She had never spoken to me other than to ask if there were any messages, and I was flattered by her interest. She was vague about what sort of pictures she was looking for, and I said I would bring in some sketches. I assumed that if she liked what I had done she would commission something larger. That my work wasn't really the type that hung in offices, those large decorative abstracts with swathes of color I was used to seeing, didn't concern me. Instead I thought of what I would enjoy seeing on the walls of an economic forecasting company. The symbol of a dollar sign for instance. I had been reading up on Ayn Rand and was aware of the gold pin in the shape of a dollar sign she wore on her lapel. I tilted mine backwards in a playful stance and gave it an amused face. Then I did a pastel of bright orange chrysanthemums to offset the gray of the cubicles.

These were pinned to my wall, but as the weeks went by and Kathryn seemed to forget about me, I turned to Greek mythology for ideas. I can't say why other than I had always liked mythology, and maybe I was looking to strike a balance between my inner world and this outer one where they poured over statistics and housing starts to predict the future. I thought to bring in a more imaginative period from the past, and came up with a drawing of Diana the Huntress in a little white tunic. This goddess of the moon was everything opposite from what I saw as the sterile corporate world. I placed her in the forest with an arm outstretched to touch a tree, palm resting on the bark as if to feel its vibrations and marking the spot. The Huntress Finding Her Tree. I did her brother Apollo next, god of the sun, only I had him straddling a crescent moon. Then Neptune, god of the sea, striding through the surf, holding his trident aloft like a giant tuning fork, and paired him with a drawing of a mermaid. She was lovely perched on a rock, combing out her hair while she sang. I no longer cared whether Kathryn saw my drawings or not. I was having too much pleasure sitting at my desk and staring at my wall, knowing I didn't have to leave part of myself behind when I came to the office.

They meant something more than that too, for it was the first time I had allowed myself to play. Until now my work had always felt serious. I didn't begin studying art until I was twenty-eight and I was in a hurry to catch up and learn everything as quickly as possible. I was concerned with improving my skills and being faithful to my subject or pleasing the client. When I finally felt confident enough to draw from my imagination, the pictures were freighted with meaning. I'd forgotten what I knew as a child, that art could also be play.

24

AN EMPTY VESSEL

You are the candle that lights the whole world
and I am an empty vessel for your light.

— RUMI

One morning my landlady knocked on the door and said her mother was visiting and wanted to meet "the artist upstairs." I walked them around what had been the living room and was now my studio, as well as the spacious dining area where the walls were covered with canvases, and the mother, who was not Hasidic, said a little impatiently I thought, "But who are these for?"

Did they had to be for someone? I almost said, 'They're for you to look at,' but instead I smiled and said, "I guess they're for me."

"But where do you get your ideas from?"

"I don't know. They just come." Then I remembered the empty vessel and said, "I like to think of myself as an empty vessel." I raised my arms and mimed pulling something down from above as I continued, "Allowing whatever it is to come through." There was no need to mention how I dreaded the emptiness when nothing came.

Then not long afterwards I had a model who gave the idea of emptiness a whole new slant. I found him in one of those 'Man With a Van' ads in the *Village Voice* when I was ready to move the rest of my studio from 86th Street. I'd left some of the furniture and canvases behind because Lenny said he was keeping the studio for when I moved back. I knew that wasn't going to happen, but I was still hoping for portrait clients and the location was so perfect I thought I could still go up there and paint. But the one time I did go back brought too many memories. And then of course the clients never materialized.

His name was Fred. "Hurricane Fred" when he played in his band. When he set down the last load of canvases and said, "I like your work," I replied automatically,

"Would you like to pose for me sometime?" I didn't expect him to say yes, and when he came by the following week I wasn't sure what to do with him. He was pleasant looking, tall and slender with light hair and eyes, but there was a blandness about him, and nothing came to mind. The canvas I had prepared was large and had a squarish shape. "We'll have to have you sitting down," I said, and he suggested I paint him meditating. He stripped down to the khaki-colored Bermuda shorts under his jeans and sat on the platform with one leg crossed and the other leg jutting out with his knee bent. Then he said, "I'd like my face to have an empty look, you know, as if I was meditating. But no particular feeling showing. Just paint me as a human animal. A male specimen. Can you do that?"

"I'll give it a try." There was more to this Fred person than I thought. By the end of the session we were both happy with the way it was coming along and made an appointment for the following week. But it was the last I saw of him. He was apologetic when he called to say his girlfriend wanted him to spend his day off with her. I said, "Of course," but I was disappointed. The canvas had been left on the easel and I'd been contemplating it all week. It would be a shame not to finish it. Then I remembered I had taken a Polaroid. In the early days I'd made it a habit to take a Polaroid of models to have a record along with jotting down what the sessions were like and if I'd achieved my intention. I thought to pick up the practice again in my new studio. The photo was poorly lit, but there was enough information to finish the painting after all. I was at a loss when it came to the background though. I hadn't known what to do with Fred either until he told me, and now I couldn't even think of a color. Backgrounds usually evolved organically along with the rest of the picture, and all Fred had given me was an 'empty look,' as empty as the white space around him. I rummaged in the paint drawer to see what color I wouldn't mind wasting if I ended up throwing the picture away. Not one of the expensive Winsor Newton tubes, but maybe the cerulean blue from a brand I bought on sale. It was settled then. Fred's background would be cerulean blue.

The space around him seemed bigger once I began the task of filling it in. I was in a hurry to get it done and switched to a larger brush, lathering on the paint with sweeping strokes. I didn't stop to see what kind of effect the blue was having, so it was something of a surprise when I stepped back to look and saw Fred was under water. The 'empty look' was now a dazed look, as if he didn't know how he got there. I changed the color of the brown platform to yellow ochre to make it look as if he was sitting on the sandy bottom. After that all it needed was some fish and undersea plant life wafting in the current. Not that Fred noticed. He was in his own world. A dazed young man at the bottom of the sea. I called him *Boy on the Sea Bed* and hung him on the wall to dry, but that was hardly the end of it. Like with the painting I once did of Martha, the *Dreamer* through the open doorway, my eyes kept gravitating back to Fred. The dreamer had drawn me in with her faraway look, making me wonder what she was seeing through the doorway, and now this *Boy on the Sea Bed* was drawing me in too. But he looked out of reach. If the dreamer was peering into another realm, Fred seemed already there. Not that I saw the connection between them at the time. She was out of sight in the stack against the wall. I saw it later though, and thought how strange the way these two models had come to me by chance, and simply by being themselves had struck a chord I couldn't quite place.

Later that summer after I tired of the Greek gods, a couple of odd little oils sprang from the empty vessel. I was experimenting with a lighter palette and different colors, but the subject matter and size were different too. Each was a young girl with red hair and a rose-pink top. The first one looked wistful as she held a ghostly white mask up close to her face. The second looked unspeakably sad behind a bowl of colorful fish. I thought she was sad because she felt alone and wanted to be with the fish. They were in their element and she was on the outside looking in. The pictures were anomalies. I didn't know where they came from or why. It would be a long time before I realized these red-haired girls in rose-pink tops marked the beginning of a connection to an eleven-year-old girl who died in the war when her plane was shot down and fell in the sea. A girl named Petra which means rose-red. Did it begin when I saw Fred at the bottom of the sea? Or when he connected me to the *Dreamer* dreaming of something beyond. Or the nymph beckoning me to *Come, follow!* Because I ended up following a train of thought. It wouldn't make sense to me for a long time, but now when I look at the girls with red hair, I can almost imagine hearing them speak.

The first one might have been saying, *I'm not really dead —this is only a mask!* The second one might have been saying, *I'm with the fishes—that's where you'll find me!* Because that's where I did find her. I had a long way to go yet, but she was starting to seep in through the colors. Maybe that was why I decided to dye my hair red. Because the colors were starting to seep into me. Also, my new boyfriend was fond of red hair.

25

SAFE HARBOR

A ship in port is safe,
But that's not what ships are built for.

— GRACE HOPPER

I met Ivan when he saw my pen-and-ink renderings in Mel's office and wanted a watercolor of his brownstone. He agreed to have his portrait done too as long as I painted him in his living room amongst his possessions. Depicting the Icart etching of Leda and Swan on the wall behind him, the Tiffany lamp on the table beside him and the richly colored Persian carpet beneath him was more than I bargained for but I was more than willing. Ivan himself, in his forties with wiry gray hair combed over the bald spot, was an easy subject in comparison. He had been in the navy and wore a navy-blue blazer with gold buttons that reminded me of a sea captain and Ivan as the captain of his ship. When I wasn't working on him he left me alone to paint his surroundings while he went out to play poker with 'the guys.' It wasn't until the portrait was finished and he took me to lunch at an expensive little restaurant on Madison Avenue to celebrate that I noticed his deep gravelly voice sounded like Humphrey Bogart. And not until the oboe player left town and he invited me to come cross-country skiing upstate did I see him as a romantic interest. After skiing there was snorkeling in Aruba and golf in Virginia. I used the clubs that belonged to his ex-wife. I wore her golf shoes too. The clubs and the shoes were the only things she had left behind and it tickled Ivan that I wore the same shoe size.

It surprised me how well we got along. I wouldn't have thought Ivan was my type. A tough-talking, poker-playing, whiskey-drinking man who carried a concealed weapon in town and hunted game in the wild. But we had art in common. For me it was a practice, for him it was something to bid on at Christie's or Sotheby's. I drew buildings, he supplied the mortgages. I lived on the border of crime-ridden East New York, he lived around the corner from the Whitney Museum. Yet these were minor differences compared to being with a man who didn't want other women. A man who liked his scotch and wasn't an alcoholic. When he needed to escape the stress of work he didn't go off on his own, he took me with him. He may not have inspired my creative juices, but he spoke of marriage and a baby. I thought it was only a matter of time before he proposed.

Colleen didn't understand my attraction to him or why an artist would want to play golf. She would have been horrified to hear Ivan call me his "little artist." Yet having Ivan in my life made it easier to delve into my inner world because I knew he would be waiting for me when I got back. I still had to be careful though. Ever since the morning I overslept after staying up half the night painting and was in a rush to get ready for work, I realized certain barriers still needed to be kept in place. Because when I left the house and was in the process of locking the front door behind me, I suddenly wondered if I had remembered to put on a skirt. I knew I was wearing a blouse because I could see a puffy white sleeve from the corner of my eye. I hoped at least I had put on a slip, but all I felt against my legs was the breeze. A moment of panic ensued while I gathered the courage to look down. Yes, there it was, the white cotton eyelet skirt that matched my blouse. I locked the door and dropped the keys into my bag with a sigh of relief. But what a fright I'd given myself. As I came down the steps and crossed the front garden, all I could think of was how I never should have allowed this to happen. I promised myself that next time I would be more aware of making the transition from inside to outside. Everything would be fine if I remembered to do that one thing. I shut the iron gate behind me, and as I turned the corner up to the subway I told myself to just act like a normal person on her way to work.

I knew I was spending too much time alone, but it was the only way I could get anything done. Going outside broke the spell. I might come back a different person. I might have different thoughts in my head when I returned. I couldn't put down my brushes when everything was flowing. What if my muse slipped away while I was gone. A trip outside, however short, might change things. I had to stay with a picture until it was finished. Let time slip by, let dawn and dusk go unnoticed. Be immersed in the reality on the canvas, even if it had no more substance than a dream.

Ivan was the antidote. If he had no mystery, there were no surprises either. He liked saying, "What you see is what you get." I appreciated that, though it meant there were things I couldn't share with him like Elmer the fly. I came across Elmer when I noticed a black spot on the breast of one of my nudes and went over to investigate. It was fall, the weather had already turned cold and I was surprised a fly was still around. It made him seem special. I started greeting him when I came in the door, calling out, 'Hello Elmer, I'm home!' Being able to say hello to someone, even a fly, made the house seem less empty, and Elmer never made a nuisance of himself like buzzing around when I was trying to sleep or while I was eating. I still didn't think it was a good idea to tell Ivan though, and I probably should have kept the white light to myself too. I learned about white light from a book called *Psychic Self-Defense*, and told Ivan that if he used white light as protection, he wouldn't have to take the gun with him every time he left the house. Then one night over dinner with a couple of his friends, Ivan said, "Tell them about the white light," as if it was a party trick. I didn't want to at first, but then I thought how could I not when his friends might need to use it themselves some time. While Ivan struggled to hold back his laughter, I explained that if you ever felt in danger, all you had to do was visualize yourself surrounded by white light and the danger would disappear because light cancels out darkness.

Ivan might think white light was a joke, but he took my art seriously, encouraging his real estate friends to commission renderings. When I told him I wanted to paint his poker game, he let me come and take pictures. I managed five oils from the photos, and sold them all to his card-playing cronies, one of whom said he was going to hang his over the mantle to annoy his wife. If I hadn't met Ivan I never would have thought of painting a poker game, and I might not have carried on drawing mermaids either.

We were at a golf resort in North Carolina, holed up in our room waiting for the rain to stop. While Ivan passed the time drinking beer and watching the sports on tv, I drew in my sketchbook. Sketching centered me in my own world, and that day for some reason it was mermaids. Wispy, dream-like creatures in soft shades of pastel. I may have just been amusing myself, but later I realized *mer* means sea in French. The French call mermaids *sirène,* perhaps because they were known for calling to sailors.

I didn't think of it at the time, but considering the direction I ended up going in, I can't help wondering if they were calling to me. *Mer* was for sea. 'Maid' used to describe a young girl. Mer-maid, sea-girl. Or see-the-girl. Maybe the *sirène* were calling me into a deeper world. I didn't know anything about the *Ibis* then, the plane that was shot down in World War II, or the thirteen passengers and four crew who disappeared in the sea, yet I seemed to be giving myself clues. A mermaid who could breathe above and below the surface might tell me what was down there. I didn't think of it then. All I knew then was that I was amusing myself while Ivan watched television.

Townsend-Greenspan was lenient with giving me time off, and on my return Maria from accounting would stop by my cubicle on her way to lunch or the Ladies Room and ask, "Where did you go this time?" I'd say Bermuda, or Aruba or Costa Rica, and one day Maria said, "I wish my husband would take me on a trip instead of always buying me jewelry." She pointed out the necklace and bracelets she wore and the rings and earrings that commemorated various holidays and anniversaries. Maria seemed to think I was the lucky one, but by Christmas, when Ivan hadn't given me anything more personal than a gift card at Bloomingdale's, I thought the luck was all on Maria's side. A piece of jewelry, no matter how small, suggested permanence.

I began dropping hints that I was fond of opals, especially fiery opals, since I read they were known to increase psychic abilities and creativity, as well as luck and abundance. I went so far as to mention the name of the jewelry store where I had seen them in the window, but Ivan acted as if he hadn't heard.

I wished I had pretended I was deaf when he invited me to another one of those weddings or bar mitzvahs his friends were always having for their kids. Telling Ivan I didn't have anything to wear didn't let me off the hook; he simply gave me the cash to buy a new dress. I needed a new roll of canvas. It killed me to have to spend it on clothes. The day I went shopping I could barely stand to look at myself in the fitting room mirror. I wanted to be standing in front of my easel, not a mirror. I wanted to forget self, be in that state of blind humility serving Art.

If I was stuck going to another one of those fancy parties, I seemed to be stuck with painting too. I couldn't see what was next, and whenever I couldn't see what was next I felt like I had reached a dead end. When I signed up for a course in illustration at the School of Visual Arts it only made things worse. The first assignment was to bring in an anti-war sketch. I knew right away to draw a grief-stricken mother raising her hands up to heaven, the little boy beside her covering his ears to block out the sound of gunfire. We pinned our drawings to the cork wall and the instructor walked by giving them critiques. I noticed mine was different from the others, torn from a sketchbook while theirs had a more finished look, but I was astonished when she came to mine and said in a tone of disgust, "What's *that?*" I never went back.

Next I tried juried art shows. *American Artist* magazine had listings all over the country. There was an application fee and the cost of framing and shipping, but I needed a boost, and it would be worth it if I was accepted. Then I came to the part where you had to write an Artist Statement and I had no idea what to say. But there was also an ad in the magazine for an artist's society that helped you market your work, so I joined and received forms in the mail that were supposed to help you define your goals. I was put off though when they called art "a career choice." Art wasn't my career, it was my life. My calling.

If I were to write an Artist Statement today about the work I was doing then, I might say I was exploring an inner world of non-verbal feelings. It sounds ridiculously vague, but even that was beyond me at the time. I didn't actually have a goal. At least not one I was in touch with. The record of the Dream of '76 was stashed away in my file cabinet somewhere and I'd forgotten about it, including what I knew then, that painting or writing was the only way I'd find out what I knew inside.

My vessel was empty. I lay on the bed feeling sorry for myself until Van Gogh's swirling sky and writhing trees popped into my head and I thought how dare I call myself an artist if I wasn't prepared to feel that kind of energy moving through me. The scolding I gave myself propelled me into the studio. I told myself all I had to do was paint *something*. Anything to get the motor running again. It could even be a simple study of a flower. I put on my coat to go out and buy flowers, and on my way to the door I happened to glance at *Boy on the Sea Bed*. And maybe because I had just been picturing the swirls of Van Gogh, the water in the picture looked static and flat. It needed to move. I took off my coat and squeezed out some paint, and by the time I finished stirring up the water it was too late to go out for flowers. But I had another idea. Diana the Huntress. I could paint her.

It took me all night. I didn't have a fresh canvas and had

to paint over a picture I didn't mind losing, only it was big, so the Diana had to be big too. I felt an affinity with her, being that my sign was the archer. Sagittarians are supposed to be good at setting goals and going after them. I didn't feel like myself unless I was working, going after an idea, and it felt good to work on a big canvas. I caught her mid-stride, bow in one hand, reaching back for an arrow with the other. A dreamlike Diana, a bit out of focus. Her face was turned to the side, mirroring my own self-doubt to face head-on whatever it was. But if she was uncertain of her prey, she was reaching for an arrow. And if she was hesitant, at least she wasn't lying about, drowning in self-pity. She was on her feet, on her way, reaching for an arrow like I reached for my brush. I was so happy when I finished the painting I didn't know what to do with myself, whether to laugh or cry. I wanted to hug someone, but I was alone so I hugged the refrigerator.

When the new year came around I decided it was time to start calling her by her Greek name. Artemis not only began with the word Art, she was not only goddess of the moon and the hunt, she was goddess of the Perilous Passage. With my next painting I seemed to know that I had arrived at some kind of passage that held danger. It was a picture of a woman doing a backstroke far out to sea under a full moon. Three brightly colored fish were swimming up to her. It wasn't clear yet if she saw them. What was also unclear was whether they would guide her back to safety or drag her below. I couldn't think of a name for the picture, and I was usually good at names. 'Shipwreck' didn't sound right since there was no sign of a wreckage. 'Drowning' wouldn't do either since the woman didn't appear to be struggling to stay afloat. In lieu of a title, some lines came to me.

Something is calling me down to the depths.
I'd rather stay in daylight time
than go exploring where there's no end or
return.
But something is calling me down to the depths.
A voice heard in ancient dreams.
I plunge.

Ancient dreams and something calling. I was in awe of myself for coming up with lines like that. Especially the last one, 'I plunge,' as if I didn't have a choice. It seemed a momentous start to the new year. Then Townsend-Greenspan decided they needed someone full-time in my position who would learn the computer. They asked me to stay, but more than not wanting to work full-time I wanted nothing to do with that little black screen and its blinking lines of code. I left the company and got stuck in daylight time.

26

DAYLIGHT TIME

The two most powerful warriors are patience and time.

— LEO TOLSTOY

I didn't expect I'd be lucky enough to find something else part-time, but I could handle a stint here and there and take a week off to paint in between. When the agency sent me for a two-week gig filing and making cold calls for a brokerage firm at the World Trade Center, I thought I'd get back to painting when it ended, but then it didn't end. They liked my telephone voice and asked me to stay on permanently, promising to send me to school to become a broker. They had already invited me to sit in on some of the presentations by new tech companies looking for backers. I was hearing about new gadgets before they were on the market. I didn't understand the gadgets any more than I understood the ribbon of stock prices hanging from the ceiling, yet as unbelievably as it would seem to me later, I found the proposition hard to resist. It was like being offered a better role in a play, wearing a fancier costume. I pictured myself in a stylish business suit, carrying a leather briefcase and having a secretary instead of being one. I had a moment of doubt when they called me down to Personnel to fill out forms and I saw the pension plan. Artists didn't retire or have pensions. I signed it anyway because in the weeks since painting Artemis reaching for an arrow and the swimmer doing a backstroke, the trail had gone cold.

Then not long afterwards I began seeing a lighthouse superimposed on the bank of gray filing cabinets. They were to the left of my desk, and whenever I turned my head in that direction, the lighthouse would invariably appear. I liked seeing the tall white pillar against a clear blue sky. It reminded of the lighthouse at Montauk, the most eastern tip of Long Island. Was I supposed to paint a lighthouse? It didn't occur to me that the purpose of a lighthouse was to signal danger to passing ships. Or that it might have been a warning not to get stuck in the shoals of a permanent office job.

At the start of the golf season in April, Ivan didn't take it well when I begged off saying I needed my weekends to paint. After a few weeks without me on the links, he offered to pay my expenses if I quit my job. I gave in my notice without a second thought. My young co-worker was horrified when I told her I was going to let my boyfriend support me. "How can you give up your independence?" she said. If she didn't know that her own so-called independence came at the price of having to sit in an office all day, I wasn't going to tell her. Ivan reminded me that I was an artist. He said I should be building up my rendering business. When I left the job I left behind the vision of the lighthouse too and never got around to painting it. Neither did I have any idea of the new danger I was walking into.

Ivan set up an interview with *Real Estate Weekly* that

brought in a few commissions when they published my article and included a picture. More work came in when I started advertising in the paper, but it wasn't regular enough to support myself. Ivan wanted me to read Napoleon Hill's, *Think and Grow Rich* for more ideas on how to make a success of my work, but I never saw renderings as anything more than a way to pay the rent while I did my real work, picturing the unseen realms of imagination. Except that I wasn't doing much painting, or not anything that felt significant. Life had been simpler when I worked at Townsend-Greenspan, allocating this much time for the rent, this much time for painting, and this much for Ivan. It should have been easier now, but the borders were no longer as clear. Sunday mornings, and sometimes on a weekday before we left for the golf course, Ivan drove around downtown to point out buildings where he knew the owner or the manager so I could take down the address and call them about doing a portrait of their building. Only occasionally did it end with a commission, and Ivan said I wasn't trying hard enough. And then, because I no longer had a schedule, I was given the task of looking after his little niece and nephew when they came to visit. Setting up a lemonade stand for them on Madison Avenue meant another few days lost for painting but I didn't begrudge it. This was life with Ivan, and though he hadn't mentioned marriage and a baby for a while, everything seemed to be falling into place. He'd paid for my divorce from Lenny and taken me to his brother's family upstate last Christmas. I presided over the dinner parties for his friends and didn't mind the hours I spent cooking. I liked cooking and I liked his friends, and I had reconciled myself to living in his dark apartment that never got any sun. Even the garden in back, surrounded by tall buildings, was always in shadow. Ivy was the only plant that survived, and looking up was like looking up from the bottom of a well. But Ivan had grown on me like the ivy, and I thought it was only a matter of time before he asked me to move in. Yet after a few months into our financial arrangement I began to notice a change. How it seemed to irritate him that I wasn't more aggressive about getting new commissions. I brushed off his complaint I wasn't trying hard enough. It wasn't so easy to brush off the way he flirted with the waitress in Atlantic City.

We had driven down for the day and he wanted to stop for lunch before he hit the casinos. When the waitress came to take our order and they began exchanging pleasantries, I thought he was just being friendly. But then he was complementing her appearance and her smile, the two of them acting as if I wasn't even there. I was stunned. Ivan had never done such a thing before. I didn't know how to react. I knew he had moods and could be rude at times, and I never took it personally. But this was a side of him I hadn't seen before. I couldn't eat. When Ivan said, "What's the matter, aren't you hungry?" his tone was indifferent.

I didn't go to the casino with him. I would have liked to have taken the bus back to New York and left him there, but I didn't have the energy. Instead I walked along the boardwalk until I found a spot where I could sit in the shade. I had my sketchbook with me but I was too upset to draw. Instead of drawing I thought about all the times I'd been hurt before and made a list to drum it home to myself because this had to stop.

Ivan reverted to his old self once we got back to New York, but I didn't trust him anymore. I had to confront him, find out where I stood. I'd never had to ask anyone before because either I knew or I didn't care. But soon I would be turning thirty-four, and if we weren't going to be married and have a baby I needed to know. I was just going to ask if we were in a committed relationship or not, and even this made me nervous. I chose the night he asked me to meet him for dinner at the restaurant near his office in midtown. I was going to wait until we were having coffee, as if it was an afterthought to be curious about our relationship, but I was in such a state having to bring it up at all that I just wanted to get it over with. Ivan chuckled and said, "I'm happy with the way things are." He went on eating for another minute before adding, "I don't like having a gun at my back."

I was too shocked to think of some clever riposte. All I could do was go back to Brooklyn instead of going home with him. On the train I prepared myself mentally to call the temp agency in the morning and tell them I was available again. I'm sure I would have too if not for the disaster unfolding in Illinois that same night.

* * *

My mother had moved back to Illinois to look after Gramps when Nano died. When my father died a few years later she took in my brother Frank who had nowhere else to go. She wanted him with her anyway and Frank improved in Decatur. The mental problems that had all but paralyzed him in New York seemed a thing of the past. He repainted the exterior of the house and tended the grape vines out back. Then Gramps died and money was tight without his pension. Maybe my mother took her frustrations out on Frank, nagging him once too many times, and that was why he erupted, threatening her with a lead pipe one night. She made him sleep in the basement after that, but he only went down at bedtime, and the night after dinner when she was on the phone with my sister, he attacked her. Ellen said they were laughing about something, and maybe Frank thought they were laughing at him, because suddenly Ellen heard my mother scream. Ellen hung up and called the Decatur police. By the time the police came and took her to the hospital, Frank had run away.

Ivan hugged me and said, "You poor kid." Then he gave me the plane fare to go out and look after my mother. She was badly bruised with a black eye and three broken ribs. She said it hurt to breathe. I was shocked at her appearance and sent her to bed. More troubling was the wound to her spirit. There was a dullness in her eyes I'd never seen before. I spent the next two weeks cooking and cleaning, shopping and doing laundry. But she no longer felt safe. She worried Frank would come back, break in through a basement window. I asked Ivan to cable me the money to have bars installed.

He was out in Colorado hunting antelope. When he called from the ranch I was never so happy to hear from anyone. I could have done without his tale of shooting a defenseless antelope, but I couldn't have done without him. I felt buoyed up just hearing the strength and certainty in his voice. I could be there for my mother because I knew Ivan was there for me. His ability to provide solutions was an assurance that there was still order in the world. Thoughts I'd had of leaving him were put to the side.

If at first my mother was afraid Frank might return, it wasn't long before she was praying he would so she could get him the treatment he needed. But Frank never came back. If she had pressed charges the police might have been able to pick him up. But she hadn't wanted to do that, and all she could do now was put him on the missing person's list. My mother never saw Frank again. He was homeless for the next twenty years and lost all his teeth. He said they were shaken loose when he rode the freight trains. When he wasn't riding the trains he tramped around the countryside getting work picking peaches or potatoes. Eventually he made his way back to New York where he slept outdoors in all kinds of weather and gathered food from garbage cans and dumpsters. Rather than beg, he collected empty plastic bottles to sell for a nickel.

My mother wanted to come back to New York. The house in Decatur needed repairs she couldn't afford on her minimum wage at the mall. She could earn more in New York if she brushed up on her bookkeeping skills. I had a spare room in Brooklyn and said she could live with me until she got on her feet. Planning for the future brought back her appetite. By the time I left her eye was almost healed and she felt well enough to come out for a drink. We played Sinatra on the jukebox and she sang along—*I want to be a part of it, New York, New York.* "I'll be there by Christmas!" she promised.

My gratitude towards Ivan had already faded by Thanksgiving. His brother's family had come down for the holiday and he put me in charge of preparing the feast. I knocked myself out with all the trimmings, but as we sat around the table and I looked at his brother's family, I saw myself as the girlfriend who cooked, and all the joy went out of the day. His relatives stayed the weekend, and by Sunday night when we were finally alone again, I was seeing things clearly. We were sitting at the bar drinking scotch and Ivan was getting all sentimental, slurring his words, telling me how much I meant to him. "Well, what's it going to be with us then?" I said.

"I don't like having my back against the wall."

First the gun at his back and now his back against the wall. I wouldn't ask again. I left in the morning, and on the train back to Brooklyn I realized there was no need to break up with him yet. I could wait till my mother came, and once she got a job she said would help with the rent. I was proud of myself for being able to think it through calmly and do what was best for me. But when I came home I found a scene of chaos in the small front room where I had my drafting table and did renderings. I took one look at the collapsed shelving unit, everything in a jumble on the floor, and shut the door.

Too many things were falling apart at once. Like the brackets that held up the shelves, I couldn't bear the weight anymore. I went down the hall to my bedroom at the back and collapsed on the loveseat in tears. If only Ivan hadn't led me on, letting me think it was for keeps and we'd have a baby. I thought I'd be safe with him, have a normal life, and he'd pulled the rug out from under me. I cried harder remembering that other time I'd been duped when my mother told me Dad wasn't my father. It was like she'd severed a cord and I saw my father's face spinning away, hurtling into the void. Now I was seeing Ivan, his body spinning, turning head over heels as he was sucked into the black void of nothingness. I felt broken again and buried my face in my hands, sobbing for the past as much as for the present. Then something caused me look up.

A few feet away in the middle of the room was an otherworldly vision. A goddess of unearthly beauty. It was only her head, an enormous head floating in midair. She wore a white turban with a glowing emerald in the center. Light poured from the jewel and beamed from her eyes. She said silently to my mind, *It wasn't meant to be.* Then she vanished. As suddenly as she appeared she was gone, leaving me dry-eyed and calm, staring at the space where she'd been.

It wasn't meant to be. Those five little words changed

everything. It was useless to grieve over something that was never meant to be. I no longer felt so alone either. But who was she? A goddess, an apparition? A discarnate entity coming to me from another world? I never saw her again, but then I never saw the void again either.

A long time later a friend of Ivan's told me that he wasn't able to have children. "I'm surprised Ivan didn't tell you himself," he said. I was surprised too. Ivan used to say I was one in a billion. Maybe he thought a miracle would happen. But if there was a miracle, it was the knowledge that I was being looked after.

27

THE DRAFTING ROOM

Only art penetrates...
the seeming realities of this world.

— SAUL BELLOW

The door to the drafting room remained shut for days. I don't know what its original purpose was or what other tenants used it for, though I suppose it could have fit a bed. But for me it was a perfect fit for my drafting table. All my art supplies and instruction books went on the shelving unit along the wall. Yet it was more than a place where I spent countless hours on the hard wooden stool cranking out renderings. It was where I measured distances between windows and doorways down to the last centimeter, lining them up with a T-square, making sure all the angles were correct. It was where I taught myself how to draw perspective and find the vantage point, the angle of vision. I dreaded having to face the wreckage. The tangled jumble in a heap on the floor, everything at odd angles, none of it making sense, was a sacrilege against the order and clarity I'd worked so hard to create.

I picked up the books one at a time. They were all covered with plaster dust and I cleaned them off with a rag. *The Story of Art, How To Draw Perspective, How To Draw in Pen and Ink. How to Paint Watercolor. How To Draw The Human Form.* I went about it methodically, putting them in piles on the floor outside the room. Piles of books, piles of pads and piles of sketchbooks and different types of paper. Then I collected the brushes and pencils and pens and sorted them out so they could go back into their proper containers. And as I went about picking things up, setting them to rights again, it felt like I was picking up the pieces of my life. Orienting myself back to these solid objects, these tools of my trade that were real and purposeful. They were my life, not Ivan. When I finished I saw that nothing was damaged except for the wall where the brackets had been. The long wooden planks were still good, but I couldn't see putting them on the wall again. Stacking them on cinder blocks would be safer. My father used to have cinder blocks for his shelves before we had proper bookcases. The more I thought about it the more I liked the idea, and I took out the Yellow Pages to look up where I could buy cinder blocks. They weren't listed in the index, and when I combed through the listings of building suppliers, I couldn't see them mentioned anywhere. I would have to call Sender and ask him.

Sender had come to my aid a few months back after I started tearing up the old linoleum in the bathroom. Colleen said the original tiles underneath were probably nicer and I was curious to see if she was right. When I tore up a piece in the corner and glimpsed a white hexagon, it brought back memories of bathroom tiles when I was growing up. The thought of having them again kept me prying up the linoleum bit by bit with a screwdriver. The work was slow and tedious, and the summer heat was so debilitating I could only work on it a little each day. Weeks later the floor wasn't even half finished and I was already disappointed with the tiles, many of which were cracked and streaked with glue that had yellowed with age. It was a mess and I wished I'd left well enough alone.

When Sender came over to finish the job he lay on his stomach in the bathroom with his legs sticking out into the hallway. I had to stifle my laughter seeing him like that. The job took him no time at all and he asked if he could rest his back on one of the long wooden picnic benches at the kitchen table. I said, "I'm sorry you had to lie on the floor. I didn't know it hurt your back."

"It wasn't that. I hurt my back doing some heavy lifting. Lying on the floor was the best thing for it," he said.

We went on chatting while I leaned against the sink in the kitchen and he lay on his back, and when he mentioned he and his wife had separated, I said, "That's probably why your back hurts. It's an emotional reaction."

"No, my back hurts because I lifted something heavy and strained a muscle."

I let it go. To me it was all related, but I was still hoping Sender would pose for me and I didn't want to annoy him. He happened to be driving by one day when I was walking Colleen to the subway and he honked and called out, "I'm ready to pose for you now!" I laughed and shouted back, "I don't believe you!" Colleen thought his eyes had a mad look, but when I finally caught him in a quick sketch I saw something else.

I had gone out to draw the trees leaning over the driveway and I was sitting on a camp stool behind the house and when Sender happened by. He stopped when he saw me and I said, "Oh, please, can you stay like that? It won't take more than a few minutes!" Without waiting for an answer I flipped to a clean page, and though it took more like fifteen minutes, he didn't move. He remained caught in my gaze like a creature from the wild who might suddenly take flight. It was then that I saw the dreamy, faraway look in his eyes, and with his beard and the cap, I saw the look of Old Russia.

Sender told me I didn't need cinder blocks. "These shelves can go back on the wall," he said. "They fell because the screws and anchors weren't long enough." He had the right ones in his tool box, and I stood in the doorway watching him drill new holes in the wall. When the shelves were up and his tools put away, he took out a thermos and offered me a sip of juice he said was full of vitamin C. It was cherry-flavored, and when I said I liked it he gave me a packet to make some myself. I couldn't help thinking it was probably another Amway product he wanted me to sample so I'd buy some. I was already buying Amway soap and shampoo from him. But he didn't say anything more about the juice, and I found myself telling him about Ivan and how he'd let me down.

He said, "Would you like to come fishing sometime?"

We never went fishing, but not long afterwards he rang me on a Saturday night around eight and asked if I'd like to come for a drive to the ocean. I told him I was working, and he said he'd call back in a few hours. I felt so warm after we hung up that I had to take off my sweater, and then I couldn't paint anymore because all I could think about was the ocean. After I cleaned up my paints I showered and washed my hair.

I don't know what beach it was because we talked the whole way and I didn't look at the signs. He parked in an empty lot, and I smelled the sea as soon as we got out of the car. It was a long trek to the water's edge, and it felt strange walking on the sand wearing boots—and at night no less. A freezing cold night where it became noticeably colder as we got near the water. Moonlight reflected off the sand and made everything eerily bright. We stood at the shore, listening to the gentle lapping of the surf and watching the waves roll in. When my teeth began to chatter, Sender took off his belt and tied it around my waist. "It will keep the warmth in," he said.

On the way back to the car I put my arm through his and said, "Is it true you thank God every morning you weren't born a woman?"

"Yes, but it's so we can appreciate them more."

Before taking me home he stopped at a bar in Bay Ridge and ordered Irish coffees, "To warm us up," he said. It was after midnight when he pulled up to my house and I asked him in. He told me to go in first and leave the door on the latch while he parked the car. I thought he would park in one of the empty spaces out front, but he was gone a long time and said he parked on another street so his car wouldn't be recognized by the neighbors. The street looked deserted to me, the houses dark and locked in slumber, but I accepted it, and I continued to accept more of these nocturnal visits when he tiptoed up the stairs after midnight.

Then not long after the night at the beach I began having a funny sensation in my legs. I was lying down and thought my legs had fallen asleep, but when I got up and walked around, shaking them and stamping my feet, it had no effect. There was nothing I could do but wait for it to pass. The next day it came again when I was lying down, this up-and-down-flowy-feeling like I was sensing the blood coursing through my veins. I didn't know how that could even be possible and I knew it wasn't normal. It wasn't unpleasant though, and it didn't last long, but it was coming every day now. It worried me not to know what was causing it, and when Sender called I described the symptoms and asked if he knew what it was.

"Caffeine," he said. "You've probably been drinking too much coffee."

"Not any more than usual." I knew it wasn't caffeine. I'd had to take my sweater off again while we were on the phone because hearing his voice made me so warm, and it made me wonder if the sound of his voice could change my body temperature, what else it might do. Had something happened that night at the ocean I wasn't aware of? The feeling in my legs was liquidy, like water flowing up and down. Was it like the bends? I didn't know what the bends felt like, but Sender used to go deep-sea diving, and maybe he'd had the bends. Maybe I had picked up the feeling from him as we stood at the shore. Or maybe I'd picked it up from the sea, the waves coming in and going out. The feeling in my legs did feel wavy. Tides and waves were ruled by the moon. Sender was a Cancer, a water sign ruled by the moon. The more I started imagining things, the more mysterious it seemed. But I became so used to the waves that at some point a month or so later I realized they weren't coming anymore and I hadn't even noticed when they'd stopped.

It wasn't until later that I learned what I was feeling was vibrations and it was a sign my vibrations were changing. Such a concept was unknown to me at the time, but looking back I can see the sense of it. How it came after I saw the apparition, the goddess, the other-worldly being, telling me it was never meant to be with Ivan. Everything changed after that. Soon I would be swimming in a different sea. The affair with Sender was only the beginning.

* * *

The sea was calling to me again. After the wavy-feeling in my legs I painted a watery dreamscape where a girl floated above the waves in a crouching position, traveling from right to left. I didn't think of it at the time, how we read pictures from left to right the same as we read words, and she was going the other way, going back as it were. A gigantic moon hung in the blue sky behind her, its face aligned with her profile, so that the eye of the man in the moon was positioned as if it was her other eye, the hidden eye we couldn't see on the other side of her face, and it looked as if moon and girl were seeing eye to eye. One of her arms was reaching for something. I didn't know what, so I placed a bird on her finger as if she was following the song of a bird. He was yellow like the canary I had as a child. My bird never sang but I liked to think hers did. Or perhaps it was a silent song she could hear within the waves as the bird led her back across the water. Whether I knew it or not, my brush was guiding me back.

Renoir, re-noir, regarding the black, the unknown. The inner workings of the inner world. The intuitive plane. The judge in the dream kept asking, *Who are you?* and I pulled out a piece of my gut that looked like a dried up umbilical cord. I'd held it out as if expecting the judge could see by looking at it who I was. But he didn't, and finally I whispered, 'Renoir.' I couldn't understand why until I separated the syllables, re and noir, and saw I'd given the right answer after all. I was regarding the black. Going into the darkness of the subconscious, searching for what I knew inside. I knew I had to do it after the Dream of '76, and five years later I painted the *Dreamer* wearing green, the color of the heart chakra, had I known it. She was looking through the doorway. I didn't know what she saw or even what there was to see. But knowing what I know now, I might say she was looking through the door to her heart.

I was working on *Girl, Moon and Bird* the night Sender dropped by to deliver my order of Amway shampoo. When he asked if he could use the phone, I showed him into the other little front room opposite the drafting room where my desk and bookcases were, and when I went back to the easel I could hear him talking in Hebrew. It didn't occur to me that the girl floating from right to left was also how you read Hebrew. I didn't know anything about Hebrew, I just loved hearing other languages, listening to the strange sounds and wondering what they meant. It made Sender sound foreign, more 'other' than he already was. When he finished the call I put down my brush and was seeing him out when he said, "You have a lot of books. Have you read them all?"

"Some I've only dipped into."

"A lot of them are on writing. Are you a writer?"

"Just diaries and letters. And not many of those anymore since so few people answer them."

"If you write to me, I'll answer," he said.

"You will?" This was a surprise. "Better give me your address then." The nearest paper was my sketchbook, open to my initial sketch of the floating girl. I turned the page and handed him a pencil, but instead of writing on the fresh page, he wrote his name and address on the back of the drawing. I looked at it after he left, thinking how appropriate for Sender the Cancerian ruled by the moon, to sign the back of the girl and the moon, as if he was signing off on it. Or signing on as the man in the moon?

I wrote him a letter. There was no reply. I sent him another letter anyway. I liked writing to him. I didn't mention the moon, or how I saw him as a link to my Russian-Jewish background I knew so little about. Or that being with him was like being with a part of myself that was missing. But I told him about Elmer the fly, and how I could only express my deepest feelings through drawing or painting. When Sender didn't reply to that one either, I continued the conversation without putting the letters in the mailbox because it felt so good to tell him things. It was odd that he couldn't be seen with me, when he was the only person in Crown Heights who actually did see me. I could tell he saw me the first time we met when he came up to fix the kitchen faucet and said, "What's a woman like you doing *here?*"

I wrote 'Dear Sender' at the top, and put the letters into a folder labeled, 'Dear Sender,' which was funny since I was the sender. I might as well have written Dear Self, since I was writing to myself, but Sender had inspired me, and I told him so. "How?" he asked. I didn't know how to explain about the ocean or the man in the moon, or how it felt like I was coming back to myself. But I wanted to acknowledge him somehow, and when I happened to pass a florist in Manhattan, I decided to send him a dozen roses. I had to give the florist Sender's phone number as well as his address, and the florist called him, maybe to ask when he'd be home for the delivery. When Sender heard he was getting roses, he asked if he could have a plant instead. Then he drove all the way to the florist on the Upper East Side to choose one himself. "You don't mind, do you?" he said.

I minded terribly, the more so when he told me he kept the plant under the skylight in the hallway outside his door, claiming it was the best spot for the light. First he rejected my roses, then he wouldn't even bring the potted plant he chose instead into his home. Had he even read the letters I sent? It was a mistake to have gotten involved with him in the first place. I had to end it with him anyway; Christmas was coming, my mother would be arriving, and that would be that. Then I thought why wait, the sooner I got him out of my system the better. I'd put him on canvas, see him outside of me. I used the charcoal sketch I had done of him for reference, but the way it came out, he was looking down at his coat sleeve. Since the picture needed a bit of color anyway, I put the yellow bird on his sleeve. And then it was as if the bird from *Girl, Moon and Bird* had flown to Sender, and Sender was now communing with the bird.

After *Girl, Moon and Bird* was finished I went back to churn up the waves, making it seem they were drawing her in, trying to pull her below. It reminded me of the painting I'd done of the swimmer floating on the surface doing a backstroke. She was afraid to go below. Three big fish seemed to be coming for her, and whether or not she saw them, I did, and I didn't know what they might do to her. And now I had this other girl floating above the surface, coming in from the other direction as if she was going back. Maybe she was looking for the place where I'd left the swimmer almost a year ago when I was afraid of the deep. I'd wanted to stay in the world that I knew, the one I called daylight time. I don't know that I saw that particular connection at the time, but something was coming together in my mind because I found myself looking over at *Boy on the Sea Bed.*

He was still hanging in the same spot on the wall where I'd put him a year and a half ago. Unlike the swimmer doing a backstroke and the girl floating above the surface, he was in the water, all the way down at the bottom. I hadn't done it on purpose and had only given him a blue background because the model disappeared on me and I had a full tube of blue paint. And yet it was perfect.

Suddenly I wanted to see the *Dreamer* again. It took me a while to find her in the stack, and after I propped her against the wall I took Fred down and placed him beside her. It was uncanny how both canvases were five feet tall, the figures around the same size too, each peering into the distance, seeing something only they could see. They had been painted separately at different times and in different places, yet there was a sameness the way each appeared lost in their own world. She was looking off to the right and he was looking off to the left, and I happened to place them as if they were looking towards one another, as if they belonged together as a pair. As if the *Dreamer* was dreaming of finding the *Boy*, and the *Boy* dreamed of being found. I wondered if I could make their connection more obvious. His main color was blue, hers was green. If I put a transparent blueish-green wash over both of them it might work.

I put the canvases down on newspaper and mixed the colors with turpentine to make them runny, then poured the mixture over them one at a time, quickly raising each painting up on its side so the wash would run horizontally across. I got the result I was hoping for. A hazy bluish-green veil over each not only brought them together, making them seem part of the same story, but it gave them a sense of movement, of something happening that hadn't been there before.

I wonder now that I didn't notice how cold the colors were or how separate and isolated the figures still were, as if they were each lost in their own dream. All I knew was that I wanted the story to continue. That my own story wasn't looking very promising at the moment was all the more reason to find something on canvas I could believe in. Perhaps bringing the *Boy* and the *Dreamer* together in a third painting might do it. Uniting them on the inner plane behind the veil of bluish-green. The 'inner male' with the 'inner female,' Jung's *animus* and *anima* coming together as one.

I had been reading Jung again. He said we tend to go about looking outside ourselves for our other half, thinking this other person will make us whole, when we should really be looking within. That I hadn't found anything lasting in the outer world was all the more reason to see myself as an extension of the *Dreamer* who would find her other half within. The one waiting for her at the bottom of the sea. There wasn't any time to waste since it was almost Christmas and my mother was coming to live with me. Her room was ready and I was looking forward to seeing her, but I was all too aware I only had this brief window of time when I would still be able to paint alone.

It was a side-view of two dancers crouched on the floor, coming into an embrace. I copied the pose from an ad for a ballet I'd cut from the newspaper and saved in my picture file. The black and white photo was fuzzy enough to make white leotards and tights seem like bare skin. When I sketched them with their legs curled under them, knees almost touching, it struck me how the side-view of the woman's legs with only one of them visible looked like a mermaid's tail. The tip of her foot sticking out from behind even looked like the tip of a fin. I couldn't help seeing her as a mermaid then, and changed the narrative to a mermaid and her lover at the bottom of the sea. The story evolved then, and became one about a *Dreamer* who passed through the doorway and turned into a mermaid to find her lost love, her inner male, the *Boy on the Sea Bed* in the inner realm. The union of inner selves in the inner sea of the Great Below. The girl floating over the sea in *Girl, Moon and Bird* became part of it too. She was the spirit of the *Dreamer*, aligned with the moon. The spirit who traveled over the waves, following the song of a bird who would lead her to the *Boy*.

It was a lovely story about finding union, but I'd left something out. In my desire for a happy ending, union in the inner world if it couldn't be in the outer, I forgot there might be danger. That December I forgot what I knew in January when I painted the swimmer doing a backstroke far out to sea. She was floating on the surface, no land in sight, and three fish were gaining on her. I wrote some lines to go with it.

Something is calling me down to the depths.
I'd rather stay in daylight time
Than go exploring where there's no end or
    return.
But something is calling me down to the depths.
A voice heard in ancient dreams.
I plunge.

I'd left out the fish. It was as if I'd forgotten about them. I must have put them there for a reason, yet there was no way to tell what they were for. Would they drag her down and devour her? Or would they save her and lead her back to shore. I'd been afraid of the darkness, afraid to go deeper. What if I never came back? Yet I'd written *I plunge,* as if I knew the plunge was inevitable. The fish were inevitable too. I had been sticking around in daylight time long enough. The following month the first fish would arrive on my doorstep.

28

THE PLUNGE

A mermaid found a swimming lad…

— W.B. YEATS

I was sorting old drawings that morning and had them spread out over the floor when the doorbell rang. My mother called from her room down the hall, "Are you expecting someone?" I was not, and I yelled back, "I'll go down and see who it is!"

Sender stood on the doorstep beside a clean-shaven hatless young man who looked stiff with cold. Sender said, "This is Davyd. I'm showing him the ropes of Amway. Do you need more soap or shampoo?"

"No thanks, I'm good."

"What about this new lotion?" He told me to hold out my hand and squirted some into my palm. It smelled of almonds and cherries. I was freezing with the door open. I looked at the young man, his curly black hair framed by snow-covered branches, and said to Sender, "It's cold out here. Would you like to come in and have some tea?"

Sender begged off saying he had another appointment, and Davyd, or David, as he preferred to be called, followed me up the stairs. I forgot my drawings were strewn all over the floor. "Just step over them," I said.

David looked at down at the drawings of nudes, then up at the pictures on the wall, many of them nude also, and said, "I'm surprised to find someone like you living in this community, especially making these kinds of pictures."

His voice was soft, his accent heavy. "Oh, I'm not part of the community. I just live here," I said.

When she heard voices my mother came out from her room and her face lit up when she saw David. I introduced them and said he'd come up for tea. She said, "Why don't you pick up those drawings honey and I'll put the kettle on."

My mother made the tea. David seemed genuinely glad to meet us. He was twenty-two, just off the plane from Tel-Aviv. Apparently he had come to New York without knowing a soul. As he was leaving I said, "Maybe you'd like to pose for me sometime. Just a charcoal portrait."

"I'm an artist too," he said.

"Oh?" He spoke with such earnestness I couldn't help smiling. "Then you can sketch me too."

A few days later he came back for the sketch. I studied the sensual face with dark eyes, heavy brow, full lips and an easy smile. His white shirt sleeves were pushed up to his elbows as if he could no more bear the confinement of sleeves than the armrests of the wicker chair, which was too small for him anyway. He crossed and uncrossed his legs and kept shifting position. I said, "Can you please try and sit still?" But he could no more sit still than he could be quiet. His lilting accent made English sound foreign and I wondered what he sounded like in his own language. When I said, "Can you say something for me in Hebrew?" his whole demeanor changed. He seemed older, more worldly. I have since learned that Hebrew is one of the few spirit languages left in the world because of the flow of different meanings reaching us on more than one level. Whatever it was he was saying made me feel uncomfortably warm. I was annoyed with myself for being attracted to him. Then he started talking about Sender and the Amway meeting in New Jersey when Sender danced with "a beautiful young artist." He laughed and called Sender, "a wild guy."

My concentration was gone. I blew away the charcoal dust peppering the drawing and pronounced it finished. I felt tired and wanted him to go, but I had promised he could sketch me too. We switched seats and I handed him the sketchpad and box of charcoal. His drawing took less than half the time mine did, and when he turned the pad around to show me I was shocked at how old and unhappy he made me look. Did I seem so old to him? I don't know why he said he was an artist. He didn't have a clue how to draw. Not portraits anyway. The only thing I found to like, the only part where I saw any sensitivity, were the two little birds he drew at the bottom next to the Hebrew letters of his name. After he left, my mother told me to throw the drawing away. Before I crumpled it up, I tore off the piece with the birds and the Hebrew letters and saved it.

I would have been happy if our paths never crossed again, but my mother had taken a liking to him. She said David reminded her of my brother Frank who had run away. I didn't see the resemblance. David was lithe and muscular with a quicksilver smile. The only thing they had in common was curly black hair and a restless energy.

She said, "We should invite David for dinner. He's cute, don't you think?"

I thought he was a bad artist, and gauche besides.

She went on, "A young man new to this country would appreciate a home-cooked American meal. I'll make a pot roast."

And so it began. The young man who left Israel came to dinner because he reminded my mother of the son who left her in Decatur. Wine and conversation flowed, and the pot roast was delicious. My mother liked having a man at our table, but then so did I. When David invited me to come with him and Sender to the next Amway rally in New Jersey, I went along hoping to see the "beautiful young artist" Sender had danced with. There was no one remotely close to that description, and Sender seemed happy enough dancing by himself, stamping his feet and swaying with eyes half-closed like the mystics I'd read about in *The Romance of Hasidism*. Then David asked me to dance, and when he took me in his arms and I felt the shock of attraction again, I forgot about the twelve years between us. Sender drove us back to Brooklyn. When he pulled up to my house David got out saying he would see me to the door and told Sender he would walk home.

I asked him up for a glass of wine. My mother had gone to bed and the apartment was dark. I poured red wine into Norwegian goblets and we sat in the studio, whispering and muffling our laughter in the dim shadowy light filtering in from outside. When he leaned in for a kiss, I leaned back against the pillows on the couch that was really a bed. The pillows gave way and I gave way and it was all as natural as if we'd made love a hundred times before. He left before daylight and I would have liked to have slept on the bed in the studio, falling asleep in the place where he'd been, but I didn't want my mother to find me there in the morning and ask questions, so I went back to my room at the end of the hall and laughed myself to sleep.

The next morning when I went into the studio and saw the painting of the mermaid and her lover at the bottom of the sea, I thought of the poem Yeats had written about a mermaid. I had known it by heart once, and I went looking for my copy of Yeats to see if I'd remembered it right.

A mermaid found a swimming lad,
picked him for her own,
Pressed her body to his body,
Laughed, and plunging down,
Forgot in cruel happiness
that even lovers drown.

The poem went so well with the painting, I thought why not add the verse to the canvas. There was plenty of space around the figures. I put the picture back on the easel and painted the words in white against the blue of the sea as though I'd intended it all along.

I have no rational explanation for what happened in the weeks following. But I had just read a book by an Italian called *Falling in Love.* It was a Christmas present for Colleen and I couldn't help reading it before I wrapped it up. This Italian said that to be in love was to be in a nascent state. But in order to be reborn you had to experience the falling. He emphasized the importance of falling into the unknown, into a kind of madness where you lost your bearings and didn't quite know where you were. Nothing like that had ever happened to me before. I'd always known where I was. Yet now I seemed to be taken over by what I can only describe as a joyful madness the way I was hammering stretchers together and working on multiple paintings at once. I couldn't get them out fast enough, and started no less than five that first day. By the end of the week I had eight different pictures going at once.

My mother said, "I don't know what's gotten into you."

Neither did I. First came the *She-flame* down on one knee, her skin an orangey-fiery-pink, her arms raised as if to say, *Take me!* She was surrendering to love. Asking to be lifted up. She wouldn't feel the heat; she was already on fire. I'd read Kahlil Gibran's *The Prophet* years ago.

When love beckons follow him… He threshes you to make you naked. He sifts you to free you from your husks… He grinds you to whiteness.

Then came the *He-flame*, for there had to be a 'he' in all this. I had to paint him on a separate canvas and it was just as well because he was blue with cold, longing for her warmth but hesitant about stepping into the fire. And still I couldn't leave him like that, there had to be another one of him surrendering too. Now he was down on one knee with an arm raised, his skin burnished almost to white. So went the first week. Elemental forces seeking to merge with a pull as strong as gravity.

The second week I asked David to marry me. I couldn't help it. Like the impetus driving me to paint those pictures after only one night with him, it came from somewhere inside I had no control over.

It was evening. My mother was in the kitchen and I'd gone into my room to make a phone call. I was probably calling David when I sat on the edge of the bed by the phone. I was about to dial when a voice came through the receiver. It said in a whisper that sounded far away, *Marry him*. I dropped the receiver like a hot potato and sprang up. Who was that? Marry him? That was crazy. David wasn't even planning to stay in New York. He was either going to Australia where his brother lived, or to L.A. where he had a friend from Israel. I would have liked him to stay in Brooklyn a while longer, but marry him?

I paced around the room trying to make sense of what made no sense at all. Aside from the apparition a few months ago, I hadn't heard a voice since I wanted to do away with myself in London and was warned I'd only have to come back again and it would be harder next time. I didn't know where the voices came from or how they got into my head, or if it was simply my own intuition speaking to me from a place I had no more control over than the waves flowing through my legs that time. When my room felt too confining I paced up and down the hallway. I would have gone into the studio but it meant going through the kitchen and my mother was there. Then the voice came again. This time it sounded like, *Maaaarrrrry himmmm.* I went back to my room and closed the door. Then I called David.

He was as surprised as I was when I asked him to marry me. My mother said, "I hope you know what you're doing," because Ivan was still supporting me. But Ivan didn't want to marry me. My hand was available, why should I let it go to waste? Why not put it to good use so David could stay in the country and be with me at least for a little while.

We were married at City Hall in Manhattan on a mild, rainy February afternoon. My mother came along as a witness. David looked handsome in the black suit and tie he borrowed from Sender. He took a picture of me in the gray wool suit I'd brightened up with a pink sweater and pink tights, but it was an effort to smile. The whole thing seemed as unreal as the voice that told me to marry him. On the way home he took us to lunch at his favorite Chinese restaurant in Downtown Brooklyn which was nothing more than a greasy takeout place with plastic chairs and fluorescent lights. I had no appetite anyway. When I opened my fortune cookie I read silently, "You will be rewarded a great honor." I slipped it into my bag for safekeeping.

The rain had stopped by the time we came out, and when we passed a pet store on the way back to the train, David told us to wait outside, he had to get something. Ten minutes later he came out holding a birdcage and handed me a little box with a canary inside. I was so touched I didn't know what to say. When we got home my mother sent David out to buy a cake and a bottle of champagne and I set up the birdcage while she set the table. Then David come back, and he'd barely taken off his jacket when we heard glass shattering in my bedroom at the back. I started for the hallway to see what happened and David stopped me. Motioning us to keep quiet he whispered, "Don't move. Stay here till I come back." As I watched him move silently down the hallway I remembered he'd been a soldier in the Israeli army. A few minutes later he came back for a broom and dustpan, but he wouldn't let me see what happened until he'd closed the curtains and swept up the glass because someone had thrown a brick through the window.

The landlord hired Sender to put in new glass. I never found out who threw the brick, and decided it was someone wishing us luck. Breaking glass was the custom at Jewish weddings. Ours was hardly that, but it was still a wedding. Though who could have done it? No one knew we were married that day except Sender because he'd loaned David the suit. It remained as much a mystery as the voice that said, *Marry him.*

David moved in with us. My mother said it couldn't have been very nice for him sleeping on the floor over at Sender's, and he could contribute to the rent. She was going to help with the rent too as soon as she finished her course in bookkeeping and got a job. I determined to work harder at getting rendering commissions as I was anxious not to be dependent on Ivan any longer than necessary. David was over at our house all the time anyway. My mother liked having him around, especially at dinner when she told him about life in the Midwest and he regaled us with stories of life in Israel. Or they discussed the state of the world and the oil crisis, debating who was to blame. After dinner when my mother retired to my bedroom to watch the tv Ivan bought me because he couldn't understand how anyone could live without one, David and I had the rest of the apartment to ourselves.

Sometimes he read aloud to me from his dogeared copy of Gurdjieff. Or he might show me his book of Escher drawings, going over the plates of illustrations and explaining how the puzzles led you into another dimension. I didn't need Escher for that. All I had to do was sit on David's lap in the darkened studio, his arms around me, to feel transported to another world. The world of the *She-flame* and *He-flame*. And while I knew that what he burned for was life itself rather than me, I felt his energy as the elemental force that drew two beings together. And he was with me now, young and untried, yet with so much belief in himself.

Wherever I went with David I still had to return to Ivan's world on the weekend. I felt guilty and wanted to tell Ivan the truth, but David said no. He reminded me he wasn't staying, and he didn't want me to break up with Ivan because of him. So I went on letting Ivan think it was just my mother and me in Brooklyn, and prayed for the day I wouldn't need Ivan anymore. To speed it along I began a series of small oils of Central Park I hoped to sell to tourists at an outdoor show in the spring. Meanwhile, my mother got a job and David went about getting contracting jobs. But then my mother had to pay the water bill and taxes on the house in Decatur, and most of David's earnings went for the tools he needed, then the van to haul them around in. I soon gave up on my Central Park scenes. I never had trouble painting details in watercolor, but I didn't seem to have the knack for it in oils. They had to be oils because in order to display watercolors I would have had the expense of framing them. It was all for naught anyway once I found out how much display racks cost, even secondhand.

I had fallen into the unknown. And just like the Italian said in that book on falling in love, I lost my bearings. I didn't know how bad it was until the day I was riding with David in the van and he dropped me off on Kingston Avenue so I could do some shopping. We had been talking as usual and I wasn't paying attention to the world outside the van. When he suddenly pulled up to the curb and said, "See you later!" I was caught unawares. I automatically stepped down and shut the door, but the change from being with him in the van to being without him on the sidewalk was too abrupt. I felt beached, as if without him I had no self of my own. My legs felt so weak I had to grab hold of the fire hydrant. Then I couldn't remember what I had intended to shop for, and it was all I could do to walk the mile or so home.

I had lost the quiet of my own inner world, and it seemed I had lost myself along with it. It didn't seem to matter that my mother and David were gone all day and I had the place to myself. The space where I once found solace had become a shared space. Even when I was alone it no longer felt private. I hadn't missed it in the beginning when being with David felt like my inner world had come to life. So much so that I didn't feel the need to paint those sorts of pictures anymore. Yet not doing them made me feel out of touch with myself. As if my inner compass was gone and I'd replaced it with David.

He was having none of it. When something set me off one day and I couldn't stop crying, he sat me down, told me to close my eyes, and led me to a place inside. I breathed in the softness of his voice as he described perfumed flowers and a leafy green paradise where birds sang under an endless blue sky. When he told me to open my eyes I didn't want it to end. "You can go there whenever you want," he said. "All you have to do is decide." But I couldn't find the garden by myself. It didn't work without him guiding me. I didn't see anything inside, as if my inner screen had gone dark. When I asked him to take me there again he said, "No, it's a place inside you have to find on your own."

Then David and my mother started squabbling at the dinner table. It seemed to happen overnight, their usual light-hearted, friendly banter suddenly becoming barely disguised hostility. There was nothing to be done when they were spoiling for a fight. It didn't take much to set them off. One or the other would make a remark guaranteed to annoy and they both had short fuses. David was impatient by nature and always rose to the bait. Nothing was happening fast enough and he didn't want to hear my mother's complaints. I never knew which way the wind would blow, but I thought at least we could have a nice dinner for her birthday. There was cake in the fridge and flowers on the table and I bought a bottle of the Bordeaux she liked. Then she came home from work grumbling about the long commute and having to stand the whole way during rush hour. I thought she'd settle down once she put on her slippers and had a glass of wine, but something at work had upset her, and she didn't want to be cheered up. When David came in the sniping began. As much as I wanted to end my dependency on Ivan, those were the nights I couldn't help being grateful for the refuge he offered on weekends. I used to be able to go into the drafting room and close the door, but lately the renderings had become too big for my drafting table and I needed the long table in the kitchen to work out the perspective. There was no getting away from them then, and sometimes I worked through the night just to enjoy the quiet after the two of them had gone to bed.

I was working late the night one of their tiffs had sunk into name-calling. My mother was too upset to sleep and came into the kitchen around one to heat up a glass of milk. I was bent over the table with my back to the stove listening to her go on about how unhappy she was, and I made what I thought was a reasonable suggestion, one I probably should have made sooner. "Maybe it's time you found your own place," I said. But she took it badly, maybe because of the late hour and the state she was in. "I never thought you'd be the one to betray me," she said bitterly. She went back to her room with the warm milk and must have stayed up the rest of the night packing her suitcase because she left early the next morning. She didn't speak to me for months, but later she thanked me. She'd found a room in a residential hotel in the Murry Hill section of Manhattan that had a French window with a tiny balcony. I knew she'd felt marooned in Crown Heights, and now she had an easy commute along with all sorts of conveniences my neighborhood lacked like a coffee shop on the corner and a deli nearby where she could pick up a sandwich on her way home from work. She was even taking a class in accounting.

The atmosphere lightened considerably when David and I had the place to ourselves. For a while it was like playing house. One night when we were laughing and clowning around we put sunglasses on and took our picture in the mirror. I looked at us being silly in the mirror and saw no difference in our ages. We were the same, and it struck me that I would always be the same inside. My face would age and my body would grow old, but I would always be me on the inside, however many birthdays I chalked up. It was a revelation, and though my thoughts didn't go any further that night, I think with David I must have located the place in my being that would never change. The place that would always be me because it was the very livingness of being alive. It felt like the secret of happiness, and I wanted to hold onto that moment seeing ourselves in the mirror, bitter-sweet though it was, because I knew he wasn't going to stay.

Not that he seemed in any hurry to leave. He was reading a book about getting into real estate and talked about how much money he could make buying and selling buildings. Or he was taking a course to get his license as a contractor so he could have his own business. All this while his immanent departure for L.A. remained in the foreground. Then at some point he began finding fault with me. When my mother was around he often commented on my artwork with suggestions how I could improve it, but he never criticized me as a person. It didn't occur to me that he might be pushing me away because I was becoming too attached and he felt guilty he wasn't going to stay, and that was why he said, "I don't want to have to think about you. I want you to be like the air, so I can pass through you or around you, and not be obstructed by you." It was like Ivan accusing me of putting a gun at his back or his back against the wall. David was more poetic about it, but when had I become such an obstruction?

Another time we were talking in the studio when he

swung his arms out to make a point and bumped against the canvases stacked carefully against the wall. I had recently double-stacked them to have more floor space, and when his arm knocked one off balance, the whole top layer began crashing down like dominoes. I screamed and David yelled, "What are you screaming for? These are not your babies!" Maybe not of my flesh, but they'd come from my spirit.

Then the bird died. David named him Mickey. He said, "Mickey doesn't like being caged in," and one of the first things he did when he came home from work was to open the door of the cage. "Come Mickey, come!" he cooed. "It's time to fly!" David wanted him to fly and I wanted him to sing. I bought a record of canaries singing, hoping it would encourage him to join in. But Mickey never sang, and rather than spread his wings, he preferred hopping about on the floor, probably because he had been caged his whole life. When the exterminator came on one of his twice-yearly visits courtesy of the landlord to spray for roaches, the smell was gone after a few hours and by evening I'd forgotten all about it. Then David let the bird out as usual, and after supper when I got up to clear the plates I noticed something yellow under the table. Poor Mickey. He was lying on his back with his little toothpick legs sticking up. David said it was my fault for not telling him about the exterminator. I could have said it was his fault too for letting the bird out, but I knew it was David who felt caged.

He cared for me though. I knew that. One night I happened to cough when he was asleep, and it wasn't even a loud cough, but he was instantly awake, leaning over me, holding me in his arms, saying, "Are you alright?" as if I was in danger of slipping away. I still had to tell him to go. It was because of everything until it was about just one thing that was too much.

It didn't seem too much when he asked to use the spare bedroom for refinishing some cabinets with his new machine. He said he would take the carpet out and put it back by Monday, assuring me that everything would be cleaned up and put back when I returned from Ivan's. If I had seen the size of his new machine or the size of the cabinets, I would have realized it was the kind of job you did in a workshop or a garage, not your home. I came back Monday afternoon to find Eris, the goddess of chaos and destruction, had taken over in my absence. The apartment reeked of varnish and nothing had been put back. The cabinets, larger and more numerous than I had been led to believe, leaned at odd angles on the kitchen floor and on every available surface. I might have overlooked the rolled-up carpet propped against the refrigerator, the overflowing garbage, the answering machine on pause and the sink full of dirty dishes. But when I saw the five-foot-long two-by-four leaning against a painting on the wall, denting the canvas, and David shirtless and sweaty, a drill in his hand and a belligerent look on his face, I said, "I want you to leave. I want you out of here by the end of the month!"

He shot back, "I'll leave when I'm ready." Then he smiled and said, "Meanwhile, you're stuck with me."

He was gone a few weeks later. I came home one day and he wasn't there. I broke out in a rash. Colleen, whom I hadn't seen in a while, said that I'd aged. I could no longer sleep in our bed so I got rid of it and moved into the guestroom. The bedroom where someone had thrown a brick through the window on our wedding day became a storage room for canvases. It wasn't enough. I started painting his portrait from photographs, thinking to get him out of my system that way, but after I had done three I still cried myself to sleep. A month or so later when he began dropping by with takeout and a couple of beers, we talked and laughed. He'd come and go, and if each time he left I went through another wrenching withdrawal, I didn't have it in me to tell him not to come anymore. He never said that he missed me, but one day when we drove to the ocean and sat on the beach, staring at the water and listening to the gulls wheeling overhead, he said he realized what he had lost. "Would you like to come back? I said. "You can come back you know." If only he would come back.

It was a long time before I could look at the painting of the mermaid and the swimming lad. Longer still before I could read between the lines of the poet, "…forgot in cruel happiness that even lovers drown," and know that a heart breaking open was cruel happiness too.

29

THE WAY OUT IS THE WAY IN

When one door closes, another opens.

— ALEXANDER GRAHAM BELL

Rachel, the first Hasidic woman who spoke to me other than my landlady, sent me to the rabbis. She lived up the block and I'd often seen her from my window, the slightly heavy woman pushing a stroller with several more children trailing alongside. She wore glasses and dark colors, and her hair in a pageboy always looked as if she'd just had it done. I didn't know it was a wig. Nor did I know why she stood out more than the other women who were similarly dressed with numerous children. It wasn't anything I could put my finger on. One day we happened to pass each other on the street, and when she smiled and said hello, it didn't seem like a small thing. I stopped and said hello back, then looked at her children and said, "Your children are beautiful. I'd love to paint them sometime!"

"I'd love that too!" she said. "I've been meaning to ask how much you charged."

It was silly of me to think I'd gone unnoticed, the shiksa carrying stretchers and rolls of canvas home from the subway, yet I was amazed she knew I was an artist. David must have stood out too since he didn't wear a hat or a beard, and his battered orange van parked on the street was hard to miss. After all this time I was still thinking my Brooklyn neighborhood was like Manhattan where people didn't know your business.

I photographed the children separately in front of their house. I was going to do the head and shoulders of each and paint them in oil while charging her what I'd ask for a charcoal drawing. Even then Rachel could only pay in installments, and I let half of them go because by then we were friends and I was doing them for my own pleasure anyway. The youngest was two, the oldest ten, and Rachel herself was only thirty, younger than me with five kids. I invited her to come by anytime to see how the portraits were coming along. I had been feeling isolated since David wasn't around anymore and I'd finally broken it off with Ivan, but Rachel was even more hungry for conversation than I was. She called my place, "a house of free expression," and the first thing she did when she came in the door was remove the scarf covering her hair. She didn't come from a religious background, and had taken it up at twenty when she was disillusioned with secular life. We drank wine and listened to records. Her favorite was "Ecstasy," the album I bought when I used to go down to the Rajneesh Center in Tribeca. But mostly we talked about poetry and painting. After ten years of marriage she had come back to her first love, poetry, and said I inspired her. She brought over the neatly typed pages that were written in secret and hidden in a drawer until she could smuggle them out and read them aloud to me on nights when her husband stayed home with the children.

One night I told her about my Jewish father Milton, how my mother met him on a cross-country bus and would have named me Rachel too if they had married. "You should write a letter to the Rebbe and ask him for a blessing!" she said. I couldn't imagine the famous Lubavitcher Rebbe having an interest in me, but Rachel said, "Everyone writes to the Rebbe, why not you? You're half-Jewish and you've already lived here for three years. It's hardly a coincidence don't you think? I mean, maybe your whole purpose in coming to Crown Heights was to connect to your Jewish roots. Have you thought of that?"

Of course I had. But I never felt I belonged, and I wasn't sure about inserting myself into a world I had little knowledge of and had only observed from the sidelines. Rachel brushed my doubts aside and we drafted a letter she translated into Hebrew. "The Rebbe doesn't read anything that's not in Hebrew," she said. I stared in wonder at the page of indecipherable symbols that was somehow about me. "There's a box where we put them. I'll deliver it myself," she said. So the letter went off to the Rebbe, but asking for a blessing was only Rachel's first idea. Once I told her about my quandary whether or not to start divorce proceedings she said, "You should speak to a rabbi. Ask his advice."

Involving a rabbi seemed a big step. I was still having a hard time accepting the separation. I was tired of being the empty vessel and sometimes wished I'd had a child with David. He was still in New York. Sometimes I thought it might not be too late. "Are you sure a rabbi will see me?"

"He has to. They're not allowed to say no. I know just the one you could talk to. He has consultations with non-

Jews and he's young. He'll be understanding. You could ask him about converting too."

Rachel had been talking to me about converting. I envied her sense of belonging and being part of a group. If she admired my 'house of free expression,' the artist's life she had missed out on, she had the husband and family that had eluded me.

My appointment with the rabbi was at the community center. I don't know what I expected, but not a small sterile windowless white-washed room with orange plastic chairs. He was young with a red beard and a manner as uninviting as his surroundings. When I briefly explained why I was there, he said curtly, "Get a divorce, the sooner the better." Such self-assurance. Such matter-of-factness without knowing a thing about me. "I've been thinking of converting to Judaism," I said. But again there was to be no discussion.

"You don't have to become Jewish. Read *The Seven Laws of Noah*. The Noahide Laws are for everyone. That'll be enough."

I was dismissed. His lack of interest in me was disheartening. But there was no question of not getting the book, and on my way home I stopped at the religious bookstore on Kingston. The slim volume didn't do much more than go over the Ten Commandments. The only law that was new to me was the one that forbid eating the flesh of a live animal. Who did that anyway? I wanted more than laws and mandates; I wanted a course correction that would keep me in check when I didn't know any better. Those with a religious conviction may have had a lot of restrictions, but they seemed to know who they were and what they were about. I wanted that too. I wanted to change, be better than I was.

The answer seemed to be in taking the next step towards

conversion. This meant applying in person at the Rabbinical Alliance in Manhattan, and it was there I found the atmosphere I'd been hoping for. One that hinted at the mysterious goings on of an ancient order. First it was the right sort of building, old with decorative carvings from the late 1800s on Lower Fifth Avenue. Then the classroom with high ceilings, tall windows and old wooden desks, all of it suggesting not only a place of learning, but imparting the knowledge of some other time. The desks were empty that day, and in front by the blackboard were clusters of white-bearded elderly men in long black coats and hats talking amongst themselves. I was given forms to fill out at one of the desks while they conversed in low voices and milled about at the front of the room. A few weeks later I received a letter saying that I had been assigned to a rabbi in Borough Park.

The Borough Park section of Brooklyn didn't look far from me on the map, but to get there I had to take three different trains and walk the last mile. The lessons were on Sundays when trains didn't run as often so I gave myself plenty of time and was never late. I didn't want to be late for Rabbi Josephy, a rotund, fatherly man who always seemed happy to see me. I learned the Hebrew alphabet and the Shabbos prayer while we sat at the polished dining room table and Mrs. Josephy in headscarf and wrapper pottered about in the kitchen. At my dining room table at home I delved into one of the Aryeh Kaplan books the rabbi recommended, and it was there I came across a concept I'd never heard before, that of asking God what *His* purpose for you was. It took me by surprise. I remembered how Lenny sometimes got down on his knees and said, "Okay God, what do you want from me *now?*" I'd never done it myself. I'd only thought about what I wanted. What

I thought my purpose was. I put my head down on the table and wept.

That winter when the divorce was in motion and David finally left for L.A., my thoughts were on redemption. This didn't turn out to mean conversion. What the fates had in store wasn't nearly as radical and was more in keeping with the role I already had. It seemed rather than celebrating Shabbos myself, it was enough for me to commemorate the ritual on canvas for others. The commission came from Rosenblum, the exterminator. The last time I'd seen him was six months ago when the canary died. Now he came by not only to spray but with the happy news that his wife had given birth to their sixth child and they were ready for a family portrait. I had no idea he was even interested in my work. He didn't know how one went about such things, and he looked relieved when I told him I would come to his house and take photos and do the painting at home. We made an appointment for a Friday before Shabbos when they would all be dressed in their best.

The table was covered with a spotless white cloth. The plates were laid out with a silver candelabra in the center and a loaf of challah off to the side under an embroidered velvet cloth. Rosenblum, red-cheeked and burly, sat at the head with the baby in his arms while his petite and slender wife stood at the other end preparing to light a candle. The children, three boys and two girls, were arranged standing or sitting around the table. The boys looked grave while the girls smiled at the camera. I had a good camera by then with interchangeable lenses so that I could take wide-angle shots and zoom in for closeups. Their dining area wasn't as large as mine and even with the wide-angle I couldn't step back far enough to get them all in one shot. I felt guilty for having a bigger apartment than this family of eight, and when it came to making the sketch I was even sorrier because not having them all together in one shot made it difficult to get the proportions right. But as I found their size in relation to one another, I was finding my place in relation to them.

When my mother came over to see the portrait she saw something different in me. "There's more soul in your eyes," she said. "I think you draw strength from this neighborhood." Sender saw the painting too. The landlord and his wife had a new baby as well, and Sender had been invited to the bris downstairs. Afterwards he came up to say hello. Maybe because he knew I was studying with a rabbi he said, "How do you feel about God?" My eyes filled with tears and I started to cry. But mine weren't the only tears. After Rosenblum collected the portrait he came back to tell me about all the complements it received and how one of his neighbors cried when she saw it. My paintings had made me cry more than once, but that portrait of a family with candles about to be lit and bread about to be eaten was the first time I'd brought anyone else to tears.

It wasn't me of course, it was the scene I'd brought to life. Now I was offered another commission. Avraham Kass, a teacher at one of the yeshivas, asked if I was interested in illustrating a children's book he'd written. Those weeks of collaboration when he would come over to discuss the drawings brought back happy memories of my theater days when I worked with others. I'd forgotten how much I'd enjoyed it.

The story was about a boy who was given a small boat for his birthday and went rowing down the river. First he came upon a farmer who needed his help carrying water to the strawberry patch. Then he met a carpenter who needed to borrow money for a new hammer. Finally there was the old rabbi who'd wrapped himself in a blanket because he had no more wood for the fire. The boy took an axe to his boat and gave the wood to the old man. Now he had to walk home, but on the way the carpenter built him another boat with his new hammer and the farmer gave him a basket of freshly-picked strawberries. That night after supper the rabbi came to teach the boy Torah. The book was called, *Torah, the Greatest Gift of All,* but it was not a gift meant for me. The rabbi at the community center had been right, there was no need for me to convert. Rabbi Josephy congratulated me on coming as far as I did. Then Avraham Kass, who had promised me a share of the royalties in lieu of payment up front, didn't sell enough copies for there to be much in the way of royalties, and gave me a tall glass pitcher with a stir instead. An empty vessel waiting to be filled.

Maybe it was time I wrote and illustrated a children's story myself. I mentioned the idea to Rachel the night we were celebrating one of her poems being accepted into an anthology, and over a bottle of wine we confessed our secret desires. Rachel's was to go back to school, finish her degree and get a job. I said mine was to write a children's story. I had taken up my journal again and had a few ideas, but I couldn't get anything going. And now I wished I hadn't mentioned it to Rachel because every time she came over she'd say, "How's that story coming along? Have you started it yet?"

When at last I did get something down, I couldn't think of an ending. It was about a one-of-a-kind fish with scales that glinted in the light with all the colors of the rainbow. A restless fish who dreamed of rivers but was stuck in a pond with no way out. It seemed hopeless until he got tangled in the reeds one day, and in his struggle to free himself he dislodged the stalks covering up a secret passage. The opening was narrow, but he was slippery enough to squeeze through, and off he went to swim in new currents. I couldn't think where he might have gone though, or what might happen to him next, and apologized to Rachel for not being able to finish the story.

"Don't be silly," she said. "At least you made a start. Maybe if you went ahead and did some drawings it might inspire you."

I couldn't bring myself to try. My mind was a blank after the fish escaped from the pond, as if getting him out of that stuck place and letting him roam free was all that mattered. Maybe I was remembering the gap I once imagined when I crossed the Atlantic. That gap or crack at the horizon between the sea and the sky. Day after day we sailed towards that far away line without ever getting closer. I had no idea what lay on the other side any more than I knew where the fish had gone. As if the water was too dark to see anything.

30

LIGHT IN THE WATER

Artists cannot tread the path of beauty
without Eros keeping company with us
and appointing himself as our guide.

— THOMAS MANN

Two whole years had slipped by since I saw the swimmer doing a backstroke far out to sea. Whether the three fish closing in on her would gobble her up or guide her back to shore seemed less important than the lines I'd written to go with it. *Something is calling me down to the deep...A voice heard in ancient dreams.* I knew it was about going deeper. I felt the pull before I took a chance with David and lost my bearings. 'Dig deeper,' said Colleen. But it wasn't in the ground of the earth, it was in the sea. I must have known it when I did the picture of a sad girl with red hair standing behind a bowl of colorful fish, wishing she could be with the fish. Or better still, become a mermaid living in both worlds and not afraid of the deep.

If David was the first fish, I was now on track to

encounter the second. I couldn't have helped myself if I tried. Certainly not that sunny day in April when I was on my way to a client for another commission. As I walked over to First Avenue from the subway at 68th and Lexington, there was a spring in my step. Commissions had been good lately and I'd smartened up my wardrobe with a designer jacket from the thrift shop that was brown and threaded with gold. The oversized leather bag from the thrift shop swung from shoulder. My new look was casual jeans and boots. The boots made me feel more sturdy if anyone tried to get my price down. Not that George ever did. Though he was younger and better looking than most of my clients, I wasn't aware he had other more interesting qualities until that sunny April day.

When I came up the stairs in one of the old tenements he owned on First Avenue, his secretary said he was on the phone. This was always the case and I took a seat where I could admire the previous watercolors I had done for him which were nicely framed on the wall. Large, 30x40-inch watercolors of entire blocks of tenements with cornices and decorative moldings and fire-escapes zigzagging down the fronts that were like slices of old New York.

The wait seemed longer than usual this time and I think the secretary felt bad for me when she said if I was thirsty I could help myself to a glass of water in the kitchen. I wasn't thirsty but I was glad to get up and stretch my legs. The kitchen was small and narrow, the counters bare except for a coffee machine and the newspaper. It was open to a story about unicorns. There was a picture too, and the caption said it was a real unicorn. I was so engrossed in the article I didn't notice George had come up behind me until he said, "Oh, you found that story. Do you believe in unicorns?"

When I looked up into his dark, heavy-lidded eyes, I

think I would have said yes to anything. "Of course," I said. "Don't you?"

He laughed and leaned towards me, and for a moment I thought he was going to kiss me. But he stepped back and turned towards the office. "Come, I'll give you the address." Then he apologized for keeping me waiting and said, "Can I give you a lift somewhere? I'm on my way to the West Side."

"I'm only going to the subway at Lexington."

"I'll give you a lift to the subway then." He grabbed his jacket from the back of the chair and I followed him down the stairs wishing I'd said I was going to the West Side too. I could just as easily have taken the train from the West Side and had a longer ride with him. He went up to the powder-blue car parked at the curb. I had pictured him more the black Mercedes type. Then, as if reading my mind he said, "It's a rental. Mine's in the shop for repairs."

As he pulled away from the curb I was aware of our sudden closeness again. With the windows rolled up, that small cramped space felt like a submarine in a sea of traffic. I racked my brains for something to say. Then I remembered George was from Iran. Iran had been in the news lately. Just the other day when I was on the phone with my mother she asked if I knew what they were fighting about in Iran and I had no idea.

"What's all the fighting about in Iran?" I said.

"Oh, the Shiites and the Sunnis have been going at it for hundreds of years. It's nothing new." His voice sounded tired and I wished I hadn't brought it up. I studied his profile as he went on talking, then at his hands on the steering wheel and noticed he wasn't wearing a ring. I was lost in thought and was unaware that we'd come to the subway until George prompted, "You'll call me when it's finished?"

"Oh! Of course!" I picked up my bag from the floor, and

when I glanced back at him and said, "Thanks for the lift!" he leaned over and said, "It was my pleasure." Then he kissed me softly at the corner of my mouth, and as I was getting out of the car I heard bells in my head. I shut the door and stood on the corner watching him drive off, his car becoming no more than a silver streak indistinguishable from all the others. My knees felt weak and I held onto the fire hydrant. Bells! I'd never heard bells before. It was like Ginger Rogers in *Tom, Dick and Harry,* when she knew which one she would marry because he was the only one who made her hear bells when he kissed her. I didn't know what to do. I had to think, but the sun was in my eyes and there were too many people, too many cars rushing by. I needed to sit down somewhere quiet. I needed to get home. The subway stairs were right there and I thought how nice it would be if I could just get down the stairs where it would be cool and dark, but I still felt weak. It was a few more minutes before I made for the stairs and held tight to the railing all the way down. Thankfully I didn't have to wait long for a train, and by the time I changed to the express at City Hall I felt almost normal again. Then the train picked up speed under the river, and when it rocked back and forth I could hear George's voice swishing back and forth in my head, asking if I believed in unicorns. This was no good. I couldn't let myself get carried away like I had with David. This had to be nipped in the bud before it got out of hand. And then I had an idea. I would take whatever this was with George and transfer it to the country he was from. Fall in love with the country instead of the man.

I got off the train a few stops early to borrow some books on Iran from the library at Grand Army Plaza. Then I had to decide between a book on modern Iran or Ancient Persia. The choice was easy. I'd had enough of the Shah and the Ayatollahs during the hostage crisis in '79, and I knew nothing about Ancient Persia. On the way to check-out a couple of books, one on the history and one on their art, I passed the record collection and found a couple of albums of Iranian music. I borrowed them as well and got back on the train. By the time I got home I'd already learned it was the Ancient Persians who came up with the word Paradise.

I put on the record of classical music first. It was unfamiliar and foreign with strange cadences and pulsing beats. I'd never heard anything like the chords that seemed to ripple through my bones. I took off my boots and started to dance. Then I took off my jeans and changed into a long flowing Indian dress and let myself go, dancing and swaying to the music that came from some other place, some other time, as if I was dancing to some long-forgotten dream. I didn't stop until I was out of breath and giddy with happiness. The effect of the folk songs was even more powerful with voices that sobbed and wailed, though whether from joy or grief it was impossible to tell. The translations on the back of the album cover spoke of unrequited love and longing, as if they were a kind of ecstasy in themselves.

The following day I got down to business and went back to Manhattan to take pictures of the block. It was another day before the slides were developed, and I passed the time reading about the Battle of Gaugamela when Alexander defeated Darius and invaded the Persian Empire in 331 B.C. I kept the records playing while I sketched out the drawing. I needed a break before I started laying in the color, and thought to walk over to Woolworths to pick up a few things. But whatever I meant to shop for was forgotten when I went down the aisle where the goldfish were. Fish! Why hadn't I thought of it before? Having a couple of fish to keep me company was just what I needed. On the way home I decided to call them George. They would be the George Fish, so that whenever I started to think about George, the fish would come to mind instead.

I placed the bowl with turquoise gravel on the windowsill in the drafting room where it caught the light and I could see it every time I looked up. The combination of blue gravel and orange fish was so pleasing that I looked up a lot at first. But as I became more engrossed in the painting I forgot about them, and when I chanced to look up later I was shocked to see one of the fish floating on its side and the other lunging to the surface, gasping for air. I ran most of the way back to Woolworths, praying they'd still be open, and said breathlessly to the clerk, "My fish are dying!"

"It sounds like you need an air-filter," he said. There was no time to be annoyed he hadn't told me this in the first place because the loudspeaker announced the store was about to close. Along with the air-filter I grabbed a book from the rack on the care of goldfish and hurried home. The fish perked up as soon as the water started bubbling. I would have been devastated if I had killed them, and now I basked in the thought that I had saved them.

The rendering kept me busy for the rest of the week. I wanted it to be a standout, better than any of the previous ones I had done for George, and rather than drawing only some of the bricks and suggesting the rest like I usually did, I outlined each one. And then, probably because of the Persian music I kept playing in the background, I let go of my usual restraint of sticking to reality and got creative with some of the colors, finding green in the shadows and pink where the sun hit. Up above, puffy white clouds floated dreamily across an expanse of blue as if the sun might break through any moment. As planned, I managed to finish the painting on a Thursday night so I could call George Friday morning and deliver it that afternoon. It had been ten days since he drove me to the subway and I could hardly wait to see what would happen next. But when I called Friday morning he said, "I'll be out of the office all afternoon. Can you come in on Monday at five?"

This was a blow. I had no plans for the weekend and no other picture in the works. I was at a loss what to do with myself for the next few days. Then I thought, just because I wasn't going to see him didn't mean I couldn't *see* him. I saw him so clearly in my mind. The straight black hair and dark eyes. The wide mouth and long nose. I put the music on while I stretched a canvas and kept it going to shut off my mind while the brush did its work. The thick bristle brush felt good in my hand after all the precise, studied strokes I'd had to make with the tiny sable brush for the rendering. Except for the sky. I'd used a big one for wide sweeping strokes of blue.

I worked on his portrait through the night and went to bed at dawn. When I came back to the studio later I was surprised what I had done. Was this George? The man with eyes shrouded in pain, his shirt so transparent you could see through it in places? You could even see through the skin over his abdomen where the organs were exposed. The loud bursts of color and jagged edges in the background suggested war. He looked wounded, yet he was hanging on. His arm was raised but there hadn't been room to show his hand, so whatever he was holding onto was out of sight. That he was simply hanging on seemed the message. Though I didn't see how the painting related to the George I knew, I didn't want to change a thing.

For our meeting on Monday I wore the black cotton skirt and jacket splashed with big pink and white flowers that Sender's wife had grudgingly complemented me on years ago. The day was mild but blustery, and when the wind picked up it blew the jumbo-size portfolio around like a sail unless I held tight to the handle on the body of the portfolio and kept it close to my side. George was on the phone as usual and I chatted with his secretary about fish. She had fish too, and I realized how easy it was to make small talk when you had a pet, even if it was only a couple of fish. When George still hadn't come out I showed her the rendering, and when she exclaimed over the clouds, calling them 'heavenly,' I could have hugged her. Then George poked his head out the door and summoned me in. I glanced at his face for any sign of the tortured soul on the canvas at home, but aside from looking a little tired, he was smiling the same as always.

I took the watercolor out again and propped it on the bookcase against the wall. "It's perfect," he said. "I love it." I was about to point out how all the bricks were drawn in this time and ask how he liked the pinks and greens on the sidewalk, but he had already turned away. He sat at his desk to write me a check, and as he waved it in the air for the ink to dry he said, "You're looking lovely today. Going somewhere?"

"No," I said smiling.

"How about having a drink with me then? I sure could use one."

Though this was what I had been hoping for I could hardly believe it was happening. Downstairs he offered to carry the bulky portfolio, and when it blew about in the wind and he struggled to hold onto it, I don't know why I didn't point out the handle on the side. We came to a bar on the next block and he looked through the window. "It's too crowded," he said. He found the next bar too crowded also and said, "I don't really feel like being around people. What do you say we get a bottle of wine and some cheese and go back to my place?"

I marveled at how fast things were moving. Too fast really, because when I followed him into the little gourmet shop and he picked out a bottle of wine and a bunch of grapes, he asked what kind of cheese I liked and I couldn't think. The display case was full of different varieties. George and the woman behind the counter were staring at me. I told myself to think of cheese, but my mind was a blank. Then I remembered that since the Ancient Greeks had eaten goat cheese, the Ancient Persians probably did too. "Goat cheese!" I said, forgetting that I didn't much care for goat cheese.

George flagged down a taxi and we piled in clumsily with the shopping and the empty portfolio. It seemed no more than two minutes later we were climbing out again. I didn't notice where we were. I was still amazed we were going to his apartment already. The lobby and the elevator ride passed in a blur, and I only knew we were on a high floor when I looked out the window at a bird's eye view of the city.

George came out from the kitchen with a tray. "Here we are," he said, setting it down on the carpet. When I saw him taking off his shoes I slipped mine off too, and we sat on the richly colored, intricately patterned Persian carpet. "Did you know that Persians invented the word paradise?" I said.

He put a grape in my mouth. "Of course." There were so many things I wanted to ask him, like had he been to Shiraz, and what was it like in Iran, and how long had he been in the States. But he was kissing me, filling my mouth with wine. Then the phone rang. "Sorry, I'd better take this," he said.

I thought he'd say he'd call them back, but he kept talking, making himself comfortable leaning against the sofa with his legs stretched out on the floor. I didn't recognize the language. It wasn't like listening to David or Sender speaking Hebrew, but if it was Farsi I wouldn't have known. While he went on talking and laughing into the phone I sipped my wine and gazed around the room. It was one of those boxy high-rise apartments that all looked the same, and aside from the carpet, none of the furniture distinguished it in any way. There were no books or pictures and I didn't see anything personal lying about. It wasn't until I turned to look behind me that I saw a picture on the wall. It was one of those generic clown paintings with sad eyes and a painted smile, the kind you saw in shops catering to tourists. What was George doing with schlock art? He was still on the phone. It had been a mistake to come. I reached for my shoes and began putting them on. Apparently reaching for my shoes was all I had to do for George to hang up the phone. He got to his feet and was pulling me up too, saying he was sorry but he had to take the call, it couldn't be helped, and before I could say anything he was kissing me again and taking me by the hand.

It was still light out. The bedroom windows were bare, and the white walls and white sheets made the room even brighter. I wished there were curtains or a shade to pull down, and told myself, never mind, you're with George. I was with George. But I wished there was some music. I couldn't hear any sound from the street so far below. All I could hear was George breathing in my ear. I tried to relax and shut off my mind, but I kept thinking, 'I'm with George.' His breathing became a moan, then a shudder, then he lay still. But only for a few moments because then he was up again saying he'd go get the wine. I covered myself with the sheet thinking I'd ask him to put on some music when he came back. But when he came back he was already half-dressed and only stayed long enough to give me the wine-glass and a quick kiss. I got dressed too then, and when I came into the living room the tray with the grapes and the goat cheese we hadn't touched was nowhere to be seen. George was putting on his jacket. We were talking and laughing and I was putting on my shoes when he picked up the intercom and called down for a taxi. I assumed he was taking me to dinner or to a club where there would be dancing. No other thought had occurred to me, so when he held the door open and said, "I have to go out. My sister is expecting me," it didn't register. When he saw I was still smiling as I looked up at him, he smiled back and said, "I adore you."

If first I had trouble taking in we were going to his apartment, now I had trouble with the fact we were leaving so soon. By the time we came to the lobby I wanted to slow everything down. George was walking too fast and I found myself hanging back, taking my time to see where I was. The lobby was spacious with marble floors and crystal chandeliers. When we passed by a wall of glass looking onto the courtyard I saw that night had finally come and the fountain was lit with colored lights. "Wait a minute," I said, "I'm going to make a wish!" George called after me, "You can't—the door's locked!" but I kept going. I was going to throw a coin into that rainbow of flowing colors and I couldn't believe they'd lock it up. But they did. I gave the door a push and it didn't budge. I pushed it again but it was no use. The fountain was out of bounds.

A taxi was waiting at the curb. George held the door open. I got in and he handed me the portfolio I'd forgotten about. "It's on my account, I'll get the next one," he said, shutting the door with a smile and a wave. The taxi took off and I burst into tears. But soon we were speeding down the FDR Drive with the wind on my face which cleared my head, and I looked out at the lighted bridges over the river. Then we were across, and I felt calm and peaceful driving through the dark empty streets of Brooklyn. When the cab dropped me off I hurried up the stairs knowing what I had to do.

I changed my clothes, opened a beer and hammered some stretchers together. The night wasn't going to end with being packed off in a taxi. I would create my own ending, and listen to some Persian music while I was at it. I didn't know what it was going to be until I drew a circle for completion. It was over with George but I was still whole. The circle was yellow, a happy color. And when the yellow circle made me think of the sun I added orange to make it fiery. I was on my second beer now, slapping on the colors with a palette knife to make it go faster. With a bottle of Amstel Light in one hand and a palette knife in the other I was reckless with the cadmiums. Normally I used them sparingly because they were the most expensive colors, but this was not the time to be frugal. This sun of fiery yellow-orange was not the personal *She-flame* or *He-flame.* It was the impersonal life-giving sun.

I turned the record over and started on the sky, but after finishing the second beer I got sloppy and added too much thinner to the blue so it dripped. The sky dripped into the sun and the sun became runny and dripped into the sky, and when it was all looking a bit watery I thought why did the sun have to be in the sky anyway? Why couldn't it be in the sea? The sun in the sea. The fire that couldn't be quenched. The light that shone from above or below. I added some fish. Small orange fish that looked like goldfish crackers swam in a circle around the circle of sun. There, it was done. And the night felt complete.

I called it *Solar Fish,* not realizing that it sounded like *soul-are-fish.* Not knowing, not having heard that each soul harbors an inner sun, the life found inside the darkness. But one day I will read somewhere that fish are a symbol of the subconscious. And at some point I will come upon these lines from Rimbaud.

It is recovered.
What? Eternity.
In the whirling light
Of the sun in the sea.

The sun in the sea. I hadn't recovered anything yet. But I'd gone below. Gone somewhere else inside myself and found light there. I liked thinking that the light which hadn't quite broken through in George's rendering, came through in *Solar Fish* the night he sent me home. And while I was nowhere near thinking of it as light in the subconscious, I'd seen light in the water, light in the depths.

I never heard from George again. I heard later that he went to jail for six months. Something to do with a real estate deal that went bad and George took the fall. It made me think of the portrait I'd done of a sad wounded man, so different from the one who smiled and laughed and had a picture of a clown hanging on the wall.

31

THE KINGDOM OF HEAVEN

There is no art without Eros.

— MAX FRISCH

June came, summer loomed ahead and I had nothing to look forward to but more work. I got what I wanted, earning my living doing commissions, but it was all that I had. For the first summer since coming back to New York eight years ago I wasn't seeing anyone. There wouldn't be any days at the beach or weekends in the country or even a night out. When the phone rang and a cheery assistant from Direct Centering said, "Are things going your way?" I didn't know the answer. Being independent seemed to mean I had to forgo everything else. But living alone and working alone made life very dull indeed.

I hadn't been to Direct Centering since I moved to Brooklyn, but they never really let you go. I would still get calls inviting me to this or that event. This time it was an invitation to take the course again. I remembered the high it had given me the last time, everyone reminding each other how unlimited we all were. Why not, I thought. I could use the stimulation. But doing it a second time was a disappointment. It made so little impression that I can't even recall what my goal was this time. It reminded me how I missed being around people though, and forgetting about work for a while, so I signed on to assist again, desperate for any kind of social life.

I was still there in August, long after the novelty had worn off. The theme for assistants that afternoon was 'Getting Completion,' the expectation being that we call someone we didn't feel finished with. I sat at one of the long tables with phones, a pitcher of water and the ubiquitous box of Kleenex because someone was always crying and needing to blow their nose. The loft was sweltering. Gavin didn't believe in air-conditioners so the windows were open to the noise of traffic downstairs, and all the ceiling fan did was blow hot air around. I had no idea whom to call. When I flicked through the pages of my address book, all I could think of was how much it needed an overhaul. I wasn't even in touch with half the people anymore, nor did I want to be. Before I gave up I went back to the beginning for one more try, and found myself lingering over a name in the E section. He had been a rendering client a year ago, though I remembered it as if it was yesterday. The commission had been an unusual one. In fact the whole thing had been odd from the start. It had been hot the day I met him. Blistering hot and humid just like today.

* * *

I was already sticky with sweat after the short walk from the subway, and coming into his air-conditioned office was bliss. The secretary showed me in and he stood and held out his hand. I glanced down at the starched white cuff with a gold wristwatch poking out, then up at his dark curly hair and soft brown eyes. He wasn't much taller than I was and seemed about the same age as me too, but unlike me he looked crisp and cool in a suit and tie. There was only time to shake hands before the phone rang and he excused himself, motioning me to take a seat. My heels sank into the deep red carpet as I made my way past the wall of windows to the chairs at the other end of the long room. I welcomed the chance to sit down, and when I felt the chilly air from baseboard vents on my bare legs I eased out of my sling-backs to get the full effect while I took in the view from the twenty-third floor. What a difference being up here in the rarified air instead of down in the devilish heat. Then I turned around, but other than bare white walls there was nothing to look at but the pedestal in the middle of the room with a bronze sculpture of a cowboy. I recognized it as a Remington because Ivan had a similar one on his mantel. I felt like crossing my legs so I put my shoes on again, as surreptitiously as possible, and found my skirt was sticking to me. I should have worn a slip, but it was so hot when I got dressed that morning that I couldn't bear the thought of another piece of clothing, especially nylon. Once my legs were crossed and I could see my foot, I wished I'd given my shoes a polish before setting out. I was still lamenting my scuffed shoes when the impeccably dressed client hung up the phone and beckoned me over. I stood and gave the back of my skirt a tug in case it was sticking to me again.

My portfolio lay open on the desk and I watched in dismay as he flipped quickly through the pages. I really needed the job and this didn't seem a good sign. Then he looked up and began talking about converting a building into a hotel. Or maybe it was a hotel into condos. He talked so fast I had trouble keeping up. Even when he got to the part about needing a rendering to show to investors, I couldn't tell if he was offering me the job or not. Then he pulled out a color brochure of an elegant pre-war apartment building and said, "This is how most people see it. It's called a wedding cake building because of the recessed layers at the top. I need you to copy it. But then I need a second watercolor of how you see it."

"How *I* see it?" This had never happened before. No one had ever been interested in how I saw their building. Neither had I ever heard the term 'wedding cake' building before. And now I had two rendering commissions when a minute ago I didn't think I had any. It was all I could do to say, "When do you need them by?" He laughed and said, "Yesterday."

I came back to midtown the following day to take pictures with Lenny's old Polaroid, which was all I had at the time, and found the building looked nothing like the glossy brochure. The bricks had darkened with age and it wasn't even the same color, but that was the least of it. At street level there was no sign of the recessed tiers with their intricate carvings at the top, the wedding cake part that gave the building its charm. And instead of a corner building as the brochure would have it, it was sandwiched between two others the same height in the middle of the block. A dark narrow block that looked as if it never got the sun. If he wanted a picture of how *I* saw it, he would have to deal with how little I could actually see as a lowly pedestrian among the canyons of New York.

Copying the brochure was a breeze compared to the small dark Polaroid shots. I wasn't sure what to do with the pyramid shape. It wasn't just the Polaroid; any camera without a special lens was going to narrow the sides of the building as it rose up, and normally I corrected it in the drawing. But in this case the building would have appeared flat at the top if I straightened the sides. At least if I left the pyramid shape there would be the suggestion of more at the top even if you couldn't see the tiers.

I had to work at the kitchen table since he wanted them large, which meant listening to my mother and David offer advice since they were both still with me at the time. My mother said, "You should have charged him more money for those." David said, "You should make some of the windows dark. They shouldn't all be reflecting the light." I continued working after they went to bed, and by one or two in the morning I thought I may as well stay up and finish it. In the morning I had just enough time to shower and change to get to his office by nine.

He hadn't come in yet. His young blonde secretary in high heels and too much makeup said, "I'm sure he'll be here soon. Have a seat!" A minute later she came back and said, "Do you mind if I have a look? I love art!" I handed them to her and she gushed, "Oh! he's going to love these!" And instead of giving them back to me she trotted off saying, "I'll just go put them on his desk."

I was too tired to care. I got comfortable on the cushioned bench with my head resting on the back and fell asleep. I don't know how long I was out before I heard voices and was aware of a dark blur rushing past. To my horror I realized I had been lying down asleep with my legs curled up on the bench. How embarrassing to be caught napping. It was unprofessional, worse than scuffed shoes and no slip. I sat up too quickly and my head was throbbing. I felt woozy. The secretary came back with a check and I was putting it away when he came out and thanked me for the watercolors, saying they were exactly what he was looking for. Then he apologized for being late and offered to walk me to the door. As I was stepping into the hallway he said, "Do you have something I could read?" Even in my semi-somnolent state I thought it was a strange request, but I reached into my bag for the book I always carried to read on the train. This day it was a collection of Mark Helprin stories I bought because I loved his *Winter's Tale.* I handed it over, he thanked me, and that was that.

I went straight to bed when I got home and forgot all about giving him the book until months later when I was browsing in East West Books near NYU and *Golf in the Kingdom* caught my eye. It seemed to be about the mystical side of golf. I might have wanted to read it myself if I still played golf, but it was over with Ivan by then. I knew this client—D.E. I called him—was a golfer though. Ivan must have told me when he gave me his number and said to call him about a rendering. It was good to keep in touch with clients and I thought I might send him the book with a note asking how he liked the Helprin stories. When there was no response I called to ask if he had received it. The secretary said he wasn't there so I left a message, and when he never got back to me I forgot about it.

Now, the following summer, D.E. was the only person I could think of that had an aura of incompleteness around him. I never would have thought of calling him otherwise, and though I remember liking him at the time, I certainly wouldn't have called him if I hadn't been at Direct Centering. Now I thought, why not. I had nothing to lose. I wasn't sure he'd even remember me, but not only did he remember, he seemed unaccountably glad that I called. I forgot to ask him about the books because he was telling me how he'd had to fire his secretary. Something about how she wasn't giving him his messages. He was talking so fast again I was having trouble following. And then he was saying how much he wanted to see me and was I free that evening. I told him I was assisting at this place called Direct Centering until ten, thinking that would put him off, but he said, "I'll pick up you at ten."

I hung up the phone and stared out the window. I was in a daze trying to make sense of what had just happened. And then, instead of the red-brick office building across the street, I saw a seascape with a sailboat in the distance. Then it disappeared and a cool breeze swept over me. How strange! I had no idea what to make of it. Something to do with the phone call I supposed. Was tonight going to be like going sailing? I couldn't help watching the clock now, even though it made the time pass slower. When ten o'clock finally came I was downstairs, wishing I hadn't cut my hair. It was longer the last time he'd seen me. Then I wished I'd worn something more becoming. There was nothing wrong with the white skirt and matching gray and white top, but if I'd known I was going on a date I would have chosen something else.

A black car pulled up and a man got out. It had to be him because he was coming towards me, but I didn't recognize him. I had only ever seen him in daylight in his office when he wore a suit and tie, and this man was dressed casually, his shirt open at the neck, the sleeves rolled up to his elbows. He knew me though. Without a word he came up to me on the sidewalk and held me in his arms for what seemed a long time. I was too startled to say anything. Then he opened the passenger door, and when he got in on the other side he kissed me like a long-lost lover. I felt shy afterwards, as if I'd walked into a play I hadn't yet read. I didn't know what to say, and he didn't seem to feel the need to talk either. We took off down Lower Broadway, though by now I hardly knew where I was. I was too shy to even look at him, and I stared at the dashboard instead, wondering what kind of car it was. I hadn't been in anyone's car for ages and I'd never seen so many buttons and dials all lit up. Not only that, but the ride was so smooth with no stopping or starting as if the traffic lights had all been green. Maybe they were, or maybe it just felt like they were. And not only that, but when I looked out the window, for a minute I thought that the streets were moving instead of us. I think because as soon as he hugged me it felt like time had stood still, and I couldn't make sense of space anymore.

I didn't know where we were going, but when he parked and I stepped onto a brick-paved street, I thought we must be somewhere in Soho. The restaurant was across the street, a brightly lit place full of noise and people, yet we were shown to a table without having to wait. And then it was like everything around us fell away and we were in our own private bubble. He was sitting across from me, looking into my eyes. I thought of telling him how glad I was to see him again and how nice he looked with his shirt collar open, but words seemed superfluous when he was taking my hands, kissing one palm and then the other. I looked at his hands, and when I felt the callouses I said, "From golf?" "Yes," he said. We drank some wine and he asked if I was hungry. I said no, so we left and went for a walk.

The street was dark and deserted, the shops and galleries shut up for the night. All this time, ever since he came up to me at the curb, no—ever since the phone call when he seemed so happy to hear from me—I hadn't been able to figure out what was happening or what this was. Then suddenly I knew. I had stopped at the window of an antique shop to slow down time, make this evening never end. "This is the Kingdom of Heaven," I said, hardly aware that I was saying it out loud. And he said, "You have peasant feet."

He was looking down at my feet. I wished I wasn't wearing sandals. I didn't like my feet. If he trying to bring me back to earth it was already too late. I was barely aware of the drive uptown to his apartment. I have no memory of him parking the car or going up in the elevator. The next thing I knew we were standing in his living room. I could see it was beautifully decorated with different colors and shapes and textures, but I was afraid to look at anything particular. As if it was all made of fairy dust and to bring my eyes into focus would either make it real or make it disappear.

He handed me a glass of white wine and said, "I want you to do a painting for me. An abstract in blue and orange to hang above the bar."

A commission too? He was looking towards the far end of the room. It wasn't well lit but I could see the wooden bar and a red wall behind it. The ceiling was low and there didn't seem much room for a painting, but I couldn't think about that now because he had taken a step closer to me. He was going to kiss me again. I looked away for a moment to put my glass down on the little table beside me, and when I looked into his eyes again the strangest thing happened. The black hole of his pupils became larger and larger. They were pulling me in. I was disappearing into his eyes. The last thing I remember thinking was, *But I haven't finished painting yet!* Then the screen in my mind went dark. I have no memory of the kiss or how I got to the bedroom or how my clothes came off. I remember opening my eyes for a moment, seeing him rearing up above me like the

Remington cowboy. But the light was on and it was too bright, too much of everything, and I slipped away again.

That night I dreamed there was a terrace off the bedroom with a huge quartz crystal on either side of the entrance, guarding it like a couple of sentries. A sign I was being protected? Inside, the wall opposite the bed had disappeared. It simply wasn't there anymore, like the fourth wall in the theater wasn't there. I was in the audience, watching a scene play out on a stage that appeared to take place in the great hall of a palace. Courtiers in period costumes milled about talking to one another. They were discussing us, the pros and cons of our union. I was too far away to hear their exact words, but I could tell the general consensus was no. Then I woke up with the sun in my eyes.

I didn't know where I was at first. Then I saw the outline of his form beside me under the sheet. How did I get to the bed? It was embarrassing not to remember. I was afraid to look at him so I looked at the sheet. It had a colorful pattern of different shapes and colors, but it was too busy, too jazzy for my taste. There were too many colors, especially red. If all the lights had seemed green the night before, all I saw now was red. Red meant danger. It meant stop. I had to get out of there. I sat up carefully so as not to wake him, and from the corner of my eye I saw his stomach was bare, the skin smooth and unblemished. I couldn't bring myself to look any higher. I was afraid to see his face. I was thinking of the myth of Eros and Psyche. He only came to her in the dark, and though he forbid her to ever look at him, one night she stole a peek and he was the most beautiful man she'd ever seen. But when a drop of hot oil from her lamp fell on his arm he woke up and saw her looking at him. He flew away then and she never saw him again until he took pity on her and brought her up to heaven. I wouldn't make

Psyche's mistake. I wouldn't look at him. Not looking at him felt like the only chance I had of ever seeing him again.

I crept slowly from the bed and dressed hurriedly in the living room. I didn't feel safe until I was standing on the corner across the street watching the trucks roll down Second Avenue. Then I looked up at his building and thought what have I done? Was it too late to go back? I looked at my watch. It was only six-fifteen. He was probably still sleeping. I didn't want to wake him. I would go get a coffee, get one for him too, then come back.

But I didn't go back. I might have gone back if there had been somewhere to sit at the bagel place on the next block, but it was only takeout and I needed to sit down. I got a coffee and a cinnamon raisin bagel, and as I walked to the subway I told myself I'd call him later, tell him I was sorry I left without saying goodbye. And though I did call him later and left a message, he didn't call me back. Each day that passed without hearing from him felt more and more strange. Even what I wrote in my diary was strange. *He whisked me off the sidewalk and flew me off to Venus, and I let him in.* I had been helpless not to. But I wished I hadn't run away. Was it the color red? Red meant stop, but it could have meant stop, *don't* go. Green meant go. But there had been the dream too. The message of no. And it was true I hadn't finished painting yet. I knew that if I stayed with him I wouldn't feel the need to paint anymore. I'd be too happy just living life. Then I thought of the vision of the sailboat, and wondered if it was a message that he would take me sailing just for the night and that would be that.

For a while I thought he might still want the abstract painting of blue and orange to hang above the bar. I had never painted an abstract before but I knew about blue and orange, and dealing with his colors felt like a way to deal with his silence. I began doing a series of small watercolor sketches where blue was the water swirling towards fiery streams of orange. I had to keep them from touching because if you mixed blue and orange they turned gray. Like the way water put out fire, and fire turned water into steam, neither could survive if they merged with one another.

The sketches gave me another excuse to call him, and a week later when I rang his office he picked up and spoke as if nothing had changed. I was relieved, then delighted when he said he wanted to show me his beach house in the Hamptons. I was sorry now that I'd signed up for a week-long retreat in Pennsylvania with Direct Centering, but he said we'd go when I got back. Then I never heard from him again. I couldn't believe it at first, and thought I'd get a response if I sent him the sketches of blue and orange, but there was nothing. I was sorry that I hadn't looked at him that morning before I rushed out, because now I couldn't even remember what he looked like.

But I could stay with him in the colors. Since I was a fire sign I would be orange and he would be blue since he was an air sign. Blue and orange were complementary colors. Seen together, each strengthened the hue of the other. Blue was cool, orange was warm. A warm color made an object appear closer, cool colors made them recede. Orange and blue, the colors of near and far. Sometimes blue was the air giving life to the flame. Other times it was the water giving chase to the fire. The flame rose up and the water threatened to envelop it. Or the fire heated the water, changed it into steam—into air. Orange and blue could be anything. They could be a pattern, a wavelength, a frequency, a sound, a feeling, a combustion. When the colors seemed about to devour one another, I wouldn't allow them to go gray. I kept them separate but together, each intact, true to itself.

The passion for his colors went on for months. It was the only way I knew how to deal with a meeting that no longer seemed tethered to ordinary space and time, but part of some timeless inner space I didn't want to lose touch with. It no longer mattered that he didn't want a picture; painting the colors kept the connection alive. Not to him; he was gone, I accepted that now. But the connection to what had happened that night. I still couldn't explain it. It had nothing to do with regular life. It was in a category all by itself, something to look back on and treasure, the feeling of being in heaven while I was still here. And so I found more ways to keep the memory present, like buying blue and orange lightbulbs for the staircase outside my door, as if the colors had seeped out of my studio. To open my door was to step into a pool of blue light and walk down the stairs towards an orange glow. When I came in from outside and opened the door to my stairway, an orange light welcomed me in, and I walked up towards the blue.

When I ran out of ideas for small sketches, I decided to paint a large abstract in oil, bigger than any painting I had ever done before. There was a six-and-a-half-foot-long swathe of canvas left on the roll, too big for the stretchers I had, so I stapled it to the wall. Then I covered the surface with a light-blue undercoat, and while I waited for it to dry I noticed shapes in the weave of the linen and the uneven brush strokes. I saw a large bald head and a staircase coming down from above as if into the head. Then I saw a small figure coming down the stairs with a candle as if she was bringing light down into the head. It was too good to pass up, and the idea of a formless abstract was put aside in favor a picture that seemed already there, waiting for me to bring it into focus. The staircase itself was a source of fascination, suggesting levels in terms of making a descent. I hadn't thought in terms of levels. In pictures I had done before, you were either above the surface or below it, nothing in between. Stairs, on the other hand, presented the idea of stages, of taking one thing at a time. Still it was only the upper half of the canvas. I had yet to think of what was below. The canvas was smooth on the lower half and didn't offer any clues. Then something made me think of attaching a cutout from some other painting I'd already done and making it into a collage.

Even before I cut them from their stretchers, I knew the *She-flame* and *He-flame* surrendering to each other would be the right size. They were the right colors too, one orangey-pink, the other white tinged with blue, both down on one knee, on fire with love. Love and union. That was what lay at the bottom of the staircase. The light from above came down into the head, down to the lovers below. When I sewed them onto this new canvas with a needle and thread, I brought them together as they should have been from the start, facing one another, joined in a single work. I'd only painted them separately because I didn't think of a him until after I painted a her. But I got it right now. The figure venturing down with a candle seemed to be doing more than bringing light to the mind; she was bringing light to the depths. Light, to the inner world of *animus* and *anima*, the inner man and woman and the marriage within. Wholeness below. I got there in the end. Psyche means soul. The encounter with the man I still called D.E. had been green-lighted, so to speak, because all the lights had been green that night. I knew it in my soul. But it couldn't last. I saw his red wall that night, the wall behind the bar where he wanted a painting. And I saw red in the morning, and knew I had to go. I knew it that night too, when I felt myself disappearing in his eyes. Funny how the screen in my mind went dark so I wouldn't remember the love-making. But I remembered what came before it, the feeling of being in heaven.

I called the picture *Song to Jung* since it was Jung who inspired me to think of union with the inner male. I thought it was finished until I happened to notice a figure in another painting I wanted to add to it. A small figure of a girl leaping with joy on the back of a fish. I don't remember what canvas I cut her from or why I had painted her in the first place, but she was the perfect size to place lower down on the staircase from the girl with a candle, and it looked like her joy was in making the descent.

I had identified with the swimmer doing a backstroke far out to sea, and maybe now I was seeing myself not only as the girl dancing on the back of the fish, but the fish as well, because at the retreat in Pennsylvania with Direct Centering when I slept in a cabin in the woods, I dreamed I was swimming naked down a stream like a fish. Then I saw a man in a herringbone jacket standing up on a grassy knoll by a house. He seemed to be waiting for me, so I got out of the water and climbed up the riverbank. He gave me a tour of the house which was newly built with all blonde wood inside. There was no furniture but there was a bookcase filled with books. Then I looked up and saw the house had no roof, and I wondered what would happen to the books if it rained?

The dream was a promise of what was to come. The house wasn't ready yet and neither was I, but in less than a year I will be living in a place with blonde wood and a large skylight in the ceiling, like having a roof open to the sky. I've come to think of the herringbone jacket the man wore as dream-speak for 'her-ring-bone.' If a ring is a promise, a ring-bone was a promise that would ring in my bones. But the house wasn't ready yet. I had come out of the water too soon. There had been three fish in the painting of a swimmer doing a backstroke far out to sea, and I had only met two of them so far. David who pulled me asunder and George who sent me away. There was one more to go. It hadn't been D.E., the one I saw as Eros, love itself. I couldn't bear to look at him in the light of day. He was meant for the night and there he would stay. Meanwhile, I would go on painting.

32

A DEPARTURE

Great is the art of beginning,
but greater is the art of ending.

— HENRY WADSWORTH LONGFELLOW

By winter I was itching to move. I knew I'd have to pay more for even half the space I had now no matter where I went, but I wanted someplace different. During the four years I'd been in Crown Heights I'd gone as far as I could. Though I didn't have the money to move or any idea where I would go if I did, it didn't stop me fretting over what I would do with all my paintings. Whenever I stretched a new canvas the last thing on my mind was that I was creating something else to take up space and tie me down. I never wanted to let go of anything and I had work going back to my days at the League. Rachel said she envied the immediate visibility of my work while she had to wait to be published, but at least paper was easy to carry around. And then, because I didn't like feeling stuck and I remembered how easy it had been to cut up a few paintings to make the collage for *Song to Jung,* I thought of cutting up more pictures to collage. That way I could keep the paintings and just get rid of the stretchers. It was the stretchers that took up all the space.

I began with the portraits. It was hard at first because they were people I'd known, and I felt like I was vandalizing them when I cut them away from their backgrounds. But it became easier as I went along because I wasn't throwing them away, I was storing them in the flat file for collaging later. As more and more pictures went into the flat file and the stack against the wall dwindled, I told myself the pictures were going to look even better and have more meaning when they became part of something bigger. If a canvas on its own was a sentence, having multiple images collaged together would be a whole paragraph. I had to keep cheering myself on because opening the drawer to the flat file, seeing all those unattached heads and figures piling up was starting to seem like I was opening the drawer in a morgue.

The empty frames presented a different problem. I had been stacking them in the dining area thinking I'd take them apart and tie them together to dispose of them in bundles, but now there were so many it was out of the question. I didn't have the stomach for taking anything else apart just then. I hoped I wasn't making a mistake cutting up the pictures, but at least I could leave the frames intact. I could put them out on the sidewalk and see if anyone else wanted them. I began draping them on my shoulders and in the crook of my arms, and I was up and down the stairs more times than I could count until they were all in a row leaning against the iron railing five or six deep. Then I kept going to the window to see if they were still there, the frames I'd abandoned that now looked like so many empty husks, remnants of what had been. Finally I saw a man loading them into his car, and I went down to introduce myself as his benefactor and find out where he was taking them. I'm glad I did because it turned out he was not only a painter but an art teacher in the public schools where they were always short of supplies. He couldn't thank me enough, and it made me happy to think I'd done a good deed. There were too many to fit into his car and he said he'd come back for the rest. It didn't hit me until they were all gone that half my work was in pieces and I didn't have a clue how I was going to put them together again.

Then on the first of April the landlord gave me the push. He was very apologetic when he came up to collect the rent but he said he had no choice. The community was growing and space was at a premium. The long and the short of it was he wanted the apartment for a Hasidic family. I totally understood. I was surprised they'd let me stay as long as they did. He didn't give me a deadline, but moving was no longer wishful thinking. It also happened that just at that time my sister was about to lose her apartment too, and she did have a deadline.

It was a year since Ellen quit her job in statistics at Citibank and went off her meds. I begged her not to, but she'd made up her mind and nothing I could say made any difference. She didn't want to be dependent on drugs anymore and was going to live on her savings while she weaned herself off them. This sounded perfectly reasonable to her, but everything went to pot without the chemicals that balanced her. Her savings ran out and the phone was cut off. Then the gas and electricity too. When I came to visit I was shocked how thin and unkempt she'd become. The apartment was a shambles with flies buzzing around the dirty dishes and overflowing garbage. Still there was no walking her back. She said she left the door open at night to get the light from the hallway. The gas stove was no loss since she didn't cook, and if she wanted to make a call she went to the phone booth at the corner. I gave her some money for food and spent the next day calling different city agencies who all said the same thing. They couldn't intervene without her consent unless she was a danger to herself or to others. There was nothing I could do but bring her food and whatever money I could spare. She didn't tell me she had fallen behind in the rent. If I asked too many questions she got angry and told me to stop interfering in her life. I only learned about the pending eviction when the management company called me as next of kin. Aside from the rent, the neighbors had been complaining about her smoking in the hallways and roaming the stairwell at all hours, sometimes yelling and screaming. But they were fond of Ellen and had known her for years. They hoped I could help.

It was all on me. My mother was back working at the mall in Illinois. Frank had been gone for three years and my brother Howard was living with her now. Howard had been living in a squat on the Lower East Side until he was beaten up in Tompkins Square Park and the police called me to come pick him up from the Emergency Room. His head was bandaged, his arm in a sling and he had hepatitis. I took him home with me and took care of him until he was well enough to be put on the train to Decatur. My mother was happy to have him. If Frank was still alive he was probably homeless, and I couldn't bear the thought of Ellen being homeless too. But neither could I have her living with me.

I was in survival mode for us both when I wrote to my old friend Toshi in Japan. Ten years ago he had given me the money to move back from London and get settled in New York while I looked for a job. Five years ago when he came to New York he gave me the money to leave Lenny and move to Brooklyn. I hadn't seen him since, and I wouldn't have had the nerve to ask for his help this time if it was just for me. But I had Ellen to think of, and if I didn't come up with her back rent she would become another crazy bag lady on the street. I asked Toshi if I could work for him again. Do the job I sort of did for him in London, researching film copyrights for Japanese television. I sent the letter off to Tokyo with a hope and a prayer, and a week later the money was in my account. He said I could have the job again too, and it would be for real this time. I didn't know what I had done to deserve a friend like Toshi, and could only think I must have been good to him in another life. Before the end of April I had Ellen's rent squared away and a new place lined up for myself in Manhattan. When I told my landlord I was leaving, he said, "Already?"

"I thought you wanted me to."

"But I didn't think you'd leave so soon!"

Neither did I. I had even managed to get Ellen into the hospital. I came over one day and found she'd been cutting herself. I wanted to cry when I saw the wounds on her arms. But it was a blessing because it made her eligible for help from the city, and I left her in the care of social services. It seemed a miracle how quickly things had all turned around.

When the movers finished loading everything up and I climbed into the van to hitch a ride, Rachel and her children stood on the sidewalk and waved goodbye. Rachel said she'd come visit me and she did, but the only time I ever came back to Crown Heights was in my dreams. It was always the same dream. I was alone in the empty bedroom where someone had thrown a brick through the window. It was peaceful now with a soft pale light filtering in through the curtains as they fluttered in the breeze.

33

THE LAST FISH

The spirit is hidden in water like the fish.

— C.G. JUNG

I made it to the Village at last. Not Greenwich Village where I once wished I could live, but the East Village, which was the place to be if you were an artist in the 1980s. I could hardly believe my luck when I saw the studio on Ninth Street that had once been a carriage house. The hook for hauling up bales of hay was still embedded in the brick below the window. Developers had already started moving in, but for now it was much the same as it had always been with quaint little shops and cafes from the old days, and new galleries seemed to be opening every other week. I was around the corner from St. Mark's, one of the oldest churches in New York, built over the remains of the early Dutch settlers of New Amsterdam. Peter Stuyvesant himself had owned the land when it was a farm, and here I was, living in what had once been a hayloft. All this plus unheard of luxuries like my own door to the street, and not only a built-in air-conditioner but a walk-in closet. The bathroom was so big it had room for a washer-dryer. But the skylight was what made all the difference. An opening to the sky that opened up the space with unfettered light from dawn till dusk. The move itself couldn't have gone smoother. There wasn't room for much more than my studio furniture plus books and the secretary desk I'd brought over from London. I didn't bring a bed. I was going to sleep on the picnic bench that first night and buy a futon sofa the next day.

After spending the afternoon unpacking I went out to explore the neighborhood and find something to eat. It was dark when I came home and found a dumpster blocking my front door. Who would do such a thing? I had been so happy coming home thinking of a hot shower and spending my first night in the new studio. I could only think the apartment had been vacant for a while and they didn't know someone had moved in. I hadn't thought to leave a light on because it was still light when I went out. The container was small, more of a skiff really, but it was as high as my shoulder, and even if it wasn't filled with garbage bags it would have been too heavy to move. I threw my weight against it anyway and it was like trying to shove a boulder. I looked around for someone who might help, but the street was deserted. The catering place on the ground floor was gated and so was the carriage house next door. I thought of going to the police but they'd probably want proof I lived there and I didn't I have the landlord's phone number or anything on me except the key. I thought having my own front door on the street was a perk and now it seemed like a curse.

I went to the pay phone across the street to call Ivan. We had stayed in touch and I didn't think he'd mind if I slept on his couch. I would rather have asked Colleen, but she was always at her boyfriend's these days. Ellen was in care upstate and I had the keys to her apartment but I hadn't been up there to clean yet. I dialed Ivan's number praying he'd be home, and he picked up, but it was only to give me a curt, unapologetic no. I fought back the tears as I came back across the street, angry with myself for being so helpless. Then I was angry at whoever put the dumpster there. And finally I was angry at the dumpster itself, going after it with a vengeance, pushing and shoving and swearing at it. I don't think I'd ever been so angry at anything in my entire life. And somehow, with all the grunting and groaning and straining every fiber of my being, I managed to budge it a few inches and squeeze through. To this day I don't know how I did it but my limbs felt like jelly and it was all I could do to drag myself up the stairs. I didn't have the strength to undress, much less take a shower, and as soon as I lay down on the hard wooden bench with my head on a pillow, I was out. In the morning when I looked out the window and saw the dumpster was gone, I might have thought I had dreamed the whole thing if my body didn't ache so. Ivan would have called it a mettle tester. He was big on things that made you see what you were made of. Maybe the move had been too easy. Maybe I had to prove I deserved it. Or maybe the fates were warning me in advance what I'd be in for on Ninth Street.

A week later I wouldn't have known I was still angry about the dumpster if I hadn't done a self-portrait. I had been planning to christen the new studio with a still-life of the yellow-orange tulips I bought that morning. But when I put them on the chest of drawers to be at eyelevel and caught a glimpse of myself in the mirror, the yellow-orange tulips against the bright pink top I was wearing, I decided to put myself in the picture too. I hardly recognized myself though. The woman in the painting had indigo hair streaked with blue, and rather than blend the shadows on her face, I left them like bands of war paint. The colors were warm but her eyes were cold and her face had a hard look I'd never seen before.

I couldn't stay angry though. My new setup was too wonderful. Aside from an art supply store just a few blocks away and being surrounded by places to get coffee or take-out, the location was so convenient I had friends stopping by. And still this was nothing compared to the joy of painting under a skylight or the thrill of sleeping so close to the easel that I'd wake up to the smell of paint. Those first few weeks when I'd open my eyes in the morning I'd wonder if I was still dreaming.

Then I decided it was time to go back to my maiden name. I had taken Lenny's name when we married and kept it after the divorce because I'd been signing my work with it and thought I should be consistent. But since I had been looking into Numerology, finding that names had vibrations since each letter represents a number, I wanted to have my own vibration again. Going back to the name I was born with felt like going back to my true self. I had to send clients my new phone number anyway, and I put in the name change along with it. I was using my middle name too, and when I ordered new business stationary and they left out the e of Louise, the printer did the job over, but I kept the first batch and started thinking of myself as Nancy Louis, pronouncing it *Louis* like the kings of France because it reminded me that I'd gone to war with a dumpster and won back my kingdom. The fish got a new name for their new home too. I'd bought them a new aquarium that came with a built-in air-filter and room for a castle surrounded by rubbery greens. They were the Ralph Fish now because I didn't know anyone named Ralph and I wanted them to be their own selves too.

None of this would have been possible without Toshi and I was anxious for an assignment to start making it up to him. When he said he wouldn't have anything for me to do until the fall, I got to work on the collages. Now that I lived near an art supply store I found I could order custom-made canvases and have them delivered. The two for the portraits were so large they had to be made to fold in half to get through the doorway. The only problem was how to attach the cutouts. Floor space was limited due to the wooden pillars separating what I called the living room area from the studio area, so laying the large canvases on the floor wasn't possible. They would have to be attached while the canvas was vertical. To reach the top I had to stand on a stepladder, which ruled out sewing them on since I wouldn't be able to get to the back. The only other thing I could think of was rabbit skin glue, the smelly, slimy concoction used for priming raw canvas, but it seemed to work. I put the women on one canvas and the men on the other as best as I could without planning the layout in advance on the floor, and told myself it didn't matter, that I was enlarging their scope, making the whole seem greater than the sum of its parts. A few years later when the glue made them ripple and bend out of shape, I told myself it had been worth it. That for a time I'd been able to see what I'd done with portraits all in one place, which had enlarged my scope too.

The rabbit skin glue doomed the other collages as well, but for now the enormous canvases were a new, expanded stage for the stories I had been telling, and each set of cutouts represented a different chapter. In the one I called *Alchemist's Dream,* there were different couples leaning into one another in different ways to find the right balance in their connection. The paintings in *Transformation* signified the different phases I went through in Crown Heights. At one end, the lonely girl sat having a picnic on her own. At the other end was the girl floating above the waves, following the song of a bird. Between them the dancing sprite beckoned me to follow, and the uncertain Artemis reached for an arrow. I painted a completely new figure for the center, a sort of hermaphrodite leaping with joy, embodying the *animus* and *anima* in union with itself. A figure breaking free after the trials of Brooklyn. A new being from the ashes of the old. To bring the figures together and make it seem as if I had planned it this way all along, I changed the color scheme to blue and orange and connected them with a circuit of webby lines to show they were part of the same energy field. The fish was there too, larger than life, drifting in from the left like a guiding spirit. Maybe he was the fish in my story who squeezed through the hidden passage and escaped from the pond. Maybe he'd come back to show me the way. Or rather show the woman in *Self-portrait with Tulips.* I don't think I would have made it without her cold hard stare.

The commission came from Henry, one of Ivan's poker buddies. In the series I did of the poker players, Henry was the balding man with a receding chin and a cigar hanging from his mouth. Ivan must have given him my number. All Henry said on the phone was that he had a picture of a painting he wanted copied in oil. When I came to his office he handed me a glossy print torn from an art magazine of a young woman sitting on a rock by a stream. She was dressed, but her knees were apart so you could see up her skirt. It was schlock art, the technique as crude as its subject matter, and if I didn't need the money I would have said no thanks. But I was always short of cash and depended on commissions to supplement my income from Toshi. I could have turned Henry down anyway, but he would only find someone else to do it and give them the money. He might as well give it to me. It looked like an easy job if I could manage to put my prejudice aside. There was no point in judging Henry, and I could hardly judge the model since I had posed for cheesecake photos myself when I was younger. As far as she was concerned, she unbuttoned the top of her blouse because she was out in the country on a hot sunny day. She put her foot in the water because it's always pleasant to put your foot in the water when it's hot and you're sitting by a stream. There was no reason to think she knew she was being spied upon. I could pretend I didn't know either.

The job went quickly. The original seemed to have been done more with a palette knife than a brush, and there were few details. When it was finished I turned it to the wall to dry so I wouldn't have to look at it anymore, and then I delivered it wrapped in brown paper so I wouldn't have to carry home an empty portfolio to remind me what I had just taken money for. And still I couldn't wipe her image from my mind. I could wash my brushes and scrape the palette clean, but there was no getting rid of the fact I'd created a picture for someone like Henry to ogle. I was disgusted at myself for giving him what he wanted. Then I thought, why not paint my own version to counteract his. It would be a palette cleanser for the mind. I couldn't change the Henrys of this world, or the enablers like myself who needed the cash, but I could make amends. If she had to sit with her knees apart, she could be wearing a dress that fell between her legs. Nothing to see there. Nothing to see above the waist either, once I made her flat-chested in a dress that came up to her neck and opened in the back. A dress I painted the color red for Stop, don't go there. And rather than long blonde hair tied back in a ponytail, I made her a redhead with short curly hair. I had to have known what I was doing, making her too young and innocent to be looked at sexually. It's so obvious to me now, yet I don't remember putting two and two together, connecting how I felt about Henry's painting to how I felt the night of the Oscar thing when my mother's boyfriend looked at me in a way that he wasn't supposed to.

Maybe that was why I couldn't get her face right, and struggled to find the right expression. At one point she had a sly, knowing look, which was all wrong, and I put her aside thinking to finish it later. This in itself was unusual since normally when a picture wasn't working I didn't waste any more time with it. I may not have gotten back to this one either if I hadn't happened to glance at the stacks one day and see her peeking out from behind another canvas with that knowing look still on her face. I couldn't leave her that way. Once she was back on the easel her expression went through several more stages before it came together. The picture as a whole came together then, maybe because I placed her in water. It hadn't been my intension. I'd only painted the background blue to contrast with her red dress and hair, which was actually more orange than red, and it reminded me of how Fred had become *Boy on the Sea Bed* because I had a lot of blue paint at the time. She would be *Girl Under Water* then. I already knew she was going to be the last of the pictures having to do with water, and it seemed fitting that this last one should be that of a child since I hadn't done a child before.

For this ending of sorts, I spent a lot of time working on the water of dark cobalt blue, filling it with odd shapes and squiggles, mingling them with flecks of orange. None of the shapes were recognizable except the one that could have been a starfish and the one that was either a plus sign or a cross. I kept adding more brushstrokes and shapes until the girl appeared to be sitting in a whirlwind of currents. There was a fish too. The last fish I would ever paint as it turned out. He had stripes and was outlined in orange to make him stand out while he hovered near her face with his mouth open as if to whisper something in her ear. Maybe he was saying, *I've found you at last.*

Could she hear that? She was looking away, calm and thoughtful as if she was resigned to her fate. One of her hands fell across her thigh like the girl in Henry's picture, and I didn't know what to do with the other hand until I gave her a leafy branch to hold. Then I couldn't decide if it was laurel for victory or an olive branch for peace. Maybe it was both, since making peace with oneself is a kind of victory. I seemed to know that at the time, though it was all intuitive. On a conscious level I knew nothing. I was pleased at what I'd done though, and she went on the brick wall. A girl, a child under water. The last in a series.

Little did I know that she was really the beginning of something else. I may have hung her on the wall thinking only of defeating Henry and his ilk, but she was much more than that. I know that now, just as I know the last fish had led me to her. But I couldn't see she was me. I could only paint her. And the fish had no voice. He couldn't say, *Here you are—you've found yourself at last!* My hand knew the way but my eyes were blind. Yet it wouldn't be long before she led me to connect with my childhood nightmare, the No Exit dream of drowning in a steel box. And eventually to the night of the Oscar thing when I pretended I was drowned at the bottom of a pool. For that to occur I needed far more awareness and self-knowledge than I had at the time.

I was due for it though, now that I was in the house of

blonde wood with a roof open to the sky. I'd seen it a year ago when I slept in a cabin in the woods and dreamed I was swimming down the stream like a fish. I came out of the water to meet the man in a herringbone jacket who showed me the house of blonde wood. The house wasn't ready yet, and neither was I. But that was last year. This year I was living in the house of blonde wood. And in dream-speak, it was time to meet the blonde-haired man who 'wood.'

PART III

A GATEWAY 1986-1987

Crossing over sounds exciting,
but in order to do that
you have to give yourself away.
It's a bit like dying.

— STUART WILDE

34

GENE THE GENIE

Say Yes. Say yes to everything.

—OSHO

He found me through People Resources, the video dating club I joined while I was still in Brooklyn and didn't want to get involved with any more men in real estate. It was exciting in the beginning, coming up to midtown to browse through the possibilities. There were so many, a whole shelf of thick binders full of photos and bios of men and their interests. You'd look at the photos and watch their video interview, and after you gave a handful of names to the receptionist you'd wait until they came to the office to pick up their invitations. Then they'd look at your photo and watch your interview to decide whether to call you. All this could take weeks, and half the time you'd forget whom you'd invited because you were too busy dealing with the ones who'd invited you. But I was out there again, going for drinks or for dinner with some very nice men, though none of them were for me. This was not a concern in the beginning because there were still so many others in the binders I hadn't opened yet. But after a while no matter how pleasant it was to have dates, it was beginning to feel like a waste of time and I put my membership on hold while I moved and got settled on Ninth Street. It wasn't until the end of August that I stepped back into the fray and found the invitation from Gene.

I was surprised he picked me. He was in advertising and I never got picked for those commercials in London my agent used to send me up for. I thought the men were slick and superficial and I hated the falseness of it all. But Gene wasn't like that. When I watched his video he came across as shy and self-deprecating, vulnerable really. I found his hesitancy to talk about himself appealing, and liked the fact he was a dozen years older. Then I wondered what he liked about me, and said yes to his invitation more out of curiosity than anything else because of all those other times I hadn't been picked by men in advertising. When he called and asked me out for a drink he said he'd pick me up at my place. Now, scarcely a week after I finished *Girl Under Water* he was ringing the buzzer. I hadn't planned to ask him in, but when I opened the door and saw him standing out there on the sidewalk, a step lower than me, broad shouldered in a jacket and tie, better looking than he'd been in the video, his thick yellow-blonde hair made me think of a Viking. Yet he still had that look of uncertainty. It was so incongruous with his appearance that without giving it another thought I asked if he'd like to come up.

Viking hair. It seemed an odd connection to make. If you asked me what Vikings symbolized I would have said power. A northern race who had thankfully died out since I thought of them as merciless adventurers and marauders ruled by strange masculine gods. What I didn't think of then, and what I can't help thinking of now because of the odd relationship that was going to evolve with Gene, was what else the word Viking suggested to me. For now it was all beneath the surface, but as the months passed by and I drifted into a subliminal place looking for reasons I couldn't explain, I became fixated upon what seemed a hidden communication between us.

It began not with a word but a sound he made soon after he followed me up the stairs. First he looked around the way I did when I came into someone's house for the first time. Most people gave the studio a quick once-over and said, 'Nice place,' or, 'I like your work.' Gene only said, "Are these all yours?" But the only picture that seemed to interest him was the small framed photograph of my father. "Who's that?" he said. I told him it was my father and he went, "Hmm…" as if he was considering it.

I was standing behind him and couldn't see his face or tell what he was thinking, but I felt the energy in the room change. That *Hmm…* could have meant anything, but in the silence that followed the first thing that occurred to me was he might have thought it odd for a thirty-six-year-old woman to have only one photograph out, and that of her father. Right away I felt guilty for not having a photo of Milton on display too, and it brought back all the old feelings of doubt and insecurity I once had of whose daughter I was supposed to be. And who *I* was supposed to be. All because of that *Hmm…* of a stranger with Viking hair I happened to invite into my studio.

My acquaintance with him would continue for the next year, and at the end of it I would be no closer to understanding the strange hold he seemed to have over me. It wouldn't be for lack of trying. I tried everything I knew, even things I didn't know, and still I was left wondering. It haunted my thoughts long after he was gone, that *Hmm...* I was so discombobulated by at the time, as if he was already signaling our encounter was going to be different from anything I'd known before.

It would be many years before I realized the simple sound of *Hmm...* might not only signify wonder or thinking but could be the start of someone humming. Or even someone trying to find the right key for a song. I'd done it myself more times than I can count. Yet I didn't associate it with finding the right key until I put the sound together with the color of his hair. His Viking hair, which had nothing to do with actual Vikings or even hair color, but was instead a simple sound. A frequency hidden in the sound of Viking. Or vi- *keeng.* Or vi-*keying.* Or even *by-keying.*

I would be hard put to remember the last time I'd thought of a lost key. The key to my soul I thought was lost when Milton died. It had been more than a decade ago and so much water had passed under the bridge since then! But however I may have forgotten it doesn't mean it wasn't buried somewhere in my inner being. For it was that very loss that had sent me over the edge when I realized I didn't know what love was. And after a stint in the psych ward and the Dream of '76, a whole new world had opened up inside and I knew I had to become a painter or a writer to find out what it was all about. And now here was this man Gene on my doorstep with his *vi-keying* hair and his *Hmm...* I say this now, and at the very beginning of our story, because I believe I must have known it at the time, which explains my otherwise inexplicable behavior towards him.

* * *

When Gene helped himself to the wicker chair by the window I sat down a little ways away on the picnic bench and studied him in the beige jacket, dark-blue crocheted tie against a light-blue shirt and jeans, and just as I was thinking how delightful it was meeting a man I was attracted to, he said, "How can you afford this place?"

I was astonished he would ask such a thing. I wished I'd been able to brush it off with a smile and say, 'Oh, I manage.' Instead, I found myself telling him about the Japanese company I worked for, which unfortunately reminded me of the difficulty I'd had in London when I tried to explain to people how I'd come to live in the fancy Kensington duplex. I'd say it belonged to the Japanese company I worked for and came with the job, which was true but not the whole truth. And even though the job was real this time, or would be as soon as Toshi gave me an assignment, I felt defensive, and when I added that I got commissions too, it sounded like I was trying to justify myself. When I asked about his work, he began talking about Bella Abzug and how he'd run her campaign for mayor of New York. "How do you feel about Bella Abzug?" he said.

Was this a test? I didn't feel anything about her. I barely recalled the election ten years back when I was working as a secretary and dating Lenny. I had no interest in city politics at the time, and all I remembered about Bella Abzug was her signature hats with the wide brims, which I thought best not to mention.

The evening went downhill from there. We went out for a drink on one of those balmy late summer nights when everyone wanted to be outdoors and the sidewalks were so crowded we were barely walking together. I wouldn't have worn high-heeled sandals if I'd known we were going to traipse across town to the West Village. My feet were aching by the time he finally stopped at a little outdoor café. Ever the optimist I thought the evening might be salvaged when the wine came, but he seemed to have lost interest in me by then. It was no use trying to keep the conversation going when he gave monosyllabic answers and didn't look at me. We finished our drinks, said a polite goodbye and went our separate ways. I was surprised when he called the next day and asked me out for dinner.

First he apologized for what he called his "passive behavior" the night before. At least I thought it was an apology until he said, "I was observing your show."

"My show?"

"You're exotic. Along the lines of Zelda."

I couldn't tell if this was a complement or not, but I was game, and for the second time in as many days I began the evening wrongly assuming I had the upper hand since I was the one accepting his invitations. I was in a buoyant mood when I arrived at the tiny French restaurant in his neighborhood on the Upper West Side. He hadn't arrived yet, and while I waited in the booth for two thinking how much I liked getting to know someone new, I wondered if he was going to ask me back to his place afterwards and if I should I go. Then Gene walked in with his shirt-sleeves rolled up and looking so much at home I thought he must be a regular.

He ordered a carafe of wine, and as we studied the menu, which was only the neatly typed *plat du jour*, he asked more questions. They were easy ones this time, like what sort of parts I played when I was an actress. I loved talking about those days and I was at ease mentioning Blanche in *Streetcar* since she had been the most memorable, completely forgetting her resemblance to that other neurotic southerner, Zelda Fitzgerald. As I spoke I was fingering the rim of the little pink lampshade on the table, and it reminded me how Blanche had liked soft lighting. I said that I liked soft lighting too, and when I remembered how it felt to stand in the spotlight while all around was shadowy and gray, I added that life was full of gray areas. I didn't think I was saying anything controversial, but Gene looked at me and said quietly, as if he was speaking to a child, "There are no gray areas. There is only black and white." I wondered why he would say that, and waited for him to elaborate, but he was looking down at his arms folded on the table.

"You've disappointed me," he said, dropping his head lower until his forehead rested on his arms folded on the table and all I could see was his yellow-blonde hair. I couldn't have been more surprised than if he'd suddenly slapped me, and I sat there for a long minute or two staring at the top of his head, waiting for him to look up and explain. When neither of these things happened I slid out of the booth, took one last look at him slumped over the table with his head on his arms and hurried out of the restaurant feeling humiliated and somehow ashamed.

My eyes were already smarting when I flagged down a taxi at the corner, and it was all I could do to hold myself in until I got home. When the dam burst I didn't question why I allowed this man I barely knew to upset me. Not once did I stop to consider there was something odd about him or that he'd treated me badly. Questioning me, judging me, and now saying I had disappointed him. It unleashed a wave of remembrance how I had disappointed myself. And then, maybe because it had been a French restaurant, I remembered the time my mother took me to a French restaurant when I was nineteen to give me the news that my father wasn't really my father. And how I'd sobbed in the restaurant to think how disappointed in me my father would be if he knew.

* * *

My mother waited for her dry martini to arrive before dropping the bombshell, "Dear, Frank Wait is not your father." Then she launched into the story about her affair with Milton in Tonopah, Nevada, the small mining town where she established residency when she was divorcing her first husband to marry my dad. I was in shock, laughing hysterically then crying uncontrollably. My guilt was unimaginable. I'd chosen an acting career to please Dad, and when I got my first theater job in England, I wrote him a gleeful letter how I'd been cast as Gloria in Lorraine Hansberry's *The Sign in Sidney Brustein's Window*, a play he'd taken me to see when I was in high school. I forgot that Gloria was a call girl who suicides. I can still remember her last line, *Living without your father's values can kill you. Papa —I am better than this! Now will you forgive me?* I was practically suicidal myself by the time the play ended. It didn't matter that my father never said I'd disappointed him. He was the opposite, always saying how proud he was of me. He thought I was doing so well in London. That was what hurt. He didn't know what I was up to over there. He didn't know what I'd gotten into with Lenny either. He liked Lenny. He was so happy at our wedding. The photo Gene asked about was taken at the wedding. My father was beaming at the camera. Maybe I kept his photo out because I wanted to think he was beaming at me still. Maybe I wouldn't have been thinking about my father at all if Gene hadn't asked who was in the photo and then said, 'Hmm...' It was the only thing he'd been curious about in my whole apartment, and all he said was 'Hmm…'

It was hours before I was able to calm myself enough to fall asleep. I didn't think about Gene until the next morning when I woke up happy. Joyful even. My head felt clear, my heart so light I practically leapt out of bed, as if the flood of tears the night before had washed away the last remnants of sadness and guilt I had been carrying around all these years. Only then did I remember Gene and realize he'd done me a favor. All I could think of now was how to thank him.

At Direct Centering we always acknowledged someone who showed us where we were still attached. I had been in touch with them again since moving to Ninth Street because the center was close by and they were the only people I knew in the area. When I called Gene's office he wasn't in so I left a message. When he didn't return my call I wrote him a note. Then I got to work on a watercolor for a contest they were having at the center. I no longer remember what the theme was, but I was painting a bird's eye view of a street grid. A blurry, watery view, as if I was flying above the city without my contacts, seeing it as an impressionist might. I couldn't miss the arrows though. They were big and red, all pointing up, or north. It was a blow when I hung it up at the center with the other entries and no one understood it. But I've come to see it as a message to myself to follow the signs and stay on track. I'd had to go high up to see the big picture, and even though the view below was blurry and indistinct, I could still read the signs because they were red arrows I'd put there myself.

* * *

The painting has become even more meaningful to me since then. I felt crushed when Gene said I'd disappointed him, but I wept and got it out of my system. I was able not only to thank him then, but to celebrate with a new painting about following the signs. The last thing that would have occurred to me was that other time I had followed the signs that led me to Lenny. Two days after disembarking from the ship I'd gone down to Sheridan Square in the Village, spotted a bookstore, picked up a book called *Illuminations,* and saw the 'Apartments for Rent' sign across the square.

What I didn't think about was the significance of black and white, which seems odd since I happened to be wearing black and white that night I brought up gray areas. A black top over a black and white print skirt. Gene couldn't see my skirt because I was sitting the whole time, but he could hardly have failed to notice my earrings. A pair of those large metal ones popular in the 1980s that had a black and white design. He said, 'There is only black and white,' and I was actually wearing only black and white.

It's only now I remember who else wore black and white —Catherine in *View From the Bridge* when it was playing Off-Broadway. My father took me to see it when I was studying acting at Performing Arts High School. The set was minimal, the lighting stark, and the actress playing Catherine, who was small with dark hair like me, wore a plain white blouse tucked into a straight black skirt. I can still see her standing alone in the light on that dark stage, her voice clear as a bell, and I wanted to be just like her when I grew up. But after high school came the Oscar thing and I slipped into a gray area. Two years later the borders were smudged further when my mother told me Dad wasn't my real father.

The black and white checkered linoleum in the hallway of the psych ward was clear enough though. Maybe without knowing it I'd found solace in the squares at St. Mary Abbots because they were white or black and nothing in between. No confusion, just one or the other. And where had gray areas led me if not to the hospital, much as they'd led Blanche to the asylum. I'd forgotten all about that.

* * *

Gene called on a Friday when I'd all but forgotten about the note I'd sent thanking him, and asked me out for the following Tuesday. That evening I went to the regular Friday night community dinner at the center where they only charged five dollars for a heaping plate of noodles with tofu and vegetables lathered with sesame sauce. I sat next to Karin, a woman I knew from the old days, who made a half-hearted attempt to enroll me in the event that weekend. She said, "Expanding Relationships is about moving through your obstacles instead of away from them. My new boyfriend is doing it with me." She grinned like the cat who swallowed the canary and said, "I surrender to him. I give him everything he wants."

Then another assistant joined us with his plate of food and tried to sell me on the event. The hidden cost of these dinners was listening to their pitches. I had no intention of signing up but they never took no for an answer. There was the usual back and forth with me saying I didn't have the money and him insisting I could get it. Then he said, "What are you up against?" and I didn't know. It wasn't the money. If I really wanted to go I could always borrow it. What then. The question gnawed at me for the rest of the evening. I was still thinking about it when I walked home, and it was the last thing I thought of before I went to sleep.

I had an answer right after I woke up in the morning

when I happened to look at the brick wall where *Girl Under Water* was hanging. She'd been there all the time but I hadn't really looked at her since the painting was finished, and now suddenly she reminded me of the No Exit dream of my childhood when I drowned in the steel box. The rectangular canvas not only resembled a box but she hung on a brick wall. I'd only called it the No Exit dream because of the brick wall on the cover of Sartre's *No Exit.* The book had been left out on the coffee table in the living room for weeks. I didn't have to know it was a play about Hell; that dreadful title combined with the picture was enough. I thought it uncanny that the girl in my painting looked like I might have looked if I'd drowned in the box instead of waking up in time. It was so obvious to me now I wondered how I could have missed it. But I didn't feel trapped anymore. How could I still be up against that?

Still, I decided the best thing to do would be to surrender to the fear. I learned at Direct Centering that surrendering to whatever you were afraid of would make the fear go away. So, before I got dressed or had a coffee or thought better of it, I got comfortable on the futon and closed my eyes to picture myself enclosed in a box. It didn't work. No matter I told myself I was trapped I didn't believe it, probably because nothing was at stake. And I was back where I started, wondering what I was up against.

Karin said she surrendered to her new boyfriend, giving him everything he wanted. For her, it was the way she 'moved through her obstacles.' I might have remembered I'd done that with Lenny, but that was already the past and I was concerned with the present. What was I up against *now?* If I had a boyfriend I could try what Karin did, but there was only Gene and I could hardly call him a boyfriend. Still, he was taking me to dinner on Tuesday. That was something. I could surrender to Gene. Then it struck me that we'd never even touched. And suddenly the thought of him touching me made me feel I would crumble.

35

THE OBSTACLE

To go wrong in one's own way
is better than to go right in someone else's.

— FYODOR DOSTOEVSKY

I came out when he buzzed, and after he mumbled "Hello," he strode off towards the garden restaurant across the street. As I hurried to catch up with him I wondered if he was only taking me there because it was close by and he wanted to get the dinner over with. But then why ask me out? I resolved not to care. I had been wanting to try the Cloisters ever since I moved to Ninth Street anyway. It was walled off from the street and I couldn't see over the wall even from my second-floor window. But in the evenings if a car wasn't passing by I could hear the clatter of plates and cutlery and I'd always wondered what it was like inside.

This time we not only had dinner, we had a normal conversation, though I was the one keeping it going. I wanted to know more about him. He answered readily enough, telling me he was from Tennessee and went to

Cornell, but his manner was distant. It didn't have to stop me from enjoying myself though. The food was good, the weather perfect for eating outside, and I was dining at the Cloisters. Maybe he was closed off because of a recent divorce or a relationship that ended badly. I tried feeling him out on the subject and got nowhere. But now the topic was relationships, I remembered a wonderful line I'd heard somewhere. "We're all mirrors of each other," I said, "and you can't love another person until you love yourself."

"What a bunch of New Age claptrap," he said.

I gave up then. It was a relief when the check came and we got up to go. I thought that would be the end of it, but as soon as we were out on the sidewalk he took my hand, waited for a car to pass, and without a word hurried me back across the street and up to bed. There was no talking. No asking or thinking, as if we'd been headed there from the start. To that deep wordless place where there was only need, and satisfying that need. His need for me felt urgent, primal even. His almost brutal tenderness left me feeling I was nothing. And everything.

He left a few hours later saying, "I'll call you tomorrow." Then he didn't call. Days went by, then more days. I couldn't leave it like that. If he wasn't going to call me then I would call him, tell him I wanted to see him again.

"This is getting dangerous," he said. "I'll have to think about it."

That was it then. He didn't want to get involved. But dangerous? The idea that anything to do with me could be thought of as dangerous was laughable. It didn't occur to me that he might be dangerous. Then I wondered what might constitute danger anyway, and the memory came back of something that happened last spring when I was with a date. It was early evening, still light out when we drove through the tunnel under Grand Central Station. I knew the tunnel well because if you were driving up Park Avenue South you had to go through the tunnel to get uptown. Maybe he was driving too fast because the suddenness of being on a level plane then swooping down a sharp incline caught me by surprise. That brief plunge into darkness, then hurtling up the ramp into daylight again felt like we'd crashed through an invisible barrier. I don't know why I thought that, but it gave me a moment of panic and I quickly fastened my seat-belt, though it was after the fact. I jotted down the memory along with Gene's comment about danger, and it turned out to be the last coherent train of thought I would record for weeks.

Normally my journal was for keeping track of what I was doing and how I felt about it, with all the entries dated. There was none of that now. I have no idea what I did with myself for those weeks, and later when I looked at what I'd written, I thought I must have lost my mind for a while. First I thought of Illinois, my home state, and wondered where the name came from. I called my mother in Decatur to ask if she knew, and she said she thought it was from the Illini Indians. I wrote I-L-L-I-N-I, then I-LLIN-I, which sounded like I-LINE-I. Like, 'I align myself' with my home state. Then I saw the letter L as a right angle which was even better because when I substituted 'angle' for L, Illini became, 'I-angle-angle-in-I.' Like I was angling into myself. *Right*-angling into myself since L was a right angle. Unless angling had to do with anglers, as in fishermen. I was off on another tangent then, making lists as if I was fishing for clues. I wrote down birthdays, birthplaces and destiny numbers of husbands and lovers, fathers and friends, and looked for a pattern. Then I looked at timelines to see if there was a key in the chronology that might tell me something more, though I couldn't have said what that 'more' might have been. Disjointed nonsense, that's all it was.

Looking at it now though, I don't believe I was as incoherent as I once thought. If Gene's comment about danger made me remember the feeling of crashing through an invisible barrier, it seemed that I was now trying to break through a barrier in my mind. Scrambling words, arranging letters differently as if to wake myself up to a different level of awareness. I-align-I or 'eye-align-eye,' could have meant aligning the outer eye with the inner eye. But what really intrigued me later was what happened when I played around with Milton's surname. If my mother had married Milton my last name would have been Geller. I'd written Geller and turned it into Gell-her, then Jell-her, then gel with a hard g again, and combined it with gull. Gel-gull-girl. It reminded me of the time I played Nina in *The Seagull.* Nina, who said, "I'm a seagull." I wrote sea-gull—see-girl.

It would have been something if I'd written 'sea-girl' and looked up at *Girl Under Water* hanging on the wall. But I didn't look up. I was too busy thinking of Nina who spoke about the cross she had to bear, and I drew a cross. If only I had looked up I might have noticed the cross beside the girl in the water. A cross or a plus sign. But I was looking down at my journal, drawing an x for the crossbones of death and turning it on its side, changing it to a plus sign. Which then became a crucifix, then an ankh, the symbol for eternal life. Looking back, it was as if going from sea-gull to see-girl and coming up with the ankh for eternal life, I was seeing through some kind of invisible barrier without even knowing it. But without knowing, there was no change. No epiphany. No breakthrough. I was trying though. The memory of being on a level plane, then suddenly swooping down into darkness and swooping up again into the light just as suddenly, was like going from the known into the unknown, then back to the known again. No wonder it felt dangerous. I hadn't lost my mind, only gone deeper into it, into my subconscious. Into something I knew but couldn't grasp with my rational mind. It would be years before I began writing about the painting I called *Girl Under Water*, shortening it in my notes to the initials GUW and reading it as 'Gee, You, Double-You.'

Then as suddenly and unexpectedly as it began, I turned the page on the disjointed scribblings in my journal. Three weeks later I was back recording the date and describing the weather. What a beautiful October day! What a clear blue sky with a chill in the air. I also mentioned how I'd woken up that morning after a wonderful dream, but instead of immediately writing it down like I should have, I went and brushed my teeth first. The dream slipped away, all but the last part. I remembered at the end it was about becoming real when 'my dream' became real. It didn't do me any good though because I assumed it meant my dream of becoming recognized as an artist and having gallery shows. That was my dream in those days. My outer dream I should say. If I could go back in time I'd give myself a good shake and say never mind about that, what about your inner dream, the Dream of '76 when you were shot and fell into the sea? Remember the door that opened, and how shocked you were to wake up and realize you hadn't died after all? If there was an invisible barrier, surely it was that one, going from death into life again. But the dream had been ten years ago and I'd forgotten it. I'd finished *Girl Under Water* only six weeks ago and already I'd forgotten about her.

I wouldn't get the message, *You will become real when your dream becomes real,* until I could accept that the Dream of '76 wasn't only a dream, it was a memory. I probably wouldn't have been able to deal with it at the time. Nor was there any need. But something was going on and it had to do with Gene. He seemed to bring things up in me. There was that 'Hmm…' when I said the man in the photo was my father. And saying I'd disappointed him. I couldn't have said why I felt I had to redeem myself in his eyes, but there it was. I hadn't seen him for almost a month, not since that dinner at the Cloisters, and now I had a date with him that very evening. The same day I'd started writing the date in my journal again and talking about the weather was the day I was going to see him again. No mystery there, coming back to reality on the day he'd invited me up to dinner at his place. He probably only invited me because I'd been writing to him again. I hoped it was only the one letter but it could have been more. God only knows what I'd said given the state I was in.

I didn't know Gene was rich until I came to the address he'd given me on the Upper West Side and saw it was one of those elegant brownstones and there was only one buzzer, which meant the whole building was his. It was a reminder how little I knew about him and I almost turned around and went home. But I told myself not to be silly. I'd come this far and I might as well go through with it.

Gene opened the door wearing a chef's apron and led me through the house to the dining room in the back where he handed me a glass of wine that was already poured. Then he disappeared into the kitchen. A baseball game was blaring from a tv somewhere. I looked down at the table and saw it was set for six. No sooner did I register this was not going to be the tête-à-tête I had imagined, than a couple of tall skinny young men with the same yellow-blonde hair as Gene piled into the room with their girlfriends. I had forgotten his bio at the dating club said he had children. The boys, who looked to be in their early twenties seemed as nonplussed by my presence as I was surprised by theirs, and introductions, such as they were, were slap-dash. None of their names sunk in, and after having said hello, they sat down at the table with their respective girlfriends and forgot about me. Then Gene came out with bowls of food and took his seat at the head of the table. I sat at the only place left, the one on the side at the far end, the odd one out. The merry five were a vocal lot, helping themselves to the bowls of pasta and salad being passed down the line. Gene didn't say a word to me. In fact they all acted as if I wasn't there. The only time I said anything was to the boy across from me, a question he answered with no more interest than you'd give a stranger on the street. I swallowed my pride along with a few bites of food and wondered why I had been invited to observe these boisterous high-spirited young people talking and laughing amongst themselves. Clearly I wasn't there as Gene's girlfriend, but I wasn't even being treated as a guest, let alone a friend.

After the meal they dispersed, Gene to the kitchen, the young people to various parts of the house. No one offered to see me out, and I didn't feel welcome to go into the kitchen, so I wandered into the room where the tv was. The Mets game was still on, as it had been all through the meal, and over the noise of the set I heard feet clattering up and down the stairs, laughter rising and falling. Occasionally one of the boys stuck his head in to check the score and shout it out to the rest of the house. I was more interested in the bookcases lining the walls with shelves going up to the ceiling. That the wood was blonde wood didn't ring any bells. I couldn't remember the dream I had that morning, let alone the one I had a year ago in the woods of Pennsylvania when a stranger showed me around a house with a blonde wood bookcase full of books. Gene's seemed mostly paperbacks of popular fiction, and I climbed the wooden ladder on wheels attached to the shelves to see if there was anything more interesting higher up. But the ladder was wobbly and I felt silly up there, so I came down and settled into one of the deep-cushioned armchairs while I finished my wine and thought about leaving.

Then Gene came in. He took my hand and pulled me up from the chair. "Let's go to bed," he said. Still holding my hand, he led me to the corner of the room where there was a door I hadn't noticed, and I followed him down a narrow spiral staircase as the sound of baseball faded away. In the morning when he showed me out, he said, "Thank you for coming." It was the first nice thing he'd ever said to me. Then he surprised me again by putting his palms together and bowing his head like a Buddhist offering a prayer. I copied the gesture back to him, then turned and went down the steps as the door click shut behind me.

I took the long way home on the bus and lay on the futon for the rest of the day. I didn't notice the ugly bruise on my thigh until I took a shower. Then I remembered how he'd let go of me at one point and I fell off the bed.

The Mets won the World Series. It was the first time they'd won in twenty-five years and cars were cruising down Second Avenue honking their horns. I thought there had been an accident and went outside to see what happened. The sidewalks were mobbed. Traffic was at a crawl and merrymakers were everywhere, spilling out of bars, drinking on the street. There was so much joy in the air I almost wished I cared about baseball. Or cared about anything really. A dullness had settled over me since the night with Gene. I went about my work for Toshi, relieved that he had finally given me some assignments. Part of the job was going up to the film library at Lincoln Center to research copyright information for old British and American war movies that were popular in Japan. Or I'd call distributors for various other movies Toshi had an interest in and request videos to screen on my VCR. I tried to sound upbeat about the so-called plots of these low-budget action flicks made for foreign markets before I FedExed them to Tokyo, but they were a chore to watch. And no matter what I was doing, my thoughts invariably drifted back to Gene. I couldn't help feeling a sense of loss that it was over. Never mind his behavior, he'd sparked something in me. I couldn't say what exactly, only that something seemed to happen around him. Now there was nothing.

I stayed in most evenings, curled like a slug in the peach-colored quilt to watch old movies on tv. One night it was *Invasion of the Body Snatchers*, which I hadn't seen in years, and it was a new experience watching it after having been through Direct Centering. What we did there was called duplicating, getting on the other person's wavelength to feel what they were feeling. Staring into their eyes, getting into the rhythm of their breathing, letting everything go but the eyes and the breath. Staying with them until there was no more you, no more them, only being.

I used the technique with my mother once when she came for a visit last summer and started talking about Milton as if he was still alive. It had been ten years since his death, which she refused to believe even at the time, saying it was a plot to make us think he was dead. I was in London then and could hang up on her. I didn't have that luxury last summer in Brooklyn when she was standing in front of me. The day was hot and muggy and I was in no mood to humor her. I said irritably, "Mom, Milton died. He's *dead*."

"No he isn't! You're lying! He's not dead!"

When I looked in her eyes and saw the fear and panic there, I wondered why I had to insist I was right. It wouldn't cost me anything to go along with her. So rather than denying it again, I said softly, "I know." Because who was I to say Milton was dead when she still needed him to be alive. Her face relaxed, and I could see it was because she was believed. I'd let her know I was with her, a mirror rather than an adversary. We went on to talk about something else then, and she never brought up Milton again.

To be with someone, duplicating them, getting on their wavelength, was to accept them. And what was the penultimate form of duplication if not portraiture? I had to paint Gene's portrait. That was the way to move past him. I thought again about what Karin had said that night at the center—move through your obstacles instead of away from them. If he posed for me I could get on his wavelength, see who he was inside, end the mystery. It would have to be done from life though. Painting him from my imagination would just be my idea of him, and that had caused enough problems already. It had to be real. I had to see him as he really was, not how I saw him in my mind or what he represented to me. I remembered from his bio he had a birthday coming up. I could tell him I wanted to give him a portrait for his birthday. I was so excited by the idea that I called him that night in case I thought better of it in the morning and chickened out. When he answered the phone I said, "Can you talk?"

"No."

"I'll ring you tomorrow at the office then."

I didn't shy away from it the next day either. This was about painting, nothing more. "You won't even have to sit for it," I said. "I'll take photos and work from them." I was glad I'd thought of that. Knowing he wouldn't have to sit for hours increased the possibility he would say yes. I didn't think I would be capable of painting him from life anyway. It would have been too intense.

"Okay," he said.

I congratulated myself on this brilliant move, and again when he showed up to have his picture taken and I was calm and cool eying him in the hunter-green trench coat. Such confidence I had ordering him around, saying, "Stand over there please," and "Let's see how it looks without the coat now." It was a heady feeling telling him what to do. It was how I always worked, but I had never been like that with Gene before. "Would you mind taking your tie off?" "Let's move over here now." He did everything I asked and never said a word. I was able to shoot quickly with a skylight overhead and no need to use the flash. And at some point, now that I was looking at him as a subject rather than a love-interest, I saw a middle-aged man with a slight paunch bulging over his Levi's and wondered what I'd seen in him. The whole thing was over in less than half-an-hour and then it was my turn to see *him* out and thank *him* for coming. When he was gone all I felt was relief. I thought the hard part was over. I didn't realize how tough it was going to be deciding which shot to use for the painting. He was the strong confident alpha male in all of them, but I couldn't make up my mind if I liked him better in the trench coat or just the shirt, with or without a tie. Then I thought why did I have to limit myself to doing just one portrait? I could do two, and keep one for myself.

One would have been daunting enough, and I ended up doing five. It was only the head and shoulders. I wasn't interested in anything but his face. Strong chin, nose rather sharp, lips thin, eyes more deeply set than I thought. I hadn't noticed these things before because I didn't really look at people unless I was drawing or painting them. I saw them, but rather than noticing anything particular, I took in the whole person to get a feeling of who they were.

The first few days alone with his image I went from one canvas to another, painting them all in tandem, proud of how objective, how cold and clinical I could be if I tried. By the third day when I was starting to get somewhere, I wasn't ready to quit when the light dimmed, and switched on my special daylight bulb to work a few more hours. The day after that I wasn't ready to quit at all, and painted through the night. That must have been when I let down my defenses, during those silent hours in the dead of night when I felt alone with him and could admit to myself that I must be in love. I hadn't thought of it before because how could I love someone who was so rude and uncaring and didn't help me up when I fell off the bed. But love has no reason, and it was a relief to finally accept it. Love and be free. Maybe Lenny was right after all, and love was the way to free myself from this obsession. He glowered at me in one portrait and looked fierce in another, but his features softened as they became more familiar to me. I wasn't able to glean a sense of who he was inside and maybe I didn't want to anymore. Or maybe he had erected a shield around himself. But I felt more compassionate towards him. Towards myself too. By the end, it wasn't so much an allowing of him as it was allowing myself to feel whatever I needed or wanted to feel. Maybe that was the way through.

Painting him in watercolor was a different matter, not only because the medium was lighter and more fluid, but because I chose the photo where he looked up and away and not at me. I used colored pencils to add more nuance, and though I could see I had idealized him, it was the only portrait that kept pulling me back to look. The only one that gave me a sense there was something else going on here. Sort of how I felt the day we met and he asked who the person was in the photo. I said my father and he went 'Hmm…' He seemed to be saying 'Hmm,' in the watercolor too.

When he came by to collect his portrait it was strange seeing him in the flesh again after such intense studies I'd made of him in paint. The paintings felt more real than he did, probably because of all the time I had spent studying him from a deeper place. The watercolor was propped on the easel and the oils hung side by side on the brick wall. I was relieved he barely glanced at the watercolor and went straight to the oils. He made his choice quickly without commenting on how many there were to choose from, and declined my offer to wrap it up. Instead, he tucked it under his arm, thanked me and left. The whole thing was over in five minutes.

Gene may have been gone, but not from my wall. I moved his portraits farther back in the room near the kitchen so that I could say hello to him whenever I passed by. I didn't speak to the watercolor I'd left propped on the easel because he was looking away. Looking at something not here, something out of sight. Maybe he was saying, 'I'll be away for a while, but I'll be back,' because six months later he did come back, not as a date but as a client, which was so much worse. But first there was getting through the winter.

36

A CLEANSING

There is another reality, the genuine one, which we lose sight of.
This other reality is always sending us hints,
which without art, we can't receive.

— PABLO NERUDA

When snow covered the skylight, a cold eerie light filtered in like the half-light of dusk or dawn and lasted all day. The vents along the baseboards never gave off more than a trickle of warmth. I wrapped myself in the peach-colored quilt, too sluggish to move, or sat around in my coat and warmed my hands on a mug of hot coffee. I missed the old steam radiators I was used to. They hammered and hissed but they could make a room so hot you had to open a window. I even missed those small gas fires in London I used to feed with coins. I could have bought a space heater of course, but my electric bill was already absurdly high. I had to pay for the heat myself, which I'd never had to do in a rental before, and I wouldn't have minded if I actually had any heat. When the first bill arrived I thought it was a mistake and called the electric company. They sent a man over and we went down to the basement. He showed me the meter and explained how it worked. According to him it was working just fine.

"Why don't I have any heat then?"

"That's a question for your landlord," he said. But my landlord wasn't helpful and I didn't press it because I was late again with the rent. Toshi sent a bank transfer at the beginning of every month, but because it was international it could take days to show up in my account.

I resigned myself to the cold, then resigned myself to being sick half the time. It wasn't like me to get colds or the flu, barely recovering from one before I was laid low with the next. I even had cramps which I'd never suffered from before, and when the bladder infection came back it was the last straw. I got down on my knees and prayed.

I wasn't in the habit of praying, yet this was the second time in the last few months I'd been driven to my knees. The other time was when I was reading about healing a wounded heart, cleansing it of pain and sorrow. The first step was 'purgation.' I had to look it up. *Purgation: to make clean or pure.* Had the prayer for a cleansing unleashed all this illness? I'd feel better if I knew it was doing some good.

My friend Darla thought I had balls. "Why do you say that?" I asked.

"Because you're a painter and you live in a studio with a skylight."

Darla with her dimpled cheeks and curly fair hair always cheered me up when she stopped by after class. She was only nineteen, a student at NYU. I made us hot buttered rums and thought it best not to mention the loneliness of painting or the scramble to get by till the end of the month. What good would it do to tell her about the dragon of self-doubt that was never far from the surface. When I was nineteen studying acting and dreaming of a life in the theater, I wouldn't have believed it if someone told me what the life of an actor really was like. But I always knew art would be lonely.

When Darla posed for me I did two full-length views of her on the same canvas as if she was looking into a mirror, both views identical. It made me think of the 'Two Selves' I did of myself when I first moved to Brooklyn, which were not at all identical. One light, the other dark. One hopeful, the other despondent. I had been proud of myself at the time for being so honest and revealing, but I couldn't stand the sight of it later. I didn't want to be reminded of my dark side and destroyed the picture as if I could obliterate my own darkness. It was the second time I'd thrown a picture away because the truth was too painful. The first one had also been two views, contrasting the cityscape above and the subway below. One warm and inviting, the other murky and ominous. I didn't want to look below if it was going to be like that. I wanted to be like Darla. Happy, bubbly Darla, light and refreshing and at one with herself. Why on earth would she want to be like me? It gave me an idea though. Seeing the outer and inner, above and below, in terms of different views of Nature. The one no better than the other, differing only in terms of time. Beautiful, impersonal Nature rather than the Self, and in watercolor instead of oil this time.

I contrasted a barren winter landscape above with what might be happening under the ground, out of view. Above were bare skeletal trees under a milky-white sky, while in the ground below a burgeoning spring was biding its time. The seeds were asleep, but I pictured their dreams. I saw them dreaming of their summer glory as if it had already manifested. I put them in layers like a geological cross-section. Below the layer of ripened fruits and another of flowers in bloom, there was a stream of human-like figures white as roots, cavorting like wingless fairies as they stirred up the earth for the coming spring. It wasn't their time yet, but what they would be, they already were. I named it *Winter*, a reminder that no matter how bleak things appeared on the surface, new life was bubbling up underneath. I had to do one of spring then. *Spring,* when the birds had flown back and leaves were beginning to sprout on the trees. Now the forms below were rising up, breaking through their proscribed layers as they made ready to break through the surface and come into the light. Which is not to say there wasn't light below. That dark murky underground I once saw as the subway was a thing of the past.

Seeing stages of growth in terms of layers, and growth as a flowing stream hidden from view, put me in mind of streams of consciousness. Of the subconscious mind as a layered terrain. A third watercolor called to me then. Layers of history buried in the human mind. There were statues and old coins. Pyramids and pillars. Windows of a medieval church and windows of a mosque. Relics of civilizations from the pharaohs to Alexander, from Ancient Greece up through the Middle Ages. Ancient artifacts as stages of cultures, layers of awakening spirits. Each had their season in this vast stream of memory, the collective unconscious. It wasn't until I was finished that I noticed most of the symbols were masculine. I had to do a fourth then, and base it solely on feminine symbols. Prehistoric figurines from Africa and the Middle East. The colors were different too. Whereas the masculine images were golds and yellows in an airy-blue background, the colors of the feminine world were dark rich earth tones of orange and maroon, umber and ochre. There were statuettes of fertility and the Three Graces. There were women squatting in childbirth and goddesses with bulging breasts and bellies. I felt I was onto something, but I couldn't see where to take it next. A winter slumber, a spring awakening, masculine glory complementing a fertile feminine earth. What else was there?

I fell into another slump. Then Rachel came over and bawled me out. I wouldn't have recognized her from the woman in Crown Heights who hid her poems in a drawer. Since she'd enrolled at the New School to finish her degree she'd chopped off her hair and no longer wore a wig or a scarf, at least not in Manhattan. The New School was an easy walk to Ninth Street, and if she came by before class in the morning she brought coffee and croissants. If it was an evening after class she brought a bottle of wine. We had already drunk most of it the night I confessed I didn't know what to paint anymore and despaired I would ever paint again.

"Oh what crap!" she said. "How about painting the thing you haven't dared to do. The feeling behind the paintings."

I drained my glass. Someone else had said recently that my work lacked passion and was too intellectual. "Okay," I said, jumping up from the couch. "I will!" And while Rachel called her husband to come pick her up because it was too late to take the train, I stretched a new canvas. By the time she got off the phone I had already sketched a woman splayed across it.

Rachel studied the figure for a minute, then plucked a brush from the canister and dipped it in red paint. "Here, I'll show you what I mean," she said, and proceeded to make the woman bleed. Blood flowed from her crotch. It dripped from her nipples. Even the tears running down her cheeks were the color of blood. I was only half in jest when I shrieked, "Oh no!" Rachel laughed and cried, "Oh yes!" I laughed too then. It was the wine, and knowing this mother of five was more connected to the physical side of life than I would ever be. But how ghoulish it looked in the morning.

It was the first thing I saw when I got up and it made me shudder. I couldn't leave it like that. I doused a rag with turpentine to get rid of the blood, but the paint was still wet and all I did was smear it around. When I tried painting white over the red it turned pink. It would have been easier to just wipe the whole thing off, but I didn't want to lose the figure I'd drawn with arms raised, knees bent and legs spread apart, her body completely open. The only way to keep her would be to paint stronger colors over the pink. In deference to Rachel I put back some of the red, which no longer drew attention to itself amidst the orange and blues, the greens and gold. By the time the picture was finished, the background had spirals and triangles along with leafy greens and a flowing stream, all of it as free-wheeling as the figure herself. A primal creature with a fiery halo suspended in a kind of orderly chaos where it was impossible to tell if she was falling backward or hurtling forward. The part I liked best was the triangle behind her that bored a hole through a wall causing sparks to fly out the other side.

When Rachel saw it she said, "You've got to call her *Freude*. It's German for ecstasy. Or joy!" I could just as easily see her shrieking with pain as with pleasure. But Rachel had inspired her, so *Freude* she would be.

Her loud boldness wasn't really my taste though, and when Rachel left I began a companion piece, a goddess of grain lying back contentedly on a bed of golden wheat, reaping the rewards of her harvest, balancing the energies of her wild, untamed sister. If *Freude* broke free from restraint, this was the peace that came after.

And still nothing in me shifted. After the rush of excitement of these new works I was back on the futon, bemoaning my inability to think what was next. Maybe sending slides out to galleries was next, but I wasn't ready to face the risk of rejection. A negative response, or no response at all would only hobble me further. Not for the first time did I consider how this life I'd set up solely for painting was ruinous when I ran out of ideas and it all seemed for naught. One despairing thought led to another and crying only made it worse. I drank a bottle of wine to stop crying, and was so ill the next day I couldn't get out of bed. I stayed in bed the next day too, and unplugged the phone and the answering machine to keep the world away. Two days became two weeks of shutting myself off, passing the time watching old black and white movies on tv. My favorites were those with Charles Boyer and anything with Jean Arthur or Barbara Stanwyck. Why weren't there men like Charles Boyer around anymore? Then I got up and went on a cleaning binge, tackling the stove and the top of the refrigerator for the first time in a year. I went on dates again to get out of the house and did my work for Toshi and read books about art and books about consciousness, and none of it made any difference. I felt stuck in a never-ending repetitive orbit where nothing changed. Then I remembered something Colleen had quoted to me when I was stuck another time. It was Walt Whitman who said, "I came, I saw, I wrote." I came and saw myself stuck. I could paint that.

I was out of canvas so I did a watercolor of a woman pinioned between two giant boulders. They were closing in on her but she had big hips and strong thighs and she pushed back. She refused to be crushed. When had I stopped pushing back? I pushed back the day someone left a dumpster in front of my door. It took all my strength but I did it. How had I let myself become so weak? I put on one of my new Philip Glass records and turned up the volume while I did a watercolor of another woman stuck somewhere. Then another and another. She was stuck on a spike, stuck in a scream or a fire, or in a noose around her neck. In one she cut off her head so as not to be stuck in her thoughts. In another she brandished a knife while she crawled over the jagged edge of an abyss, bridging the gap with her body, refusing to be dragged down when the earth opened up. How far I'd come since my shrink in London told me to picture a bridge over an abyss and I kept seeing myself falling in! How far I'd come from the woman lying despondent on the bed in *Aftermath,* the picture Lenny thought was wonderful. In this carnival of pain women screamed and burned and bled rivers of red. So much red! But the pictures were hardly dark, they were vibrant and alive with color. If it was a purging, it was also a celebration of feeling. If the pictures were exaggerated and overwrought, it was because I'd kept the feelings hidden from myself. And now it was as if I was saying yes. Yes to feeling. Yes, like I'd said yes to Hades Cave all those years ago, no matter the hurt. There was no looking away from what was inside. But I could paint the feeling now. I could acknowledge it, transform Hades Cave into Pluto's Horn of Plenty. And I didn't stop until I painted a woman sitting in a pool of blood, a screwdriver in her hand as if she had aborted her own being. That was taking it too far.

I wanted to keep the pictures in sight but there was no way to hang them since they were on paper. So rather than stash them away in the flat file, I laid them out in rows on the floor and got used to stepping around them. Anyone who came by could see them too. Rachel loved them which was no surprise, and I even sold a few. Colleen bought the woman on fire that reminded her of Joan of Arc. The friend she brought with her, a novelist with writer's block, chose the demonic woman brandishing a knife as she crawled over the abyss. Colleen said it was time I had a show. I thought she might be right, and after I took slides I sent them out to a few galleries. I didn't hear back, but the purging was over. Winter was losing its grip.

37

DOUBLE VISION

Since we cannot change reality,
let us change the eyes which see reality.

— NIKOS KAZANTZAKIS

April came and I was riding uptown on the Madison Avenue bus to visit Colleen. The subway would have been faster, but after all those years in Brooklyn when the train was my only option, I took the bus whenever I could just for the pleasure of looking out the window. The bus was crowded but I had a seat. If I hadn't been sitting down looking out the window that day, or if I'd been sitting on the wrong side, I wouldn't have seen the archways. They were several stories high, not rounded but square at the top, in a row right up against the sidewalk for an entire block. I'd never seen anything like them before. As the bus kept moving and I craned my neck to see back, the last glimpse I had was of pale brick glowing pinkish-gold in the late afternoon sun.

When I got to Colleen's I told her about the arches and said, "Have you seen them?"

"That's the new Philip Johnson building for AT&T," she said. "Did you see the Chippendale ornament at the top? That's what it's famous for."

I went back the next day with my camera. To get a view of the top I had to walk back to the next avenue, and there it was, an empty cavity shaped like a bowl. A feminine, receptive space, the opposite of the usual squared-off flat surfaces of the rectangular boxes soaring through midtown. The crescent shape made me think of the moon, as if the moon had dipped down one night and left a crater behind. I began taking pictures whenever I saw a different angle or a juxtaposition of shapes, which was all the time. The pedestrian walkway in the back was covered by curved glass in a steel grid. Circular windows like portholes were cut through the brick under the squared-off arches. Most astonishing of all was the angel behind the glass of the center archway. He was a marvel. A vision in gold standing atop a round pedestal like a globe. I didn't see him until I crossed the street to photograph the front, and there he was, brandishing a bolt of lightning over Madison Avenue! Even when I learned he wasn't an angel but Mercury, the god of communication, my first impression of an angel was hard to dispel.

In all my years of doing renderings I had never fallen in love with a building. There were many I admired like the Louis Sullivan building over on Bleecker with a row of angels carved in stone under the roof line. It was Sullivan who coined the famous axiom, "form follows function," and I couldn't help wondering if he had summoned the angels to hold up the roof. Now I wondered what function the portholes in the AT&T building served. The initials stood for the American Telephone and Telegraph Company. The prefix 'tele' means 'at a distance.' Phoning a distant place. Graphs are for giving us visual information—from a distance? But it was the portholes that were the most mysterious. Portholes belonged at sea. I wasn't used to seeing them on land, and certainly not in midtown Manhattan, so incongruous in this angular metropolis of squares and rectangles. The AT&T was special. I knew it as soon as I caught a glimpse from the bus, and I was going to paint it.

I shot two rolls of film, one for prints and the other for slides, then I couldn't make up my mind which view to paint first. I already knew there would be more than one, maybe a whole series from different angles. I'd had enough of looking within. Looking out at the world had become exciting again. But which view to tackle first? Then I thought, why not put two views on the same canvas? I had to remind myself I wasn't working for a client and could do whatever I pleased. Two views at slightly different times then. The view of arches I saw from the bus, and the following day when I went under the arch and saw a porthole. One view would be what a pedestrian saw from across the street, the other would be when they crossed over and went under the archway. First you're here, now you're there, at slightly different times in space. It would be like having double vision, a bit like my watercolors of *Winter* and *Spring* that showed a cross section of above and below, two views at once. Except those were imaginary landscapes, and the AT&T building was real.

Double vision was real too. I came across the expression last summer when I picked up a copy of Kazantzakis' *The Odyssey*. I quickly lost interest in the eight-hundred-page epic, but I kept coming back to the introduction where he talked about the Cretan Glance. He described it as standing in the middle of a bridge over an abyss, looking forward and back at the same time, "In an ecstasy of tragic joy." He said it was like having double vision because you knew ". . . that nothing exists, neither life nor death." Tragic joy reminded me of *Freude*. The ecstasy beyond happy or sad when everything small falls away.

I worked slowly and methodically, painting every brick, wanting the picture to be as perfect as if I was working for a client. The work was tedious and repetitive, but with Philip Glass on the stereo I could keep going for hours without a break. Music and architecture went together. Goethe called architecture, "frozen music." If Philip Glass could make his repetitive notes into an art form, I could make art from the repetitive bricks and windows of a thirty-seven-story skyscraper. One painting became two, then three, and by the fourth I was starting to mix up the views, fragmenting them, showing some of the surrounding buildings as well. The disjointed angles made it seem like you were viewing multiple planes at once. I liked this world of angles. It made the issue of above and below, upper and lower, simply a question of angles. In this world of straight lines converging, a circular window would pop into view, so that being on land was also to imagine being at sea, seeing through a porthole. Or perhaps a portal. A hidden opening in plain sight that led to another world, another reality.

I saved the angel, the statue of Mercury, messenger of the gods, or Golden Boy as he was called, or the Spirit of Communication as he was also called, for last. In keeping with the theme of double vision, I did two of him side by side, the golden messenger of the gods imprisoned behind the glass and steel of the modern world. Then something strange happened. I took a break and had a nap, and when I came back to the easel I noticed tiny nicks in the wet paint. They appeared in bunches, as if a swarm of miniscule insects had flown into the canvas. Except there weren't any bugs in my studio, flying or otherwise. I got out my magnifying glass to see if whatever it was had left behind a telltale sign like a wing or a hair. But there was nothing, not a single clue. I assumed it was a freak occurrence, and went on with my work, but I was annoyed at having to paint over the nicks, finding the exact colors to match, and the following day when fresh marks appeared, I was beside myself. This time the nicks were cropping up while I was painting. It was maddening. When Rachel called I told her about the nicks and wailed, "I don't know what's going on!"

"Don't worry. I know what to do," she said.

Rachel thought the markings had been created by a dybbuk. She came over the next day with a talisman to scare it away. A sheet of yellowed plastic with Hebrew letters and numbers from the Kabbalah had been made to look like aged parchment with simulated burn marks at the edges. Rachel promised it would ward off evil spirits, especially if I hung it on the wall facing east. She said, "I think you should stop painting for a few days, and if the markings appear again, remove the canvas from your house. Just get rid of it."

That sounded a bit drastic. Though the painting wasn't finished it was already one of my favorites. What if it wasn't a dybbuk. What if Mercury, messenger of the gods, was sending me a message through the markings. He was purported to deliver messages between the conscious mind and the unconscious realms. I thought of my father. The seventh anniversary of his death had just passed and he had been on my mind. What if my father was sending me a message? Still, I hung the talisman on the wall facing east as Rachel suggested. I wasn't going to stop painting though. That was too much to ask. After she left I picked up my brushes, and it wasn't long before I discovered that I was the culprit. I had been making the nicks myself. What an idiot! The explanation was simple. Instead of using a mahl stick which I didn't have, I kept my brush steady while doing the delicate and precise work of outlining bricks by resting my left hand with the brush on the wrist of my right hand. To keep the right hand steady, I touched the canvas with my fingernails, completely oblivious that the paint was wet and my nails were leaving marks.

Oddly enough, not long afterwards I did get a message from my father. That it came in a dream did not make it any less real. In the dream I boarded a plane, and everything was normal until we took off, not gradually rising, but lifting off vertically like a rocket ship. When we leveled off, the plane began making stops in midair. The flight attendant summoned me to the front when it was my turn, and when the door slid open like an elevator door, my father was standing on the other side waiting for me. "Dad!" I cried, "I thought you were dead!" He laughed and gave me a hug, then he gave me a tour like the old days when I used to come up to the various offices where he worked. Only the atmosphere here was more like a cocktail party than a workplace, with people standing around chatting in groups. After a while my father drifted off to join the group clustered around a television set. This didn't seem unusual since he used to work in television, and I went back to the elevator to catch a lift home. When I woke up I was happier than I'd been in ages. My father wasn't gone, he was merely on another *plane*. What a relief. What a gift I'd been given! My sister and brothers and I were together with him before he died when he said, "I'm going to miss seeing how you all turn out." It was one of the last things he said, but maybe he was able to see us after all—on that television screen in Heaven. Decades later when I saw the movie, *Astral City, a Spiritual Journey*, this seemed entirely plausible when a man on the astral plane was able to see his family by tuning into a special monitor that looked like a tv screen or a computer.

I seemed to be tuning into something myself that spring what with visiting my father and then dreaming I was Rudolph Nureyev's sister. I had no idea why. Even if there had been an internet in those days and I had been able to look up Nureyev and learn he had a sister named Rosa, it wouldn't have meant anything to me. Funny how I had been painting roses though. A man and a woman with blue roses for hair because blue roses symbolized the impossible. They were the lovers who would never meet except on my canvas. They weren't looking at one another, but his mouth was open as if he was calling to her. An impossible call, impossible to hear, but something I could imagine in a painting. I didn't think of it then, but maybe they were each on a different plane, and that was why they didn't see one another. And maybe I was trying to call the impossible into being because early in the next century scientists would create blue roses in a lab. I had no way of knowing this then. I would have said it was impossible to visit my father in heaven too. It only happened in a dream of course, but I felt like I had really been there.

Those two planes, dream and reality, seemed to be coming closer together. I had been drawing things in twos for a long time. There were the two selves, inner and outer. They could be identical like with Darla, or diametrically opposed like I'd seen myself. They could be Adam and Eve or the He-flame and She-flame. They could be two different views of a landscape, above and below, or the masculine versus the feminine layers of the psyche, buried somewhere in the collective unconscious but never truly forgotten. Or you could be on two planes at once, in two different realities just by going to the movies. It happened to me a lot when I went to the movies, getting so involved in the action onscreen that when it was over and the lights came up it was hard to make the adjustment back to my own reality, especially if I'd gone alone, like when I went to see *Rosa Luxemburg*.

A long time later I would realize that the day I saw *Rosa Luxemburg*, June 1, 1987 was the forty-fourth anniversary of a plane that was shot down over the sea in World War II. I would learn that among the passengers was Petra, a young English girl whose name meant rose-red. I had no way of knowing any of this then. Neither had I started referring to *Girl Under Water* by her initials, Gee, You Double-You.

38

A QUICKENING

We are like islands in the sea, separate
on the surface but connected in the deep.

— WILLIAM JAMES

My air-conditioner gave out on the first of June in the middle of a heatwave. It was a Monday and I couldn't get a repairman until Thursday. I thought I could work despite the heat. A rendering commission had finally come through and I was anxious to get on with it. The heat had never stopped me from working in Brooklyn, but then my drafting table hadn't been under a skylight that baked the room like an oven. It was still morning and already 90° on the thermostat. I couldn't keep my focus and I finally gave up. But the day wouldn't be a complete waste if I managed to paint something. The easel was under the skylight too, but it had wheels. I rolled it over to the shady area by the futon and squeezed some colors onto the palette. The heat separated the oil from the pigments, and when I saw it circling the blobs of color like tiny moats I decided to paint the heat. Three figures emerged, the three phases of woman, maiden-matron-crone, wilting under the blaze of a fiery orange sun. I wasn't a maiden, I didn't feel like a matron and I was far from being a crone, but with paint dripping down the canvas and the sweat dripping from my brow, I felt myself melting like all three.

I took a break and sat under the fan by the window with a mug of hot coffee since I didn't think I could get any hotter than I already was. Snatches of conversation floated up from people walking by. Across the street couples were lining up outside the Cloisters waiting for it to open for lunch. It made me wish I had someone to meet for lunch. Once that thought took over I couldn't work anymore. I wanted to be with people. I thought of going to the movies, being with people while cooling off in an air-conditioned theater. I scanned the listings to see what was playing and the only film that looked interesting was *Rosa Luxemburg*. I didn't know much about her other than she had been a revolutionary around the time of the first World War, but I was familiar with Jane Lapotaire, the actress playing her. I'd seen her Portia at the Young Vic, and more recently as Madame Curie on tv. That today was the last day settled it. I changed my clothes, left my brushes to soak and hurried to the subway to catch the next showing.

The small theater below ground at Lincoln Center was delightfully chilly. I don't know why I had the idea Jane Lapotaire played Rosa. As soon as the movie began I must have realized it was in German with subtitles, yet somehow I still had the idea I was watching Jane Lapotaire because when they murdered Rosa it felt like they were killing Madam Curie too, which added to my distress. I had no idea beforehand that Rosa Luxemburg was going to be murdered. Kidnapped in the middle of the night by a couple of thugs who shot her point-blank in the head and tossed her into the canal. Then the screen went dark and silent. It all happened so fast that I burst into tears when the credits started scrolling. I shivered in the cold and tried to muffle my sobs because I wasn't seeing the credits, I was seeing her body sinking slowly to the bottom of the canal. The cold dark underground theater suddenly felt like a tomb and I scrambled out of my seat, desperate for heat and light. I was still crying when I went up the escalator and walked out into the blistering sunlight. I fumbled for my sunglasses, and sobbed all the way back to the subway at Columbus Circle.

I hardly knew what to do with myself when I came home. All I could think about was the merciless slaughter of a brilliant woman, an idealist, and how cruel people could be. Brutal men with their useless barbaric wars creating so much misery! To take my mind off death and killing I began a new canvas. I didn't have the energy to do more than sketch it in that night, but I couldn't go to bed without doing something positive. It was a drawing of a naked woman crawling on all fours back to the cool shelter of the forest. Her head was turned slightly as if to see if she was being followed.

The next day not only did the temperature return to its normal range for June, but the air-conditioner hummed back to life for no apparent reason. I canceled the repairman and moved the easel back under the skylight. The rendering could wait; I had to get on with the woman crawling back to the forest. When the phone rang I picked it up without noticing the green paint on my hands.

It was Gene. I was so surprised I said, "For heaven's sake," an expression my grandmother was fond of saying. I couldn't remember ever saying it myself before, and hearing myself sound like my grandmother who'd been in heaven herself for the last decade was as much of a surprise as hearing from Gene. He said he wanted me to do an illustration and asked me to meet him for lunch. When I hung up the receiver I saw it was smeared with green paint. After cleaning it off and washing my hands I called Rachel to tell her I'd heard from Gene. "Isn't it strange?" I said.

"He must still like you."

"No, I'm sure it's not that." It couldn't be that. I wasn't sure he liked me all that much before. "He just wants me to do a picture, that's all."

"But out of all the artists in New York he picked you."

"Maybe I'm the only one he knows." Though how could that be true for someone who ran an advertising agency. Gene had never even mentioned my work, let alone that he liked it. I hadn't thought about him in months and now he was upending me again. There was no question of turning him down though. I told myself just to see it as another commission, but I couldn't help thinking why did it have to be him giving it to me. And why did I say *for heaven's sake.* I never said that. It didn't even sound like me. It didn't occur to me that Nano's voice might have been coming through, telling me to do the job 'for heaven's sake.'

39

THE COMMISSION

(The heart) ...admits of no boundaries, and yearns
to pierce beyond phenomena and to merge
with something beyond mind and matter.
And so discover the essence of things.

— KAZANTZAKIS

The Japanese restaurant in midtown was packed, but as soon as I got past the throng at the entrance his yellow-blonde hair stood out like a beacon. He laughed when he saw me. What was so funny? I glanced down at my long pink tee-shirt with the large colorful parrot on the front and wondered if he thought the parrot was funny. I had never seen him laugh, or even seem happy before, and when I took the stool next to his at the sushi bar I wished I wasn't so happy to see him. He was drinking white wine and ordered a glass for me. "I need an illustration to go on the cover of my screenplay when I send it to agents," he said.

He wrote screenplays? I had no idea he was a writer.

That must have been why he was happy. Finishing a screenplay would probably make anyone happy.

"It's a picture of a zoo-keeper and a panda bear having a beer."

I jotted this down in my notebook. "The bear is drinking beer too?"

"It's after hours. His beer is in a bowl on the ground, but the bear should be standing when he talks to the zoo-keeper. He's more of a caretaker really."

"What are they talking about?"

"Relationships between men and women."

"Oh."

Our food arrived. I didn't care for sushi and had ordered a salad which was a mistake because between taking bites and taking notes I kept looking down to check I hadn't splashed salad dressing on my shirt. Gene said not to put bars on the cage, and make it look more like a stage set with bamboo trees painted on the back wall and the sky painted on the ceiling. The stone slabs on the floor should look real though.

"How should the zoo-keeper, I mean caretaker look?"

"Can you make him look like Harrison Ford?"

"Any particular movie?"

"Your choice. How soon can you do it?"

I said I could have a sketch ready the following week. Outside the restaurant he handed me a couple of books with pictures of panda bears to use for reference. We shook hands goodbye and he headed one way while I headed the other. I was planning to go to the picture section at the Mid-Manhattan Library since it was nearby and would save me another trip uptown to look for pictures of Harrison Ford, but by the time I reached the corner I felt sleepy from the wine and decided to have a nap instead. Then on the train home I remembered there was a shop on St. Mark's Place around the corner from me that sold movie posters. I stopped in to ask if they had anything with Harrison Ford. The only one they had was from *Witness*, and as soon as I saw it I realized Harrison Ford looked the same in all his movies.

After my nap I couldn't bring myself to get started on the sketch. Not the next day either or the day after that. I was afraid to let Gene into my head again. Why did he have to come back into my life? One minute I was cursing him because he did, and the next minute I was blessing him because he had. But how odd he should call me for a picture of a bear standing on two feet while I was painting a woman crawling on all fours. What were the chances of that? I took out my deck of tarot cards and shuffled them to see if they offered any kind of insight into what this was all about. My knowledge of the cards was rudimentary but I didn't know where else to turn. The first card I picked was number 13, Death. That was bad. I put it back and shuffled again, this time choosing five or six cards before turning them over. Death showed up again. That the card was more about transformation and endings, death to an old way of being rather than death of the physical body did not reassure me. I reminded myself that I hardly knew this man and hadn't even seen him for the last six months, so it made no sense to have such a foreboding. Unless I'd known him in another life. I hadn't thought of that.

Past lives had been on my mind since I'd gone to a past life regression just the week before. I had never been to one, but after seeing a flyer on a lamppost I suddenly wanted to give it a try. The woman conducting them had a wonderful name, Joy Ann Juvalis. In the photo she posted on the flyer she looked warm and inviting. I chose the group session with fifteen or twenty others because it was cheaper. The instructions were simple enough. After relaxing the breath and counting backwards from twenty, we stepped into the light. Half the group said they went back to Atlantis. I only got as far as the Middle Ages, seeing myself high up on the scaffold of a gothic cathedral to work on the stained-glass window. I could believe it since I worked with color and light in this life too. When she regressed us again I saw myself as a music hall singer, then a bus driver. Yet no particular feeling had come up with any of them, and I came away thinking I could imagine myself as anyone.

Now I thought, why not regress myself, see if I remember Gene in another life. I did the breathing, and no sooner did I finish the countdown than a scene appeared. We were sitting by the fire in a dark little hut with a dirt floor. Gene was a weary battle-scared warrior in a leather breastplate and sandals laced up his calves. I sat barefoot on a low stool beside him with mending on my lap. He gazed silently into the fire, then reached down and gently stroked my hair. I wondered if he had been wounded and I was his servant, nursing him back to health. I opened my eyes. That was it. His servant! I'd get myself to do his drawing by seeing it as a way of serving him. Serving his idea.

And still I delayed. What if he didn't like it? What if I disappointed him again? I knew all I had to do was be willing to apply myself and let go of the outcome. Willingness. All I needed was the willingness. I thought of painting a picture of willingness before I did anything else, and looked for a pose to copy from my reference book. It was full of black and white photographs of artist models. The one that caught my eye was a woman sitting on the floor with her legs apart and her knees up. Her arms were slightly out from her sides, her hands open to receive. The lighting was dim and she was in shadow except for her face which was lit up with the hint of a smile. I painted her sitting on the beach at the shoreline, welcoming in the tide. It was how I wanted to see myself, welcoming in Gene's vision.

I could get to his sketch now. A man and a bear having a beer in the bear's cage that was more like a stage set. I drew a table that was actually a log resting on a couple of trestles. The bear was at one end with a bowl by his feet, while the caretaker stood at the other end with his beer on the log. It was only a sketch, an idea of the layout, with no need for a likeness of Harrison Ford or details of the scenery. When I called Gene and told him the sketch was ready, I thought he'd come by in the next day or two, and was disappointed when he said he couldn't make it until the following week. I had been obsessing about getting to work on his drawing and finally I had some momentum going. I didn't know what to do with myself now. My head was so wrapped up in his sketch that I couldn't imagine working on anything else. Then I thought why not do another sketch? I had used markers for the first one and I wasn't that good with markers. I could do a better one in watercolor, maybe even develop it further. Then Gene would have two pictures instead of one and could compare them.

The following week he sat at my drafting table silently studying the sketches laid out side by side. I wished he'd say something. I'd never known anyone to examine my work for so long, and for so long without saying anything. His back was to me and I couldn't tell what he was thinking. I didn't want to hover so I went to the kitchen and washed the pint of strawberries I bought that morning. Then I placed them in a bowl and set it on the counter thinking I might offer him some later. I should have asked if he wanted a coffee when he came in, but he went straight to the drafting table, and now he looked so engrossed I didn't want to disturb him. But I didn't want to just stand around either so I went to the couch and reached for my sewing basket that had a couple of socks needing mending. It wasn't until I was threading a needle that I remembered I'd been sitting in that same spot a week ago when I regressed myself and saw us in a hut, and I was sewing there too! No sooner did I register this odd coincidence than Gene cleared his throat and swiveled the chair around to look for me.

I put down the sock and stood beside him at the table where he was holding up the watercolor. He said slowly as if measuring his words, "I don't know, there's something missing. Can you make the bear look more like a man in a bear suit, less like a real bear?"

"Uh-huh."

"It needs to be darker. Can you bring the atmosphere down a key?"

"Uh-huh."

He let out a sigh. We were both staring at the picture. The silence felt endless. Then he said, "It needs an air of enchantment. You had it in the sketch, but you seem to have lost it in this one."

I saw what he meant. The sketch with markers had an unfinished look, but there was a lightness, a suggestion of possibilities. I had gone further with the watercolor and filled in all the spaces which made it look dense in comparison. Gene had a few other ideas, like adding a door with a barred window to make it look more like a cage—but not a real cage he reminded me. I said I could have it ready the following Monday. He said he'd come by at noon.

Enchantment. What a vague, intangible thing! After he left I looked it up in the dictionary. Enchantment: *To attract, delight, cast a spell over.* And he wanted an *air* of this? The man who went out of his way to tell me he was "observing my show" when we first met, as if to assure me he wasn't taken in, wanted me to cast a spell? A few years ago I had been able to create something enchanting with the rendering I did for George without even trying. George didn't notice it particularly, but it was there in the clouds. It was there in the pinks and greens on the sidewalk. Of course George had enchanted me himself when he asked if I believed in unicorns. Hearing bells when he kissed me added to the feeling I was under some kind of spell. Gene, on the other hand, had never offered a hint of magic. It was up to me then. I would have to get my own self into a state of enchantment.

I don't know how I could have failed to see I was already under some kind of spell with him. It was as clear as day in my journal.

* * *

Journal Entry, June 17th

> *I was lying immobile on the sofa, laid out like a corpse, thinking about death of the ego. Surrendering and letting go of self. Maybe writing these things down will enable me to go on. I've been reading "The Story of O," but it was too much. Before putting it down I skipped to the end where she was wearing the head of an animal. I prefer thinking of the O as a circle. A portal through Time and Space to become nothing and no one. But not an animal. Please, not that.*
>
> *Before I worked on his sketch, I painted a woman as*

vulnerable looking as I could make her. When he finally came over today, I put on choral music from the Spanish Renaissance that sounded like angels singing. He stared at the drawings with his back to me. A person must trust someone very much to give their back like that. I tried to feel his vibrations while I mended a sock. I don't understand why I feel I have to keep giving up more of myself to be around him. Why am I even interested in him when he gives me nothing in return? I was peaceful with him today, but I have no peace. There's a lesson here, and whatever it is, I'm going to give it to myself as fully and completely as I possibly can. I have to wait till Monday to see him? Very well. O joyous wait! O happy me, waiting for him to come! I'll bake zucchini bread. I'll find a way to sit on the floor while he's here—like the model's pose I copied from the book to signify openness—and not judge myself for it. I'll experience whatever it is, and if I want to cry because I'm happy, I'll do that too.

* * *

The next morning when Rachel came by with coffee and croissants, all she talked about was her new poetry teacher. "He keeps telling me to whittle my poems down to their essence," she said dreamily, as if it was the most wonderful advice she had ever been given.

Whittle. Could I whittle Gene's picture down to the essence of enchantment? After she left I took out the watercolor I did of him last fall and propped it on the easel to feel his presence in the room with me. Then I played the record of angelic choral music again. Now that the scene was set and only needed a change in key and an air of enchantment, I felt more confident when I started this third drawing. I chose the same paper I used for his portrait, which wasn't proper watercolor paper because the color stayed on the surface and didn't sink in. You could put color on and lift some of it off again even after it dried, which created the impression of layers, of something happening underneath. To make the bear look more like a man in a bear suit, I straightened his posture and had him cross one foot over the other. To make it look more like a stage set than a cage, I lowered the lights at the edges so they'd be brighter center stage where the figures were. I knew about lighting and stage sets from my theater days. It was the lighting that created the magic. I didn't care if Gene thought there was no such thing as a gray area. The line between reality and imagination was most certainly a gray area. A bear that could talk and drink beer was absolutely a gray area. The bear looked sad, but then pandas couldn't help looking sad with those black ovals curving down around their eyes. The man didn't look that much like Harrison Ford, but he had a strong jaw and he looked sympathetic as he leaned in to listen to the bear.

* * *

Journal Entry, June 18th

> *When I remove color with a brush there's always some left behind and it feels like I'm revealing something deeper, allowing it to become more transparent. When Gene planted the idea of his picture in my mind, I had to allow it to pass through my system, feel it in my whole being in order to bring it to light. The feeling it gives me is as deep as my soul, and it doesn't seem like it's going away anytime soon. I can't imagine it suddenly coming to an end when he picks up the*

painting on Monday. How could it be possible that I'll never see him again after Monday?

This is not unrequited love. There is only LOVE. I feel it coursing through me, knitting my bones together. I don't have to be physically whipped like "O." I feel it spiritually, and I want to be whittled, pared down to the core. I want to BE the core. This isn't like fireworks, it's more like an underground stream, too deep even for me to know. Love is a gift. Eros makes us grow. Enjoy the strife for it will cleanse and purify, and you will let go of yourself. You are in battle with the Great Combatant. Nothingness. Give in to it. Say yes to being the receiving ground. Lie naked on the rack. Become as new as a baby fresh from the womb.

June 19th

I've been afraid of love, never fully surrendering because I thought it would mean annihilation. Like my childhood nightmare of being trapped with no way out. I remember last year when I decided to just be in the trap and turned it into a surrender to Gene. He would be the toughest, most critical person to surrender to. The most judgmental, the most demanding. This year he called after I went to the movies for a release and found only more pain. But it made me realize I had to get into my humanity on a different level. So I painted a woman crawling on her knees. Confronting Gene is like confronting myself. How foolish to think I could get complete by going to bed with him or painting his portrait. It was another illusion, because here I am again and nothing has changed.

. . .

June 20th

I'm trusting this, intuiting everything. The walls and the barriers I was so eager to get past were all in my mind. I don't feel the need to be any particular way anymore. It feels like the opposing forces of Yin & Yang are meeting, becoming one in me. There is no separation. No self, either. No self and no other. No outer or inner.

June 21st

My friend John came over last night as planned, and as soon as I saw him I knew it was a mistake. I was restless, bored with our conversation. I had nothing to say and it was exhausting listening to him. Going for a walk was an even bigger mistake. The air outside was hot and fetid. We went too far and had to walk all the way back again. I couldn't wait to be in the rarified air of my hayloft again. I told John I felt sick, which was true, but I only felt sick while I was with him. As soon as he left my energy returned. But it was a negative charge. I cried and called out to God. Then I poured a glass of wine, and when I played the overture to The Flying Dutchman *it unleashed me. I went back to work feeling more spontaneous, less careful, less fearful of making a mistake.*

* * *

Even when I had the bamboo trees painted on the back wall, the clouds floating across the painted ceiling, the stone slabs placed unevenly on the floor so they'd look more real, everything Gene asked for, I kept smudging lines and softening borders, then redefining them, but not all the way. The final touch was the beer on the log table. A bottle of Amstel Light, as if to say, Am-Still-Light, Gene!

I spent Monday morning vacuuming and mopping the floor with the new oil soap I bought for wood floors. The painting was laid out on the drafting table, paints and brushes put away so there would be nothing to distract him. It was signed, but still taped to the board in case he wanted any changes. I was about to pop in the shower when the phone rang. It was him. Something had come up and he wasn't able to make it. He said, "Would tomorrow be okay, same time?"

Now I had the chance to make zucchini bread. I hadn't made it in years, not since I was with Lenny, but I still had the loaf pan. That afternoon I went shopping for ingredients, and Tuesday morning I made the bread. It was cooling on the countertop when the phone rang. Gene said, "I've been unexpectedly called out of town. I'll give you a call when I get back next week."

Next *week*? Not even a future appointment, just some nebulous time to expect another call. Such open-endedness did not bode well for me. It's easier to see in hindsight how his failure to pick up the work left me still in its flow, unable to come back from the place I'd had to be in order to create it. There is an energy that goes into a picture, latches onto your insides to make you keep going until whatever it is, is realized. The idea and the materialization of the idea. I had done it, caught that magical something between the man and the bear. But the case wasn't closed until the third factor kicked in, delivering the fruits of my labor. Normally I delivered work in person, but nothing about Gene had ever been normal. As far as I was concerned it was done. I didn't see anything more I could add or take away, but I couldn't be sure until he saw it. Until he came to pick it up it was still an ongoing proposition. Transferring the energy to some other work of my own was impossible. I was too tied up in Gene's propellers, and all I could do was keep spinning while I waited for him to call.

* * *

Bear it, said the bear. Get your *bear-rings. Bear-the-rings?* A ring was a promise, a boundary, a limitation like the rings of Saturn. I should have known. After all, it wasn't the first time I'd had to deal with him, and it wasn't the first time I'd had to deal with a bear either. The one who appeared in my crib when I was two.

* * *

The house was dark and silent, everyone asleep when the huge bear appeared sitting with his back against the headboard. I crawled to the other end of the crib as fast as I could, but it had bars and it was like being in a cage with him. I remember thinking if I stayed very still and didn't make a sound, maybe he wouldn't eat me. And it seemed to work because in another moment he disappeared. Apparently that was when I started screaming and they told me it was just a bad dream. I've since heard it's not uncommon for young children to dream of wild animals, but I knew I'd been awake the whole time. I can still see him sitting there and me crawling away in my baby pajamas with feet, helpless except for staying absolutely still and not making a sound. I could never understand why he'd come in the first place though, unless he was some kind of spirit guide with a silent message even a two-year-old would remember—*bear*. A word that would come to mean *bear* your life, no matter what happens. It's the only interpretation that has ever made sense to me.

40

TO BEAR

YOU ARE NEVER ALONE OR HELPLESS.

The force that guides the stars, guides you too.

— S.S. ANANDAMURTI

The vibrations had come back at some point, much stronger than four years ago when Sender took me to the ocean at night, and this time I knew what they were. I don't remember exactly when they started again. I had a brief case of them last fall when I was doing Gene's portrait but they were so mild I didn't take any notice. I had to now the pulsing waves were spiraling through my whole body. As soon as I lay down my solar plexus would start swirling. Then it would gravitate up and down my torso and through my limbs, up into my face and head. I didn't mind, it was quite pleasant really, and if I got up and walked around a bit they stopped. But it wasn't normal and it worried me. I didn't know who to talk about it with until Suzanne, a woman I was friendly with at Direct Centering, came by to say hello. Though I'd stopped going to the center ages ago, now and then one or two of them would drop by for a chat.

Suzanne was one of the few assistants who was older than me and I felt I could trust her.

"Your vibrations are too high," she said. If you want to bring them down eat some meat and potatoes. That'll do it."

I almost gagged at the mention of meat. The vibrations seemed to have taken away my appetite anyway. Yogurt was the only food I could stomach, and it might take an entire day to finish one of those small containers. I didn't tell Suzanne I was also seeing things with my eyes closed. I could be sitting up completely awake, but if I closed my eyes, often as not I'd find myself part of a crowd hurrying somewhere like it was New York at rush hour. Where were we all going? Then I started seeing the head of a wolf. I had no idea why, so I looked up wolf in the dictionary and it said a wolf might represent a guardian. I liked the suggestion that I was being looked after. What with the visions and the vibrations I was starting to feel I'd lost control over myself. Having a guardian reminded me of the caretaker in Gene's picture.

He still hadn't called, and leaving me with the picture felt like another burden I had to bear. I felt stuck with the painting no different than the bear who was stuck in a cage. It didn't matter that Gene said it wasn't really a cage. The door had bars on the window the same as I had bars on the bathroom window. They were there when I moved in, a safety measure since the roof below was only a few feet down. But bars were bars, and I was starting to feel caged in my studio. My mind really took off then, for wasn't I caged in my skin, caged in my body? My human-animal body, bearing life, only to die someday. Bearing what has to be borne, then dying. I didn't need a cage to feel trapped, I had skin! The ultimate barrier, the ultimate trap, was skin! To be alive was to be enclosed in a body, trapped in skin. The only real freedom was death.

I went back to looking up words in the dictionary, the hefty *Funk and Wagnall's Deluxe Edition* I bought from a salesman during my first job as a secretary. Those were the days when salesmen were allowed to go around office buildings selling their wares. I was alone at the reception desk when he came in and said, "You *need* this dictionary." He was so persuasive I shelled out fifty dollars, a quarter of my weekly salary at the time. It weighed a ton and I had to carry it the mile home, but he was right, I did need it, especially now that I had so many words to look up. Even the simplest words I thought I knew the meaning of had other meanings I was unaware of. Or I might find new interpretations of words I did know, like the word 'dictionary' itself. 'Diction,' the act of enunciating words, was attached to 'ary.' Diction-airy, which is what actually occurs when you speak words into the air. I noted this down.

The dictionary was now permanently open on the coffee table since I never knew when I'd want to look something up. My name for instance. Nancy was a derivation of Ann which means grace. Wait didn't mean waiting around passively as I'd thought. 'To wait' was an active verb meaning to be in constant readiness. I liked that, and I liked this new world of meaning that was making sense of things in a new way. It made everything more interesting too. 'Create' was a combination of cre and ate. 'Ate' described how I ingested an idea by taking it in and feeling it in my sensory body. 'Cre' could be short for Crete, like the Cretan Glance of Kazantzakis, standing on the bridge over an abyss, looking forward and back at the same time. Like the double vision I cre-ate(d) with the AT&T paintings. A 'T' and a 'T.' T as in Tartan, as in plaid, a pattern of vertical and horizontal lines intersecting on a grid of right angles. Tartan plaid, as in Scotland. Gene was part Scottish. Scots-Irish, he said. I couldn't figure him out, not even with his portraits. That 'Hmm…' when I said the man in the photo was my father. Maybe I was just imagining there was something in the 'Hmm…' Maybe it was nothing. Or maybe it was.

I continued with the letters AT&T. T was the 20th letter of the alphabet, but zeros have no value in Numerology so it carried the vibration of two. If T was two, then AT&T meant 'a two and two.' I studied its shape and turned the two Ts on their sides, placing them stem to stem to make an H. An H looks like a bridge. A T and a T could represent a broken connection made whole again by bringing the two Ts together as an H. It was another sort of double vision of the AT&T building again. And in New York, New York no less. Or T as in tartan plaid. When the stem of the T met the horizontal line at the top it made two right angles. Tartan plaid had lines with right angles intersecting.

There were so many angles to consider! There was *Angleterre*, the French word for England, which translates as Angle-Land. The Angles or the Angli, were a Germanic tribe that invaded after the Romans left. I was an angler too, fishing for clues. I couldn't say for what, so everything was starting to seem important. My notebook was filling up with words and their meanings as if I was doing research. Or maybe just communicating with myself from a different angle.

Then I happened to come across Oscar's name in the dictionary. I was looking up something else when his name jumped out at me. 'Oscar' was from the Old Norse for "divine spear." *Divine?* Something that came from the unknowable? From God even? I was taken aback. This was a completely different angle. The Oscar thing was already in the realm of unknowable things and I had never understood why my mother did it. The why of it was the most difficult part to contend with. That night when I asked her why, all she could do was say she was sorry. I asked her again years later and she said the same thing, how sorry she was and that she'd made a mistake. I'd long since forgiven her without ever having to say so. I knew she loved me, and I'd always assumed she didn't know what she was doing, the same as when I was a child and she said she wished I'd never been born. *Divine spear* though. That was different. And I'd said no. Then I pretended I was dead.

Was that why I'd said yes to Lenny all those times? Because I'd said no to Oscar? It was all over and done with, all in the past, but was it a mistake to say no? No, I'd been right to say no. It wasn't right what they did. Marrying Lenny though, who would give me away to his friends like my mother did. I'd gone along with it until it didn't mean anything anymore. Had I been trying to make what my mother did seem right? Was that what broke the spell? When it became easy to say yes? How sad it all was. But if swinging broke the spell then it hadn't been a waste. Who could say what came from the divine and what didn't. Maybe that was why Rajneesh said, "Say yes to everything."

Old Norse though. That was the language of the Vikings. When I first saw Gene I thought he had Viking hair. But what did that have to do with anything. The feeling of being trapped though. When the assistant at Direct Centering said, "What are you up against?" I knew it was being trapped. I knew the only way out was surrendering to the trap so I surrendered to Gene since he was the only one around. When Gene said it was getting dangerous I remembered the feeling of crashing through an invisible barrier. And now I was feeling trapped again like the bear in his picture. No matter it was more like a stage set, there were still bars on the window. And I was still trapped in my body.

Something was trying to come together in my mind. As well as looking up words, I was looking through the pages of my sketchbook, crowing about what I found.

* * *

Journal Entry, June 23rd

> *I've connected the outer with the inner. I no longer seek, I find. It was in my sketchbook. It was terrifying to see what I already knew in the drawings. I knew EVERYTHING. But I didn't know that I knew, that was the difference. Being able to see it is like being on another PLANE. I feel like I've come home. I have to find my footing in this new place though. I have to keep grounding myself. Eating, cleaning, baking bread.*

What other plane? Coming home to what? I probably didn't have words for it at the time, but I wish I could have been more specific because when I looked at that entry later I had no idea what I had been talking about. When I look at those drawings in my sketchbook now, all I see are various figures wandering about and being stopped in their tracks by a jumble of unspecified geometric shapes. It's hard to tell if they are lost in another dimension or trying to get out of this one. There were grids too. A grid like a curtain in one. In another there was a figure trying to cope with a number of grids coming at her from different angles. I hadn't explored the theme further. I seemed to have drawn them without any conscious thought since I couldn't explain them. Yet they had to have been significant to cause such a reaction, writing in my journal that it felt like I'd come home. 'Connecting the outer with the inner.' 'Being on another plane.' Was I teetering on some kind of threshold? I don't even remember how the drawings came about or what I was thinking at the time. They were interspersed with drawings I did of my mother and Howard when I went to Decatur last Christmas. On one page I drew figures trying to find their way in another dimension, and on the next page was a drawing of my mother sitting at the dining room table paying her bills. Figures lost in the grid, then my mother and brother watching tv. Or there was the view of neighboring houses out the back window. Two different worlds, one cozy and familiar, the other strange and unfathomable. Yet both were about different ways of being in space. A few days later I became obsessed with being in time.

* * *

Journal Entry, June 27th

> *I guess it's when you are totally connected to TIME – is when it no longer exists (for you). For instance, I sat here to write down the fact that some time ago, though fairly recently, the beautiful gold clock from my London days at Ansdell Terrace suddenly started ticking again. I couldn't believe it. The clock stopped working years ago but I could never bring myself to throw it away and kept it out for decoration. Had the energy in the room affected it? The ticking didn't last long. The clock had been set at 4 and it stopped at 4 minutes past 4 which struck me as odd because lately when I looked at the time on my digital clock, whether it was morning or afternoon, often as not I would catch it at exactly 4:04, or 4:44 which seemed quite a coincidence.*

* * *

What I didn't know and couldn't have known was that June 1st, the day I saw Rosa Luxemburg shot and thrown in the canal, was the 44th anniversary of the downing of the *Ibis*. It was also the day I started the painting of a woman on her hands and knees, crawling back to the forest. *Four-est?*

Nor did I consider that in looking at the tarot for insight into Gene and picking the Death card, number thirteen, I was also picking the number four since thirteen breaks down to a four. I didn't take into account that the letter M was the thirteenth letter of the alphabet. The M which had so bedeviled me eleven years ago when my shrink said, "Are these men with an uppercase M or a lower-case m," that I wanted to die. But whatever I knew or didn't know, or thought I knew, it would seem I believed things were coming together at last.

* * *

Journal Entry, June 27th (continued)

> *Each day more and more is falling into place. I'm no longer afraid. I know I'm not in control, but have I ever been in control, really? I'm not making a fuss about it. I'm just enjoying myself. I'm FULL of TIME now. When you are filled with time, you BECOME time. Everything happens in the right way. Funny how when you get into a-line-ment, you are on-line, and the system works. Tom Torpor from across the street told me it wasn't until people discovered how something worked mechanically that they could discover how it worked in themselves. Like when they developed a pump*

they discovered the heart was a pump too. I must write him a note to thank him.

July 2nd

Only for me it still feels like July 1st because I haven't been to sleep yet. I feel so awake I don't even remember when I last slept. I'm so happy I don't know what to do with myself these days (and nights) since I realized that everything I thought I was doing wrong turns out to have been right. I've been going back over my paintings and my paintings of pictures. Looking at pictures of my paintings too. It's hard to believe that I know what I know. Is my search over? It's scary. I feel like I'm in Heaven, like my dream is already here, and the music sounds more beautiful all the time.

41

PERILOUS PASSAGE

Let everything happen to you, beauty and terror.
Just keep going. No feeling is final.

— RAINER MARIA RILKE

I went out to buy milk on July 3rd and ran into Cynthia, the owner of the deli-catering place downstairs. She was coming up the walk carrying a large oblong box with a picture of a barbecue grill on the front. As I moved to open the door for her I said, "Getting ready for the Fourth?"

"Yep. Did you hear Barbara Stanwyck died?"

"That's a shame. I always liked her."

"Have a nice Fourth!"

I called back, "You too!" and continued down the block. Barbara Stanwyck. Barb-e-que. Stan-wick. Wicks were for burning. Barbecues too. I'd forgotten tomorrow was the Fourth until I saw Cynthia's grill. People all over the country were going to be cooking hot dogs and hamburgers over burning hot coals. I pictured slabs of raw meat sizzling over grills, fat dripping, charcoal hissing, and swallowed back my revulsion. Then I remembered that today was *Fry*-day. I shuddered at the thought, and for no reason at all it flashed through my mind that I was going to be fried.

I crossed Second Avenue and went into the grocery store on the corner. I was heading down the aisle towards the dairy section at the back when I caught sight of the beer and thought I might as well pick up some Amstel Light. While I was looking around for it I caught sight of a label with a panda bear on it. Panda beer? How strange. I bent down for a closer look. The writing was in Chinese. Chinese beer? Pandas were from China, why not beer too? Panda beer. Now I was confused. I thought the connection of a panda and beer was only in Gene's screenplay, something he'd made up. But it was here in the real world too? Or did someone put it there on purpose. Maybe it was a message of some kind. I worried I was getting paranoid. That was no good. I had to stop it, but this was freaking me out. It felt like my inner world was now outside. It was a scary thought. I'd already forgotten that days ago I'd written how happy I was connecting the inner with the outer and how it was like being on another plane. But now it was like they'd somehow collided and I couldn't tell which was which anymore. All I wanted to do was go home. I grabbed a six-pack of the panda beer in case I should need it and went to get the milk. I would figure it out later. I told myself not to worry, everything would be alright as soon as I got home.

But the place I came home to no longer looked like the place I had just left. I felt it as soon as I came up the stairs and saw my work hanging all over the walls. First it was the sheer amount of pictures that was overwhelming. They covered every inch of available wall space without any order to them at all. Then it was all the colors and discordant images. Faces and figures hung next to buildings or landscapes, new work beside old. This had never disturbed me before, just the opposite in fact. Until now I used to come home and be comforted by this world of my making, knowing I could relax and be myself. But something had changed. I couldn't say what, but I didn't like it, and can only think it had to do with mixing the outer world with the inner. It was one thing to quietly mull over such things in my mind and write them in my journal, and quite another to have to face the consequences of such a possibility.

I couldn't stand looking at the pictures now. It was like I had been wearing blinders, and now for the first time I was actually seeing what I had done. What's more, I was seeing that my search was over. That's what it felt like. Like my search was over. Though to this day I'm unable to say what it was that I saw exactly. If I had been looking at *Girl Under Water* it might have made sense, but I don't recall seeing her at all that day. All I knew at that moment was that my search was over and I didn't want it to be. My identity, my life had been tied up with being an artist for so long that I wouldn't have known who I was if I stopped painting.

I was looking at *Amy Rosenberg Dressed in White* when I started to panic. She was from years ago and I'd only hung her up again recently, giving her pride of place between two of the windows. A young woman at her dressing table, a frightened bride-to-be who turned away from the mirror to look at the viewer. She was looking at *me* now. She had always been looking at me with those big sad brown eyes, but now they looked accusing, as if she was saying, *I see you. You thought you were seeing me, but it's me seeing YOU!* No-no-no—that was all wrong!

I was too distraught to understand what was going on. How seeing Panda Beer in the outer world had confused me and the confusion had followed me home, upsetting my observer status. It was all inside out, as if I was the subject now. It was unbearable. I didn't know how to deal with suddenly feeling what I was seeing. Amy had to come down. I had to hide her somewhere. The canvas was large, the frame made it cumbersome, and it took me a while to fit her into the stack against the wall. The relief in stashing her out of sight was short-lived. As soon as I sat down I saw the other portraits were looking at me too. Even the innocuous landscapes had something to say. There was nowhere safe to look. They all seemed to be looking back at me, telling me what I didn't want to know—that I'd seen all there was to see and I was finished with painting. But I wasn't ready for it to be over. I loved the search. I wanted to keep searching! Then it came to me that if I took all the paintings down and hid them away, had them facing the wall or facing each other and not facing me, I could pretend I'd never seen them.

I don't know how only the day before I could write that I felt like I was in Heaven and then wake up today feeling it was Hell. It was as if some kind of protection had slipped. Some kind of shield that had been there for a reason. It was how I kept my sanity, knowing dreams were dreams, reality was reality and pictures were just pictures. A little seepage may have been necessary for an artist, but I'd taken it too far and slipped through the railings. The outer and the inner were so turned about I couldn't tell which was which anymore. Gene's picture had done me in. This wouldn't have happened if he'd come to pick it up in time. I was at sea, feeling I'd lost all control.

I felt better once I'd taken all the paintings down so I didn't have to look at them. Except for a few framed prints that were done by someone else, the walls were finally as bare as the day I moved in. I sat in the wicker chair to survey the new emptiness and feel how peaceful it was. Peace. Finally some peace. Then I spotted a nail jutting out from the wall. All I had to do was see one nail sticking out from the white plasterboard before I started seeing the others. I had been in such a hurry to get rid of the pictures I hadn't bothered with the nails. It reminded me of the phrase I used to hear all the time at Direct Centering, "You're being nailed," or, "I'm nailing you." It meant the game was up. You were finished. No! It couldn't be! I had to get rid of the nails.

I was on my feet again, grabbing my hammer from the tool shelf, hauling out the step ladder from the kitchen to reach the nails higher up. Prying out nails in the plasterboard was easy compared to the ones I'd hammered into the brick. I couldn't believe how many there were. I was up and down on the stepladder, breathing heavily, racing around as if I was getting rid of evidence. Finally I stood back to look. The walls were now dotted with holes but I could deal with that later. Right now all I felt was the weight of the hammer. My blood was up and I wanted to hit something with the hammer. Smash it to smithereens.

It wasn't like me to want to break something. Every time I saw Connie smashing dishes in *The Godfather* I cringed at the waste of good plates. Not dishes then. The framed mirror? No, it was the one I bought at the used-furniture store on Second Avenue when I was with Lenny and it might bring me bad luck. Not the window either. The glass would fall on the street and might hurt someone. I'd have to pay to have it replaced too. My eyes fell on the framed print of Sagittarius, the centaur. It was my sign and I was fond of it, but I'd had the print for years and wouldn't miss it. I carried it into the bathroom where there was a large straw mat, the only floor covering I had in the place, and got down on my knees. And somewhere between closing my eyes and swinging the hammer down, it flashed through my mind that I wasn't so much breaking the glass as breaking through an invisible barrier. There was no time to ask myself why, or why I would want to do it at that particular moment, but I think it was about taking back control. The barrier had already been removed. But it was by acting it out physically that I could feel a sense of self again. *Smash!* Shards spilled onto the mat. A web of shattered glass remained in the frame but I resisted the impulse to hit it again. It felt too good that first time, and I got up quickly to return the hammer to its shelf before I went around smashing something else.

I suddenly felt hungry. All this unexpected exercise had given me an appetite. For the first time in ages I was actually hungry! I thought of going down to Cynthia's for a sandwich. I couldn't believe I'd lived above her restaurant for over a year without ever going in. I resolved to be a good neighbor from now on. I could ask her up to my place too. We might even become friends.

The restaurant was brightly lit and spanking clean but I couldn't read the menu. It was in squiggly script on the wall above the display case, more artful than legible, and the variety of choices on display made my eyes glaze over. I was starting to think I wasn't hungry after all when a voice behind the counter said, "How about an avocado and salad sandwich?" I never would have thought of it myself. She was wrapping it up when Cynthia came out from the back and I called out, "Hello! Would you like to come up for tea later?"

"I get my break around three," she said. "Would that be good?"

The girl behind the counter handed me the sandwich and I said, "Please come too!"

Guests for tea. The sandwich was delicious but I was too

excited to eat more than a few bites and I put the rest in the fridge. There was so much to do to get ready for guests. I had to get the canvases out of the way, rearrange the seating in the living room and clear off the coffee table. Then I had to go out again to buy cookies. But the tea was made and all was in order when Cynthia and her assistant arrived promptly at three. I don't remember what we talked about, only that tea parties were fun and I should have them more often. Then Cynthia said, "Are you taking your meds?"

"Meds? No, I'm not on any medication," I said cheerfully. Why would she ask such a thing. Had I been acting weird, said something strange? I couldn't remember. Cynthia got up saying they had to get back to work. They thanked me for the tea, and as they were leaving she said, "Remember I'm only downstairs if you need me."

She was probably just being friendly. I went about clearing away the tea things and forgot about it. I also forgot the mess of broken glass in the bathroom until it was time to take a shower. I wasn't ready to clean it up though. Broken glass was a reminder of breaking through a barrier. I stepped on it with my bare feet and it didn't even cut me.

My mother called shortly before eight that evening. "Are you all right, honey?"

First Cynthia, now her. Toshi had called too at some point, though it could have been yesterday, asking if I was alright, and he hardly ever called. My mother used to say she had ESP, but I thought that was part of her craziness. "I'm fine!" I said. "But I can't talk now. Someone's picking me up any minute."

"Who? Anyone I know?"

"No." I didn't know him either, other than he was an Israeli from Russia with a dry-cleaning business and a wife and kids up in White Plains. I only agreed to have dinner with him because I was hoping to interest him in a family portrait.

"When are you coming out to see us?" she asked.

"I'll be there for Thanksgiving."

"Good. I have something to tell you."

I wished she wouldn't do that. If she had something to tell me, why couldn't she tell me now? But she was talking about the roses out back, how well they were doing that summer, especially the red ones, and she wished I could see them. She had planted five different colored rosebushes, one for each of her children, and assigned the red ones to me. Listening to the familiar warmth of her voice made me want to tell her that I loved her and I understood everything now, and it was okay about the Oscar thing. But just then the doorbell rang.

"He's here—I have to go!"

"Be careful!" she said.

I didn't have to worry about Dave. He stood at the curb, a short stocky man with black hair and a beard. He held the door open to a black sedan and said, "I'm taking you to my favorite Middle Eastern restaurant." It was a beautiful night, the Friday before a holiday weekend, and the streets were teaming with revelers. I lowered my window to feel the breeze, and while we were waiting for the light on Fifth, a blonde in a convertible pulled up on my side and called out, "Do you know where the Old Homestead is?"

I had never heard of the famous steakhouse on Lower Fifth Avenue, but I had just been talking to my mother in Decatur, the house we called "the old homestead," so I laughed and yelled back, "It's everywhere!"

We were going down a side street when I saw the giant movie poster lit up on the side of a building. It was the head of a mummy wrapped in gauze except for the mouth where the gauze had peeled away. There was just a black hole there now. The caption said, "The Mummy Speaks." Was it a message I was going to have to speak soon? Maybe it referred to what my mother was going to tell me at Thanksgiving.

Dave found a parking space in front of the restaurant, and we went down into a dimly-lit cavernous underground space where a belly-dancer performed under a blue light. Dave ordered champagne and a platter of humus that arrived when the dancer finished her set and women from all over the restaurant began going up to the dance floor. Ordinary women in street clothes were writhing and rolling their hips under the blue light. Dave was buttering a roll. "They're dancing for their men, you know. It's a Middle Eastern custom. Will you dance for me?"

I laughed and said, "I don't think so."

We didn't stay long. When Dave drove me home I asked him up for coffee. I could see how pleased he was at the invitation, but the only thing on my mind was showing him my work and discussing a family portrait. I forgot I'd taken all the paintings down. I went to the kitchen to start the coffee and Dave asked to use the bathroom. When he came out he said, "What's with the broken glass?"

"Oh that! I'm sorry for the mess. It was an experiment. Breaking glass, breaking through barriers, you know?"

"Barriers?" He laughed. "I'm a Jew from Russia. What do you know from barriers?"

I tapped my head. "The ones in the mind, Dave."

He asked for a broom and swept up the glass while I finished making the coffee. I brought it out on a tray. Then I sat next to him on the couch and he said, "How about a kiss and we break through these barriers together?"

"Can't we just be two human beings and not this man-woman stuff?"

"You're a funny woman. But I *like* artists!"

He left shortly afterwards. I went to bed early, and for the first time in weeks I slept the whole night through. I registered this as soon as I woke up. I also noticed that my body felt unusually hot.

42

JULY 4, 1987

One day you wake up and your life is over.
But it doesn't mean you have to die.

— MARY RUEFLE

I sat up in bed and turned the table fan on. It blew with enough force to make my eyes tear, but after a few minutes I realized it wasn't cooling me off. How could that be? I didn't understand it. I didn't feel sick or feverish, I felt good after sleeping the whole night through. So why did I feel like I was burning up inside? Or at least smoldering. What a horrifying thought. I couldn't help looking down at my arms in the sleeveless white nighty, wondering if my skin would start turning color. What did flesh look like when it cooked? Did it turn black like a burning log? The phrase 'spontaneous combustion' came to mind. I'd read somewhere just recently that a person could suddenly explode. I didn't know how or why, but the heat wasn't going away, and it occurred to me that the fan might be fanning the flames. I switched it off and hurried into the bathroom.

I felt safe sitting on the edge of the tub with my feet in cold water, and stared at the cool white-tiled wall as I listened to the comforting sound of running water. The water was inching up my legs and my feet were starting to feel numb, but I still felt hot as a toaster. As soon as I thought of a toaster I wished that I hadn't. What if the heat was electrical? Immersing an electrical appliance in the bath was the last thing you wanted to do. I looked down at the water half-fearing I would see steam rising. But that was silly. I was letting myself get carried away. All the same I didn't feel quite as safe as I had a moment ago and swung my legs back over the side. My feet and ankles were red and stinging with cold. I padded back into the studio on wet feet, and by the time I closed the windows and turned on the air-conditioner, my feet felt as hot again as the rest of me.

Burning to death was my worst fear. When I was growing up we lived on the ninth floor and I used to plan in advance how I would escape if there was a fire. The room where I slept with my younger sister and brother was miles away from the front door as well as the backdoor in the kitchen. We could make a dash to the other end of the apartment, but what about my baby brother? My mother had taken to putting his bassinet next to my bed at night because I could always get him to stop crying and fall asleep by stroking his forehead and singing to him. Then I'd lie awake picturing smoke filling the room. I rehearsed in my mind how I would grab up the baby and cover his face with a blanket while I ran through the smoke to the backstairs off the kitchen. A few years later when Ellen and I had our own room I turned the fear into a game before we went to sleep, asking her if she preferred burning to death or freezing to death, and went over the pros and cons of each. We both preferred dying in a snowdrift, and I never changed my mind even when I saw Oliver Reed freezing to death in *Women In Love.*

I leaned against one of the wooden pillars, wondering if I should call someone and thought no, they'd probably tell me to go to the Emergency Room. Then I realized the pillar was wood and I should probably keep away from it. Of course the floor was wood too and I'd be safer in the bathroom, but I didn't want to have to go back there just yet. I wanted to get a handle on whatever this was and stop being afraid. But why was it even happening? I ran my mind over recent events and remembered I'd had cable tv installed last week. The man drilled a hole in the wall and pulled a thick black cord through it from somewhere outside. The cord probably held a lot of current. Maybe there was a leak and some of it had radiated into the room and I was absorbing the voltage and that was why I was so hot. Thoughts of electricity and wiring reminded me of the plugs in England that came with a wire for grounding. That's what I had to do, think of myself as a conduit. If I could direct the heat to pass through me and not build up inside, I might be alright. I closed my eyes and stood with my feet apart, then visualized the heat flowing down from my head, down through my body and down through my feet into the floor. Then I recited the Serenity Prayer, mouthing silently, *God, grant me the serenity to accept the things I cannot change, the courage to change the things I can, and the wisdom to know the difference.* But I *could* change this. I went back to the bathroom with its white-tiled walls and cool white porcelain and turned on the shower.

For the next few hours the bathroom was my sanctuary. That day I was never more grateful to have such a large bathroom, and one with a big window that let in the light. The vinyl shower curtain was clear with a pattern of white squares that enabled me to see out and not get claustrophobic. At first I made believe everything was normal and I was having a normal shower. I washed my hair and conditioned it, then repeated the process. I soaped up and rinsed a few times too. After that there was nothing to do but keep rinsing. The detachable showerhead with an extra-long cord made it more fun than it might have been, but it still got boring after a while. I couldn't tell if I was still burning or not, but why take a chance. I was better off where I was.

The thing to do was distract myself so I no longer thought about it. The water had been lukewarm so I made it colder, moving the dial little by little farther into the blue zone. It was shocking how cold it was, but instead of backing down I sang my favorite song from *The King and I.* "Whenever I feel afraid, I hold my head erect, and whistle a happy tune so no one will suspect I'm afraid." My whistling was terrible but I couldn't hear it over the noise of the shower anyway. When I couldn't remember the rest of the words I hummed the tune until my teeth began to chatter. I was shivering too, but rather than move the dial back towards the red, I turned the shivering into a dance. There was enough room for forward and back and turning in place, and when I put my whole body into it, it became a dance to dance away the fear. When I happened to look up at the circular white plastic curtain rings, I thought of the phrase, "Music of the Spheres." I didn't know what it sounded like or even if it was music, but I thought it had something to do with the planets. And then as the water pelted my skin and I kept bending and stretching and gyrating in place to the silent music, I felt I was becoming one with the Universe.

After a while everything fell away. Time fell away. Fear

fell away, and there was only this never-ending stream of life-giving water. I felt at one with the water, at one with my skin. No matter I was shaking with cold and my teeth were still chattering, I trusted the water. The sacred waterfall that was saving my life. I knew I would have to leave it eventually, but I could take my time, do it slowly, prepare myself mentally, even make it into a game. I called it Coming Back to Dry Land. Then I pretended I was an astronaut coming back to earth and changed the name to Coming Back to Earth. The shivering and shaking was just like I'd seen in the movies when astronauts shook from the vibrations of the space capsule. The round temperature dial became the steering wheel that I gripped with both hands as I hurtled through the atmosphere. The correct speed was critical. If I came in too fast the capsule might catch fire from the friction and that would be the end. It was worth staying deep into the blue zone even if my teeth wouldn't shut up and my legs were tired of standing. I kept telling myself, hang on, hang on, we're almost there. But after a while I began to wonder how would I know when I *was* there. And I realized there was no one to tell me but me. I could step out of the shower anytime—this very minute if I wanted to.

I turned off the water. The sudden quiet was unnerving. I missed the sound of running water, the feel of it running over me. I was freezing too, and thought sitting down in a nice warm bath would be a good transition. But not too warm. I pulled the curtain back and put in the plug, and as the tub began to fill I leaned back with my head on the rim and closed my eyes. It was glorious to finally relax, and I didn't open my eyes until I felt the water creeping up my stomach. Then I sat up abruptly and turned off the tap. The water was red. A pale rusty-red, but red all the same. How could this be? The shower hadn't been red. I wasn't bleeding;

I'd just finished my period so it couldn't have been that. It must be the pipes. Sometimes when they did work under the street it made the water rusty. I hadn't heard any drilling nearby, but the shower had been too loud to hear much of anything. The rusty color made the water look dirty. There was no question of getting out now.

I stepped onto the mat, and as I reached for a towel I realized I wasn't hot anymore. My fingers looked ghastly all shriveled, but as I patted myself dry I realized my skin was not only wonderfully soft, it was cool to the touch. And without thinking, as if it was the most normal thing in the world and all along I knew I wasn't alone, I said silently, *How did I do?*

A voice in my head answered, *Better than expected.* I heard tinkling laughter in the background like the laughter of little children. They thought I was funny! At first I thought doing better than expected was good, but as I hung up the towel it occurred to me that it could have meant not that much had been expected from me in the first place, and that wasn't good. But I took it in stride since at least I was cool now. In fact I was so cold I reached into the linen cupboard for a blanket, and as I was wrapping it around myself I looked down at the bath still filled with red water and the voice said, *You will have a son.* Oh, I thought, maybe that was why the water was red. It was a symbol of birth water.

I opened the bathroom door and came into the studio. The air-conditioner had been turned up high all this time and I pulled the blanket tighter around me. The wet hair dripping down my back was cold but I relished it. I didn't know where to sit so I sat on the floor at the back by the kitchen and stared out the window at the apartment building across the street. I couldn't see into any of the windows and wondered if someone could see into mine. Having a skylight was like having a light on. So what if they could see me. I shook the blanket off my shoulders. Let them see me naked if they liked. I had nothing to hide. If a voice could get inside my head and know what I was thinking, was there even such a thing as privacy? I almost laughed to think how surprised people would be if they knew there weren't any secrets, and covered myself up again.

I don't know how long I sat there in the stillness and the quiet before the vision came. But one minute I was staring into space, and the next minute I was seeing myself lying on my back in a field of tall grass, looking up at the clouds drifting by. It was like watching a movie and being in it too. Then the bears appeared. Three or four of them thrust their faces down at me, blocking out the light. I didn't move or try to get away. I just lay there completely still as if I had been expecting them. As quickly as the vision appeared it was gone and I was sitting on the floor in my studio wondering what had just happened. Had I died? Had I been given to the bears as some kind of sacrifice and that was why I didn't try to get away? I'd read about human sacrifices in primitive cultures, and maybe it was my turn and I had agreed to it beforehand. I had the strongest feeling that whatever it was I had agreed to it. But were they really bears? Maybe they were hairy men wearing animal skins and I only thought they were bears because they were bearing down on me. It didn't really matter though because what struck me the most was the feeling that I had died. Maybe I was already dead when they found me, and my eyes were staring blankly, seeing only the memory of clouds in the sky before the light faded. Whatever it was, the message was clear that I didn't have to be afraid of death anymore because I had already died.

This was a lot to absorb. I didn't think I was going to get any farther sitting on the floor wrapped in a blanket and I should probably put some clothes on. The clock said it was already afternoon. I went to the closet for something to wear and nothing looked right. I didn't feel like the person I'd been yesterday and I didn't know what this new self would wear. Then a voice—a different one this time, a female voice said, *It doesn't matter what you wear.* Really? This was a surprise. I must really have changed if it didn't matter what I wore. Something soft though. I wouldn't feel comfortable in a bright color either, and chose a brown tee to go with the white and faun-patterned capri pants. Then I put on beige moccasins and a brown mud-colored cardigan since I was still chilly. I didn't know what to do next so I sat on the stool by the bookcase with my feet on the rungs to think about it. Should I eat the rest of the avocado sandwich in the fridge? I wasn't hungry. Maybe I should hang up some of the paintings again since the walls looked awfully bare. Or I could always paint something new. No sooner did the thought of painting occur to me than the male voice spoke again. *You don't have to paint any more.*

I don't? Tinkling laughter sounded in the background again.

You've done enough. Now you have to write how you got here.

43

HOW I GOT HERE?

There is no remedy for love but to love more.

— HENRY DAVID THOREAU

How I got here? Today I might say that I got to that place because I lost the key to my soul and went fishing for it by delving into the dark and drawing out the shadows. Painting the feelings I couldn't say in words. Becoming an angler to fish between the planes of above and below that led me to an inner compass where I would follow the fish to find the girl under water. But I couldn't see any of that then. All I could do then was wonder where *here* was.

I got down from the stool and went to the window. 'Here' was Ninth Street. Was it how I got to Ninth Street? That didn't sound right. How I got to the planet then? I had no idea. I was shocked I didn't have to paint anymore, forgetting that I had already realized this myself only the day before. I had to figure out where I was though. Of course I was home, but where was I in my head? I reached for the green marble composition book with grid paper I'd bought on a whim and hadn't used yet, and opened to a random page filled with tiny green squares. Each square could stand for a place in time. I could put myself in any one of them, call it 'here' and outline a path to it. Create a map as it were. I outlined a square with a pen and filled it in. First I'm here. Then I outlined the square beside it and filled that one in too. Then I'm *here*. This went on for a while as the path of squares zigzagged around the page, sometimes going up, other times down or across or doubling back. There was movement alright, but I wasn't getting anywhere. It was just a design on a page of grid paper.

I'd forgotten how I once paced up and down the grid of black and white squares at St. Mary Abbots Hospital in London. Eleven years ago I'd been lost, put under lock and key for my own safety. I'd never forget how that checkerboard floor helped me to get my bearings. Life had become too confusing and now there was just one shape, a square, and two colors, black and white. The world made simple again. Though I was in a different place now and wasn't consciously thinking of those squares, I had gone to the grid again to find where I was, as if it was some kind of safety net. But what did I need a safety net for if I'd already died?

I had a sudden urge to get out of the house, see what it was like outside. When I opened the door it was like stepping into an oven. The sun baked the pavement and the heat rose up as much as it beat down from above. I crossed to the other side of the street though it was just as sunny, and didn't get very far before a young African American man holding out a pair of clogs came up and smiled and said, "Would you like these? They're new, never been worn. They look your size."

Clogs weren't my style and on any other day I would have smiled back and said no thanks, or shook my head no and walked on. But today I looked at the wooden shoes with plain brown leather attached with metal studs on the sides and thought they looked like earth shoes. I said, "How much do you want for them?"

"Is five dollars okay?" We made the exchange and he said, "Are you doing anything for the Fourth?" I'd forgotten it was July Fourth and asked if he knew where the fireworks were going to be. He said, "Down at Battery Park, the Statue of Liberty I think."

I thanked him and went back across the street to change into the clogs. I didn't think them attractive and they did nothing for my legs, but they fit perfectly. When I went out again to try them out I found each step was a clomp, a reminder I was *here*, making contact with the ground. When I got to the corner I turned up towards St. Mark's Church on the next block. A woman and three small children were sitting on the raised curb of the fence around the church. She was plump and fair-skinned, and with hair pulled tightly back from her ruddy face I had the impression of a farm woman. They looked miserable squinting in the sun and didn't look like they were from around here. I wondered if they were lost. New York was full of people who were lost in all sorts of ways, and on any other day I would have kept walking, but today I went over to her and said, "Do you need any help?" She shook her head no without looking up and I felt I was intruding on something private. I walked on, but it was too hot to be outside, and after circling the block I came home again.

The green marble notebook was still on the drafting table. I was finished with squares and nowhere near being able to write anything, so I thought of pictures. Not painting or drawing but photographs. I kept them neatly organized and separated with tabs in a shoebox. There was a section for family and one for friends. One tab was for vacations and another was for photos of paintings. The last section was photos just of myself. A visual record of who I was and where I'd been. I spent the next few hours going through the photos and picking the ones to go in the pages of the composition book. There was no order to them. I wasn't looking for a chronology, I was just making connections. But I arranged them artfully, sometimes cutting up a picture to show only my legs and feet or the legs and feet of a model in a painting as a reminder that this was about a journey. Then something must have struck a chord because I had a sudden urge to look at *Girl Under Water* again.

I can only think it must have been one of the tiny images of me at sixteen I'd cut from a contact sheet and placed at the beginning of the notebook. The photos were from the day the boy downstairs, an aspiring photographer, had taken me to Delacorte Lake in Central Park. I was wearing my favorite outfit, a blue sailor dress with white bib and red tie as I stared wistfully at the water. Maybe I was remembering the day my older sister's Ginny Doll drowned in the lake. We used to play by the lake before they built the theater for Shakespeare in the Park. In those days there were cherry trees to climb and plenty of space for picnics on the grass, and one day Kathleen decided to give her Ginny Doll an adventure. She put Ginny in a coffee can and set her afloat on the lake. I thought it was risky, but Kathleen assured me the current would bring her back. We lost sight of the metal can in the glare of the sun, and though we kept watch for hours, the doll never returned. Kathleen shrugged it off as a gamble, but I was devastated. I couldn't stop thinking about the doll in her pretty dress and trusting smile. I pictured the coffee can tipping over, filling with water and sinking to the bottom of the lake. How lonely it must have been for her, never to be found down there in the mud and the darkness!

I went looking for *Girl Under Water* in the stack against the wall. She had been hanging in the same spot on the brick wall for a year until yesterday when I took everything down, and in all that time I'd hardly noticed her. I hadn't given her a thought since that Friday night dinner at Direct Centering when someone asked what I was up against. I happened to notice the painting then, and realized she reminded me of my childhood nightmare of drowning in a steel box. Though how I could still be bothered by it all these years later was beyond me. When at last I found the painting I placed it on the easel to study it better and a strange thing happened. The red of her dress against the dark blue of the water reminded me of the dress I had been wearing the night of the Oscar thing—a mini-dress with wide red and navy-blue stripes. I hadn't made the connection before, but then I hadn't thought of Oscar in years, not until I chanced upon his name in the dictionary the other week. I could see now that she was *me*. That I'd painted her not only as a response to Henry's commission, but to tell Oscar not to look at me sexually. I pretended I was drowned that night, and now here was *Girl Under Water* actually drowned. Seeing myself in the painting was like seeing myself still down there at the bottom of the pool. Had I forgotten to bring myself back? I'd wanted to forget the whole thing and go on with my life as if it never happened. And now it looked like I was still down in the place where I'd left myself twenty years ago this summer.

I don't remember how soon it was afterwards that I saw the number five. It could have been just a few minutes because I was still by the easel when it appeared, a huge magnified version superimposed on the back wall of the Charles Demuth painting, *I Saw the Figure 5 in Gold.*

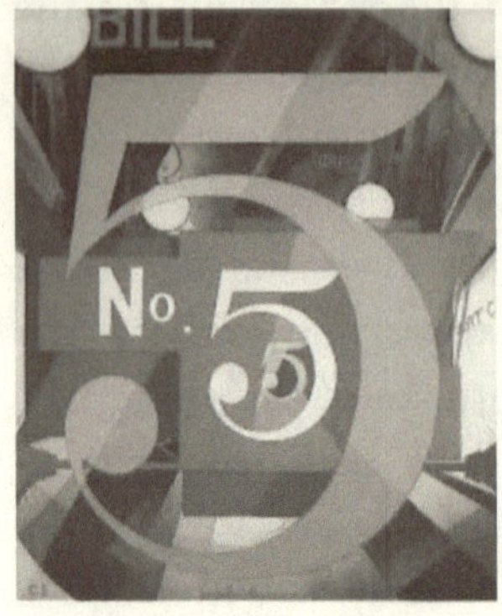

I'd seen it countless times at the Met. Five. Its message seemed to be five. The fifth dimension, 5D? It was the first thing I thought of, probably because of all the strange happenings that day. Was the vision telling me that I was in 5D, and 5D was 'here'? All I knew about the fifth dimension was that it was the Kingdom of Heaven and signified unconditional love. Only a short while ago I'd had the vision of the bears coming to get me as if I had already died. Was I in heaven now?

* * *

One day in the future I will come to know that 5D is also called the 5th Kingdom, the Kingdom of Souls. It will all become clear to me when I do what I was told and write how I got there, because I'll write about *Girl Under Water,* sometimes calling her by her initials, *Gee, You, Double-You.* And I'll look at the picture of the drowned girl, and know that there's no death when you connect to your soul.

* * *

For the present, all I could do was wonder, and I spent the rest of the day sitting on the futon listening to records. I played the Judy Collins album *Amazing Grace* over and over.

I hadn't played it in years and now I couldn't get enough of hearing her sing, *I once was lost but now I'm found /was blind but now I see.* Her voice was soft and clear, the music slow, and when she sang about sailing off to Greenland, I heard the water lapping against the sides of the boat, the gulls mewing overhead. I was with her in the boat, "threading the waves" with her as we traveled to a new Green-Land. I pictured a hand in the water, sewing the waves with a needle and thread. As if to attach waves of sound or light and bring them together as we glided along. Then I played the soundtrack of Zeffirelli's *Romeo and Juliet* and felt something else coming together.

There was as much dialogue as music in the recording, and though it was decades since I'd seen the movie, the scenes were so memorable I could watch them playing out in my mind. I was struck anew by the death scene though, their eagerness to die for one another before they'd barely lived. That I'd never come close to that kind of love made me sad. I thought of all the times I'd left a relationship, never seeing it through because there was always some hurt or other I couldn't get past. When the record finished I got up and paced around the room thinking how I'd missed out on love because I'd never seen it through. And then it struck me that love was when you stayed. I didn't think about the times when someone left me. I couldn't control their actions, but I could control mine. I would stay next time. Staying was the key to it all. Staying and waiting. If Romeo had just waited, Juliet would have woken up and they could have had a life together. I couldn't change their story but I could change mine. I would stay next time. I would wait it out.

Suddenly it felt like the most important decision of my life and I was dying to tell someone. Say it out loud, the words I'd never said to anyone before. It would feel more real then. But who could I tell? God? The universe? It didn't occur to me to go over to the easel and tell *Girl Under Water* I'd never leave her again, never abandon myself like I did at seventeen. I was too wrapped up in the story of *Romeo and Juliet* and thinking of romantic love. But who could I tell? I needed a witness who would hold me to it so I could never take it back.

Gene. I could tell Gene. He wouldn't mind. He would understand. Without giving it another thought I picked up the phone and dialed his number. When the answering machine came on it didn't put me off. I was so filled with my new resolve and the need for someone to hear it that it all gushed out, things I'd never said to anyone before. The vow I would stay and never leave. No matter what, I would stay. I would wait. However long it took, I would wait. I would stay no matter what. I don't know what else I said, or if I just kept repeating the same thing in different ways, but I felt like I was making a sacred promise, not only to Gene but to God and the Universe and the powers that be. I didn't stop until I heard the click of the tape running out. There, it was done. My relief was unimaginable, as if I'd finally said the words I had always been meant to say. To love was to stay. That was it. That's all it was. Just staying and not leaving. Accepting the bars of the cage. Accepting the trap and being willing to stay. At last I knew I had it right. It didn't occur to me then that I might have been making amends for wanting to leave my life eleven years ago by driving my car over a cliff. Then a voice said it wouldn't be any use because I'd only be sent back, so I stayed. But I had never been grateful to stay. I'd never made a resolution to stay until now. It had never seemed important until now.

I went to the window. It was dark out. Night had come and I hadn't even been aware of it. I looked out at the night and suddenly felt weary. It had been a long day after all. I hoped I could have a rest now. No sooner did I have that thought then the voice came again.

Nothing will happen for two years.

I was relieved. Two years was a long time. I could relax now. I sat down on the floor by the window and gazed at the monstera plant beside me. Until today I'd never sat down on the floor and now I was doing it for the second time. Since my eyes were level with the plant, I studied the perforated leaves and remembered the economist at Townsend-Greenspan who had given me a cutting when I left. Five years ago the plant had been small enough to carry home on the subway and now it was higher than I was when I was sitting down. Green leaves from the office of Greenspan. He had been in the news lately, smiling from the cover of *Time* as the new Chairman of the Fed. They called him, "The New Mr. Dollar." Dollars were green. Green leaves and greenbacks. A green marble notebook filled with tiny green squares. The light seemed to be green again. I didn't have to remember the painting I called the *Dreamer.* The one of a woman in a green gown looking through the doorway. Nor did I have to know that the color for the heart chakra was green. All I had to do was think of Green-land and Green-span to come up with land and span. Span was what a bridge did—spanned the distance between two points. And suddenly I knew that was it. I had to build a bridge! Never mind that moments ago I thought I'd had enough for one day, the need felt so urgent I sprang to my feet and grabbed the hammer from the tool shelf. When I came back with the hammer I realized how silly I was and I put the hammer down. It wasn't a physical bridge. I stepped up to the window again and looked out at the night sky. And as I was looking up I saw the arc of a bridge. It was small and far away but its tiny lights lit up the darkness.

* * *

In years to come I will hear about the 'lighted bridge' that leads to a higher world. I will hear about the Fifth kingdom and the Kingdom of Souls, and I'll remember the five I saw in the Charles Demuth painting, the clogs or earth shoes I bought for five dollars on the Fourth of July. And the bridge I saw that night that was so far away, as impossible to reach as the gap in the horizon I once imagined between the sea and the sky. Yet it seemed enough that I saw it, that I knew it was there. I'll remember that I saw it after I saw green, as if I was being 'green-lighted' to see it. Green, the color associated with Venus that represents love and beauty, harmony and relationships. And I'll think of the night with D.E. when all the lights were green. I thought he'd swept me off to Venus in that car of his, and *this* was the Kingdom of Heaven. I couldn't put any of it together then, but the day will come when I'll be able to bridge all sorts of things simply by writing about them. Writing will be a means of connection, no different than threading the waves like Judy Collins sailing off to Greenland. Only for me it will become the waves of body and soul. The one physical, the other eternal, separated only by an angle of vision. An angle of perception.

44

AFTERMATH II

There is another world, but it is in this one.

— W.B. YEATS

I never heard a voice again. Maybe it was because I could listen to my own inner voice now. The vibrations never came back either. Maybe it was because they had done their job of 'tuning' me up as it were. Two days later I did have another vision though. A reminder that life was not all that it seemed.

I hadn't ventured out of my neighborhood in a month, but I had an appointment with a client for a possible rendering commission in Westchester. Already it felt like an adventure just getting on the subway to Grand Central Station. I arrived during the morning rush, coming through the entrance as a horde of commuters came pouring out. And for a moment, instead of a crowd of people streaming towards me, I saw tiny colored lights. They swirled about in an orderly pattern, this world of light and energy that had no physical substance. I stood in awe for those few moments, wondering if I had stumbled into another dimension. Then it was gone, and I was making my way through the crowd again. Later though, I wondered if I had come across a portal. It had been in the tunnel underneath that very station a year ago when I'd had the feeling of crashing through an invisible barrier. What better place for a portal than a station for arrivals and departures? And in Grand Central of all places, where there was a map of the stars on the ceiling and a statue of Mercury, messenger to the gods out in front.

I took the train to Westchester only to find the client wasn't there. Maybe the important thing that day had been getting myself to the station for one last vision before they went dormant and I had no choice but to focus on this reality. I needed to now that Gene was coming by to pick up his painting. I dreaded the encounter. He'd called a few days after I'd left the message on his machine, and as soon as I said, "Hello?" he said, "Were you drunk?" I was mortified he would think that and pretended I didn't know what he was talking about. I apologized though for using up the tape in his machine.

Still, I thought he'd come, pick up his picture and go, and that would be the end of it. Only it wasn't the end because now he wanted me to photograph it for him. When he said, "Do you have a tripod?" I thought he was asking if I had 'tried pods' like in the movie *Invasion of the Body Snatchers.* I had been doing so well until then, acting as if this was just a normal artist-client meeting. But I recovered myself quickly and said, "Yes." Then he said, "Can you give me a tip-in?"

"A what?" My head was swimming. I thought he was asking for a tip into my world. He explained a tip-in was a term they used in advertising for a white border around the picture, but how was I supposed to know that? And why did I keep hearing other meanings as if we were having two different conversations. He left then, and I was still left with the picture.

But it would be fine. I was used to photographing my work and didn't hit a snag until I took the film to be developed and the man asked how many prints did I want. I couldn't remember, and suddenly it felt like a test, as if I was being asked to equate the amount of prints with the value of the picture. A hundred, five hundred? I think I settled on fifty, which was still far too many. It was costly too since they were 8x10s in color. But rather than admit my mistake and embarrass myself in front of Gene again, I said nothing about the extras.

It was another week or ten days before he came down to pick everything up, and by then I was feeling more sure of myself. So confident in fact that I could apologize for the phone call again, tossing it off as a minor lapse in judgement, a mistake anyone might make. I didn't expect a critique.

"You need to modulate yourself, not spill everything out at once," he said. To illustrate what he meant he mimed the act of vomiting. He left me with the image of myself throwing up over the phone and I never saw him again. Except for a dream I had a few months later. In the dream I was sitting in the balcony of a darkened theater when something caused me to turn around, and when I looked behind me I saw him a few seats over, kissing another woman. I knew then it was time to let him go.

* * *

The first month after July Fourth I didn't know what to do with myself. Most of the canvases had been hung up again simply to get them off the floor. Painting anything new was out of the question. Even if I'd wanted to, which I didn't, that part of my life seemed finished. The palettes were put away and the taboret was covered with a decorative scarf. Brushes stood in a vase on top like a bunch of dried flowers. Though painting may have been over, I was nowhere near ready to begin writing.

Then in August music came to the rescue and filled in the blank. I was walking home from Fourteenth Street when I happened to pass a pawn shop with a guitar in the window. That was it. I would learn to play the guitar! I found a teacher nearby who taught me folk songs and I practiced for hours each day. Yet by September, even as I sang *This Land is Your Land,* my thoughts drifted back to England. I thought if only I could touch base with London again I could move on with my life. It was simple enough to tell Toshi how beneficial it would be for our work if I met the distributors in person, and asked him to send me over on a business trip that October.

Then a week before I was due to leave I had a premonition something would happen to my mother if I went. I felt so anxious about it that I called a psychic who had been recommended, and when I asked her advice she said not to worry, my mother would be fine. I still wasn't sure, and called my mother from the airport to say goodbye again. "We already said goodbye last night," she reminded me. It was the last time I ever heard her voice. Two days later, Monday, October 12th she had a stroke. It wasn't until late on Tuesday that my sister was able to track me down in London and give me the news. I should have tried to get a plane home on Wednesday but I was in shock. I didn't know it was already too late, that she was brain dead, on life-support. Thursday October 15th, the night of the Great Storm of 1987, my brother called to say they'd pulled the plug. My mother died at the same time a cyclone with hurricane-force winds struck France and Southeast England. Trees were down, roads were blocked and twenty-two people lost their lives. I finally got a flight out on Sunday the 18th.

On Monday the 19th I was on a plane to Chicago when the pilot came on and announced the stock market had crashed. It became known as Black Monday. We buried my mother on the Tuesday. The funeral home was packed with mourners. I had no idea so many people knew my mother. I got up to say a few words, but all I could manage was to thank her for having me.

I'll never know what she was planning to tell me at Thanksgiving. Whatever she had been planning to say went to the grave with her. Maybe I was better off not knowing. Maybe it wasn't anything important, but since the last time she said she had something to tell me it was that Dad wasn't my father, I couldn't be sure. And now she had been silenced. I thought of the poster of a mummy I'd seen lit up on the side of a building in July with the gauze peeling away from her mouth and the caption, "The Mummy Speaks." It would be me now. I would speak through my writing after I became a mother. I had been told I would have a son. July Fourth when I came out of the bath of red water, the voice said, *You will have a son.* And though I can't say I thought much about it afterwards, I went about getting married again the following year and moving back to Brooklyn. Settling down into the kind of calm happy life that would make having a child completely feasible.

I met my husband when I was eager for knowledge that might give me some insight into what I had gone through that summer. He was a Theosophist and had a collection of books known as the Ageless Wisdom. I followed a course of meditation and study, learning about the soul and the Ascended Masters, and the various initiations and stages of transformation one went through to become an enlightened being. I was also taking writing courses, but I didn't have much faith in my ability and thought if only I could get back to London and finish the visit that had been cut short the previous year when my mother died, I'd be able to get on track with it. Toshi provided the funds again, and along with doing the business for him, I saw it was a trip I had to take if for no other reason than to get it through my head that the past I was looking for was no longer there. The city itself had changed the way cities do, and the friends I was still in touch with from our student days had changed too. They had homes and families of their own and were too busy to spend much time with me. I flew home on Pan Am at the end of December 1988, and the next day that same flight from London to New York exploded over Lockerbie in Scotland. I stayed put after that and let my passport expire.

It would be years before my son was born. Not long after our marriage my husband wanted to be celibate. Since I'd made the promise 'to stay no matter what,' there was no question of leaving him, and I adjusted to our new relationship, honoring it with a painting of light-bodies coming together on the astral plane. Then at night I went dancing in my dreams and woke up happy in the morning, bursting with energy. But as the second anniversary of that July Fourth approached, reminding me that my two-year grace period was coming to an end, I started having debilitating headaches. I put it down to anxiety about what would happen this time. The headaches kept getting worse. Meditation didn't help and neither did pain killers. When I finally relented and went to the doctor I was hospitalized with severe hypertension. Apparently a tiny hair was blocking a renal artery. It was a mystery how it got in there, but after they put in a stent I was as good as new. It didn't occur to me at the time that a blocked artery could have been a physical manifestation of a thwarted destiny, that of having a son. I thought it had to do with not writing 'how I got here,' and set to work before anything worse happened.

Only the story I came up with wasn't how *I* got here, it was a children's novel about how a little tree got here from another galaxy. Since he came as a seed I called him Bonzee, which sounded like 'good-zee' or good-seed,' *bon* being French for good, probably because I had once played Rhoda, the child murderess in *The Bad Seed.* He was small for a tree, only three-feet high, and was often mistaken for a bush. Worse than that, he was asleep when the instructions were given out and he didn't know what his mission was. But due to his thin, thread-like roots, he didn't have to stay in once place and could hop around on his trunk. He could also communicate with other plant-life and children if they were open to listening. The ending was bitter-sweet because although Bonzee found a measure of contentment, he was disappointed over his failure to remember his mission. When I finished the book, my husband announced out of the blue that he wanted to have a child. Of course I was elated, and though my doctor didn't hold out much hope since I was 41 and my husband was 50, destiny has nothing to do with statistics and I conceived right away.

I look back at those first two years of our son's life as the period of bliss before everything changed, for those were the two years when 'nothing would happen.' Right before the two years were up he stopped wanting to nurse, and when his need for me lapsed and my body became my own again, the visions returned.

It was such an ordinary day, an afternoon in early spring when he was napping and I was resting on the exercise mat with nothing more pressing on my mind than what to make for supper. Then from behind my closed lids the front page of *The New York Times* appeared, and splashed across the headline was the name of a client from almost a decade ago, the one I called D.E. who whisked me off to Venus one night. I was amazed to be thinking of him all these years later. It was incomprehensible and I must have gotten up and paced around the room because when the second vision came I was lying in a different spot on the floor. This time I was sitting in a coffee shop booth with three men. I couldn't see their faces. My eyes could only go as high as the collars of their white shirts. I didn't look to see what I was wearing, but they all had on long-sleeved white shirts. The mood was convivial and I thought we were friends until the man diagonally across from me, the one with his sleeves partly rolled up, pointed his finger at me and suddenly I was hurled out of the booth as if I'd been picked up by the wind. Before I knew it I was lying on my back on the floor again, staring up at the ceiling since it seemed like I'd fallen from someplace up there. Then the beams of light came. Five altogether, shooting down one at a time. One landed on each shoulder, then one on each hip, and the last beam landed on my solar plexus. I sprang to my feet. It felt like I had been activated.

I couldn't figure it out at the time, but I've come to see that D.E.'s name in the headline of *The New York Times* was a message that this time was like that time with him in New York when I felt myself disappearing into his eyes and I hadn't finished painting yet. This time I was disappearing into motherhood and I hadn't finished writing. I hadn't even started yet. Not the real story. Not how I arrived where I was that July Fourth. I can see why I needed to become a mother first though, giving my body over for a new life that would tie me down for years to come, because experiencing that kind of grounding in unconditional love, knowing that I would gladly give up my life for him, was to touch something I'd never known, yet it lay at the core of being human.

The vision of the coffee shop took longer to understand. I had to think back to my London days, to the end of the Dream of '76 when I wanted to smoke, and when I couldn't find a match, my friend Sharon appeared and held out a light. In the years since, Sharon had become famous as the "coffee girl" in the Gold Blend commercials that played over here as well as the UK. I think it was so I'd know that the lights came from the same source. The light from Sharon and the lights after I was chucked out of the coffeeshop booth. I'd been given only one light that first time, and now I was given five times as much. Taken together, the two visions that day meant it was not only time to get back to work, but the impetus was that much greater.

All I could see though was pictures. First it was one of my husband's pen and ink drawings of lines and dots. I'd been looking at it for years but only now did I see it as a map.

Much as I had that July Fourth when I went to the grid paper to try and figure out where I was and how I got there, I studied the pattern of lines and dots he'd created as if the answer might be in them now. Some people thought he'd created star maps, but for me it was more about connecting the dots. The dots themselves were clues to uncover, and the lines would be how they related to one another. But it was too abstract to keep my interest for long and I went back to painting images.

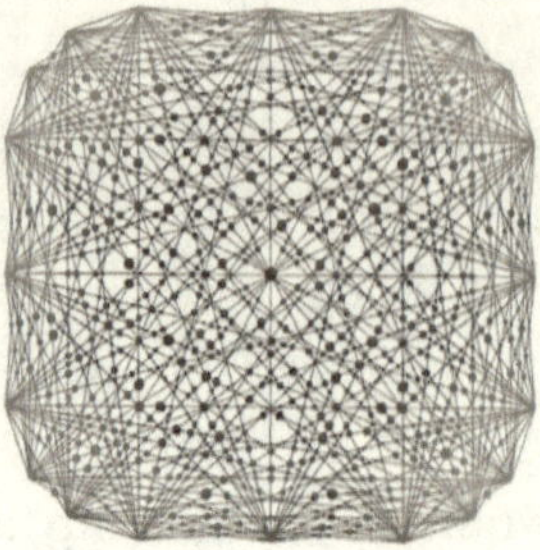

The theme was union and separation. The two figures merged to become one, but they couldn't stay that way so I took them into the etheric where they could pass in and out of one another at will. Then that couldn't last either because although they could touch, it was touching the air and they couldn't feel one another. So I made them more physical, more solid and dense. Then that lived out its course as well because the physical body has a lifespan and doesn't last beyond it. They embraced for the last time before returning to spirit in the natural order of things. All that remained was remembering the feeling of touch, which was too good to let go of. In the end there seemed no choice but to turn them into a tree that was both male and female and could propagate itself. They weren't human anymore but at least they would never be parted.

I put my paints away and went back to study my husband's drawings. He had over a hundred pen and inks dating back to the 1960s that lay scattered about in various portfolios. He said I understood the meaning of the lines and dots better than he did, but all I really saw was that they led somewhere. Where was still a mystery, like trying to recapture a dream even as it faded. But the journey was what seemed important and I wanted others to see it too. I took on the task of organizing the drawings, creating slides and prints, then rented a space to give a slide show and talk to our friends.

My energy seemed unquenchable since those beams of light had come to me. I needed little sleep to keep the household running as well as before, and found time to construct a mountainous landscape out of papier-mâché with roads and a tunnel for our son to play with his little trains and trucks. Nights were for looking up words and exploring different meanings in the pattern of those five lights. When I connected the dots of shoulders and hips I saw a square with a light in the solar plexus or center. Connecting the four corners to the light in the center looked like a sealed envelope I hadn't a clue how to open. Then I saw a pyramid from above which was more enticing, but what did it mean?

Contemplation alone at my desk was one thing, but as the months went by this search for answers began to spill into other areas. One day I followed a man down the subway stairs because of the keys jangling from his belt. I was going down to the train anyway, but when I heard the keys, suddenly it was him I was following, no more able to stop myself than one of Pavlov's dogs. If I was thinking of the 'key to my soul' I thought I'd lost twenty years ago when Milton died, I wasn't aware of it. It was just the sound of the keys and following the man with the keys down into the subterranean sub-way as if it was another sort of 'Journey to the Deep.' But it was one thing picturing an idea on canvas and another carrying it into real life.

I didn't notice at the time that losing track of the borders between outer and inner was affecting my judgement until I was tidying up my son's bookcase and realized half the picture books portrayed animals as humans. Bears and mice, frogs and bunnies wearing our clothes, eating and talking and acting like humans? I had loved reading those books to him and now I was practically hysterical thinking they were giving him the idea that animals were no different than humans. “We’re not animals!” I shrieked to my husband. I wanted to get rid of them all but he talked me down, and I could see he was becoming concerned. I would have tried harder to tamp myself down if I could, but it was impossible after the next visions came.

It was an afternoon when my son was probably napping again—he was very good taking naps—because I was alone in the living room. Only I was somewhere else too, seated in a tiny room with a glass wall like those listening rooms they used to have in record stores where you could play a record before deciding to buy it, and I was receiving visitors. Some came inside the room to talk while others stood outside watching. It was like an interview the way I was being asked about my acting experience. How would I play this, how would I play that. I didn’t know who these people were or why they were interested in my acting, but I was flattered by the attention and the way they seemed to think I was some kind of expert. It was so intense and so real that for the next few days I kept having flashbacks when I was alone in the living room, reliving the experience as if it was happening again. On one of those days the top of my head felt so hot I thought I might be on fire, and looked in the mirror half-fearing I would see smoke coming out. There wasn’t of course, but I put on a hat and wore it around the house for the rest of the day to hide whatever it was.

It wasn’t until recently that I began thinking of the tiny glass-walled room as a ‘womb-room’ where I’d received guidance prior to birth. I’d heard it can happen, though very few remember, and I’d never thought of myself as one of those who did. I imagined spiritual guides as men in long white robes, and the ones I saw wore ordinary street clothes. They were all strangers to me, yet oddly enough I recognized Bob Dylan. I couldn't for the life of me think why he would be there. He didn't speak, he was just there, standing outside the glass or sitting inside. I'd seen him a couple of times in real life though, albeit from a distance. In 1966 when I apprenticed at the Woodstock Playhouse, someone pointed to a man standing in front of the coffeeshop across the street and said, "Look, there's Bob Dylan!" But the sun was so bright that day, and it must have glanced off something because when I looked all I could see was a ball of light. The other time was when I lived in Crown Heights in the 1980s when he was studying Judaism. I saw him standing outside the next-door neighbors but his back was to me and his head was covered with a prayer shawl. I wouldn't have known it was him if someone hadn't told me.

But visions are like dreams and come from a place where anything might happen. Where Bob Dylan could appear to me in the 'womb-room' even if he was an eight-year-old boy in Duluth called Robert Zimmerman when I was in the womb. I wasn't able to reason it out until a long time later when I looked at the spelling of 'Bob Dylan' rather than at the man or the musician, and saw there was a meaning hidden in his name. It was like that day back in '76 when I took a walk up to Gloucester Road and saw the sign 'Launderette.' Launder-ette, launder-it. The *word* was the meaning.

'BOB' was easy to decipher. *Be, Oh, Be.* With 'DYLAN' I had to convert the letters to their numerical equivalent in the alphabet, which in effect was like reading their vibration. D became four since it's the fourth letter. Y is the twenty-fifth letter but I could read it as 2-5, or 'to five.' L stood for 'angle' since it looks like a right angle, and the last two letters, AN, I read as short for Ann, which I took to mean me, since Nancy is a derivation of Ann. The translation of Dylan then became, *4 to 5 angle Nancy.* And Bob Dylan, once I peeled away the association to the person, was *Be, oh be (the) 4 to 5 angle, Nancy.* Of course, in order for that to make sense I had to know that the 4-to-5 angle was a thing. Nothing less than the angle from the fourth dimension to the fifth. Or the Fourth Kingdom of Humanity to the Fifth Kingdom of Soul. The journey known as the path of ascent that led to a higher dimension, the Oneness of all beings. But the seed had been planted. The vision of a womb-room had come whether I was able to understand it or not at the time. And when I finally found an explanation it made me wonder anew about being interviewed about my acting experience. Did it mean I was being prepared psychically in the womb for a life in which I would 'act out' the search for a path to a higher realm? That July Fourth when the heat came, I stayed in the shower for hours to cool off. When at last I came out and was drying myself off, I said silently, *How did I do?* How did I do, as if all along I knew I was being tested or performing a task. Maybe even playing a role! *Better than expected,* came the silent response. If my life had been the acting job, then no wonder I'd become disillusioned with the profession, given the parts I was cast in—drug-pusher, thief, call girl who suicides. It took something drastic like wanting to drive my car off a cliff before I was given a different role. Finding out what I knew inside by becoming an artist or a writer.

The key lay in an angle of vision. Somehow I had to have known this. Or some buried part of me did because when Milton died I realized I'd lost the key to my soul. What does the soul represent if not a way of seeing oneself? Milton was part of me, and suddenly he was gone before I'd had the chance to discover who I was. A year later when it seemed to boil down to not knowing what love was, I couldn't go on.

I think I understand the placement of the five beams of light now. When I connect the first four lights that landed on me I see a four-sided box no different from the one where I was trapped in the No Exit dream of my childhood. But there was a fifth light in the middle. If I compare the first four lights to the Fourth Kingdom of Humanity, then the fifth light within the box would be the Fifth Kingdom of Soul. The eternal self within. The soul that never dies. *Be, oh be (the) 4 to 5 angle, Nancy.* If the lights were dots and the key was the angle of vision from 4-to-5, then no wonder I was drawn to my husband's drawings of the lines and dots.

I was nowhere near this kind of insight at the time, and I wouldn't be until I began putting it all into words, writing down everything that happened. It was seven years since I had been told to write *how you got here,* and it will be several more years before I begin. Three more things will need to happen first. Number one will be seeing the path with my own two eyes. Seeing that it was real and not just something I read in a book.

This occurred on a Saturday morning not long after the womb-room visions. Since my husband was home he was tending to our boy and I could take my time getting dressed. The last thing to put on was a pair of earrings, and maybe because I knew I didn't have to rush, when something else in the jewelry box caught my eye I picked it up. It could have been anything, a pin or a bracelet or any bit of metal or plastic I'd saved for sentimental reasons. Anything of value had been sold years ago to pay rent or buy paints in Crown Heights. Now, looking over these pieces of my past, these tangible things with weight and texture I could feel in my hand, each one carried me back to where it had come from and who had given it to me. Or if it was something I bought for myself then I thought back to why, and what it had meant to me at the time. As the memories flooded back I was struck by what I'd held onto over the years, and how the old cardboard jewelry box contained a history I'd lost touch with. But I was touching it now, and not only symbolically because when I held a ring or a necklace or an earring in my hand, no matter it belonged to the past, it was real and palpable in the present. Suddenly I wanted to see them in chronological order, these pieces that were part of a life that had been. They were all jumbled together and I wanted to see if I could tell how one thing led to another. I turned the box upside down and dumped the whole lot onto the bed. As a timeline began snaking around on the bedspread, it occurred to me that this was the map I'd been looking for. It wasn't the lines and dots of my husband's drawings any more than it had been those squares of grid paper I'd outlined on July Fourth when I was trying to figure out where I was. It was these treasures from the past that formed an actual path in the here and now.

When my husband came into the bedroom wanting to know what was taking me so long to get dressed, I tried to explain. I wanted him to understand that I was seeing how one piece led to another and that I'd found my Path of Return, meaning the one he told me about when we first met. The one in the books he'd given me to read about the path back to Source or Spirit. But I must have been babbling. No matter the jewelry was laid out in order and I could see their concreteness, thoughts flew around in my head willy-nilly. I know I made matters worse by throwing in my latest interpretation of the word Brooklyn. For Brooklyn had become Brook-line, then Broke-line because I felt like I had broken through another invisible barrier. Only it didn't feel invisible or imaginary anymore, not if it had to do with *real* things like the contents of my jewelry box.

What I'd done of course was I'd crossed a line. I didn't have the sense to keep quiet until I could explain myself properly, or at least in a more measured way. Gene said a long time ago that I needed to learn moderation, and here I was spilling everything out again. Gene thought I was drunk when I left him that message on his answering machine. My husband thought I was having a breakdown, and rather than soothing his qualms I became more insistent. Maybe I'd reached a breaking point and was tired of having to watch myself and keep a lid on it. Maybe I thought what if I just let go, let it all fly. I don't remember much of the next few hours, but the upshot was that he was going to call 911 and have them take me away unless I came voluntarily.

So that was the second thing, being a patient in a psych ward again. The hospital was in the neighborhood like St. Mary Abbots had been in my neighborhood in London, but there the resemblance ended. Here they put me on meds and kept me for two weeks instead of one. When I came home I was docile and repentant, and stayed that way even when I went off the meds a few months later. I was eager to make amends but a marriage where neither of us quite trusted the other anymore couldn't be saved. Divorce was the third thing that happened. It was all very amicable and we stayed friends for the sake of our son, spending holidays and birthdays together as a family, but I had to go back to office work now.

The job for Toshi had ended with the recession in Japan in the early 1990s, and after I took classes to learn the new software and went about looking for a job, I was surprised to see ads for secretarial work that said, "College Degree a

Plus!" A bachelor's degree for a secretary? Whatever for? When I asked one of the interviewers why it had become important she said, "Because it shows you can finish something." And there it was. My unfinished business. *Write how you got here.*

45

FINDING 'HERE' AGAIN

HOME IS NEITHER HERE NOR THERE.

Home is within you,
or home is nowhere at all.

— HERMAN HESSE

I enrolled at the New School, the college that in 1977 had a bulletin cover with a picture of a doorway into the light. Now, twenty years later I was back, determined to stick with the writing, show I could finish something. In the essay for admission I said my goal was to find the blueprint of my soul. I knew something about blueprints from my rendering work, and I didn't think writing a memoir would be that different from taking apart the bricks of a building to see the plan underneath. All went smoothly until my second year when I took an online psychology course and the word plum line appeared in the first reading assignment. It unsettled me. I knew what a plum line was, but I went and made it worse by looking up a more specific meaning in the dictionary.

A line or a chord with a weight attached, used for finding the depth of water.

It threw me into a panic. Even as I read the words I felt myself being pulled down into that unknowable space below. I'd been to the depths already in the series I called Journey to the Deep that began with a swimmer doing a backstroke far out to sea. I'd written, *Something is calling me down to the depths.* But I wanted to stay in daylight time, *not go exploring where there was no end or return.* I couldn't risk it again. The last thing I needed was a vertical drop, a plum line with a weight attached. To prove to the instructor that I'd been there already I uploaded half-a-dozen paintings into the chatroom and was shocked how big they appeared. Each image filled up the entire screen of my desktop. I didn't understand jpeg files and bytes and had no idea the thumbnails in a folder on my computer would turn into giant pictures, each ablaze with color. I scrolled past a woman screaming in pain, another on fire, another impaled on a spike. Was there no end to this? They were way over the top and I tried to delete this disaster but they wouldn't go away. If I'd had my wits about me I might have written some kind of explanation. I might have gotten in touch with the instructor and apologized for my mistake. But the feeling of being out of control again took over and I was too embarrassed to go back to the class, even a faceless virtual one.

Then I happened to see a rubber band lying on the sidewalk and picked it up, this piece of elastic that could expand and contract. Expand to take in more, then return to its original shape when it was no longer needed. I saw it as a message to trust myself to expand, knowing that I could always come back. At the end of the term when I got my grades and received an F in the course for disappearing instead of formally dropping out, it seemed a small price to pay for not having to deal with a vertical drop again. There would be more times when tentacles of the past would reach up to pull me out to sea again, but I kept going, putting events in order and creating a timeline to keep them straight in my head.

If vertical drops were my weakness, horizontal lines of text were becoming my strength. After three years at the New School and another two at grad school, I may not have had a blueprint but I had a solid grasp on my early life. I didn't get any farther in the story than my sojourn in England and the voyage back to New York. I didn't know how to write about Lenny yet. I tried a chapter on Gene, but when my advisor asked if I'd been psychotic, I realized I didn't know how to write about him either. I had enough pages for a first book; I would tackle my return to New York later.

Then one night I was reading over the manuscript before handing it in and wondered again whether or not to include a certain episode. I'd put it in previous drafts and taken it out because however interesting it was, it didn't relate to anything else. I was twenty-one at the time, living with my boyfriend and going to Rada. He had an interest in the occult and went to mediums at the British Spiritualist Society. Then he booked me a session too. I had no curiosity about such things, yet I went along much the same as I'd gone along with him to learn meditation or try a macrobiotic diet. The medium I saw that day was Nan Whittle, a plump, gray-haired lady who closed her eyes, tilted her head back slightly, and as her eyes rolled back in her head and her lids fluttered, she said, "Leslie Howard is looking after you." This was astonishing news. Why would the actor Leslie Howard possibly be interested in me? It was too far-fetched to take seriously. Later, when it was too late, I wished I'd asked Nan Whittle if she knew why, but I was too surprised and too much in awe to ask questions. I told myself to forget about it, which of course I never could.

Now, thirty years later, I found myself wondering how Leslie Howard died. It was the fall of 2001, not long after 9/11 when the smell of death wafted across the river to Brooklyn and the tenor of life in New York had forever changed along with the skyline. I couldn't believe Leslie Howard had anything to do with me personally, but I was curious how he died. I seemed to remember reading somewhere that his plane had been shot down in World War II, and I thought he might have been in the RAF. But I could have been thinking of one of his films so I looked it up and found it was neither. He had been flying back to England as a passenger on a civilian plane called *Ibis* when it was shot down by the Luftwaffe over the Bay of Biscay. I was struck by the date, June 1, 1943 because it was exactly six years and six months before I was born on December 1, 1949. Then I read there were children on board. My heart was pounding when I turned my head to where *Girl Under Water* was hanging on the wall a few feet away.

In the fifteen years since I'd painted her most of my work had gone into storage. But not her. I'd kept her in sight since that July Fourth when I saw her as a part of myself I'd left behind. Could she be somebody else too? I told myself not to jump to conclusions. I had to find out more information. Leslie Howard's son Ronald had written a book called, *In Search of My Father.* It was out of print but I found a copy online, and while I waited for it to arrive I went to the library at Forty-Second Street. The same library with the lions, Patience and Fortitude out front where I used to wait for the bus to my first writing class at the New School a quarter century ago. I had to go down to the basement to read the story on microfiche from *The Times* of London. The article said the *Ibis* had disappeared during its flight from Lisbon and was declared missing. Among the names of the thirteen passengers were two English girls, Petra who was eleven and her sister Carol who was two. They had been evacuated to Canada, and though the war was still on they were traveling home with their mother via Lisbon to Bristol.

Since clearly marked civilian airplanes were supposed to be off limits in wartime, Ronald Howard believed that his father had been targeted by the Gestapo for his work with the War Office and his anti-Nazi films. Either that or the plane was shot down because of a rumor that Winston Churchill was on board. There was a description of a cloudless spring morning when shots rang out and the clearly marked commercial aircraft caught fire before it disappeared off the coast of France. Petra was an unusual name. I wondered where it came from, and when I looked it up I found it meant rose-red, after the ancient city of Petra which was built of rose-red sandstone. *Girl Under Water* had red hair and wore a red dress. Was it her? Was she me?

The question would dog me for the next ten years. I thought of all the things against it, such as not remembering anything of her life. In accounts I'd read of reincarnation, people remembered all sorts of things however trivial. While it was true I'd had a fascination with England since childhood, it was because my mother used to show us old photographs and daguerreotypes of her grandparents from Yorkshire who emigrated to Illinois and the aunts from Halifax who came to visit. My mother not only collected English antiques and made Yorkshire pudding and mince pies for Christmas, she read *Wuthering Heights* aloud to my sister and me before we were old enough to read it for ourselves. When I went to London the first time it felt eerily familiar, but that could have been because of all the old black and white British movies I'd seen growing up. It didn't explain why I'd been so struck by the light though. Or the color of the sky and the smell of the air, or why it gave me the feeling I'd come home.

True, not true. Me, not-me. I went back and forth. I had a dread of over-stepping and making assumptions, putting myself where I had no right to be, and at the end of it all I had two versions. One included the connection to Leslie Howard and Petra, the other did not, and only one of them made sense. For how could the No Exit dream of drowning in the steel box or the Dream of '76 when I was shot and had a noisy fall to the bottom of the sea be explained without knowledge of the *Ibis?* I knew I had to become a painter or a writer to find out what I knew inside. And now that I was both I was able to see how the paintings combined with the story only made sense if I was remembering Petra's death.

Now when I look at *Girl Under Water* I see things I hadn't noticed before like the orange flecks swirling around in the water and in her hair. How could I not have seen they were flecks of fire? It had all been instinctive, painting abstract forms churning around her in the current, with no idea I could have been painting the debris of a plane wreckage. What was the odd patch of orange on her stomach and the white patch on her thigh if not the suggestion of burns? The orange brush strokes infringing upon her face and arms no longer seemed random. I can't say why I thought to paint her neck blue, but now that I know that blue is the color of the throat chakra and represents speech, I wonder if the only way she could communicate with me was through color. Red for Petra, orange for fire, blue for water. Blue and orange. Maybe that was why I had been so taken with those colors.

That morning on Ninth Street when I woke up with the words, *You will become real when your dream becomes real,* I thought referred to my dream of being recognized as an artist. It never occurred to me that it could have been when the Dream of '76 became real. I didn't even see it when I started referring to *Girl Under Water* by her initials, Gee, You Double-You.

Something is calling me down to the deep. Hadn't I known it when I painted a swimmer doing a backstroke far out to sea? I wanted to stay in daylight time and not go exploring where there might be no return, but I had to answer the call. Union in the deep. I'd known it all along. First it was the judges interrogating me in a dream, wanting to know who I was. I had no idea, and pulled out a piece of the umbilical cord I'd kept hidden inside. Then I said I was Renoir, meaning *re-noir,* regarding the black, the dark, the subconscious, the inner life I had yet to explore in paint. I needed symbols if I was going to access an area beyond any logical explanation. The *Dreamer* looking through the doorway was a start. She who was here and not here. And *Boy on the Seabed* waiting to be found by the mermaid who found her swimming lad. The *He* and the *She* found one another in the flame. I had to wonder though, if all that time I was looking for a soul mate, looking for union with a man, I was searching for my own soul. For Petra, the lost part of myself. My 'other half' at the bottom of the sea. The one trapped in the No Exit dream.

I look at my paintings now, the ones I said came from my 'imagination' as if I was only imagining them. How could what came from my deepest, innermost self be something I only imagined? They were no more made up than a dream. Yet the dream had to become real in order for me to become real to myself. Rather than saying the pictures came from my imagination, I'd rather say I intuited them. Still, I wasn't anywhere close to knowing what they meant until I began writing the story of what happened around them. To 'know thyself' was to know myself down to my soul.

I thought of the frozen roses then, the vision I had after the Dream of '76 of red roses encased in a cube of ice, and I looked up how ice melts. It seems that ice only has a fixed shape because the particles are so closely packed together. But give them some heat and the particles gain energy and start moving. Ice melts when the molecules of water break apart and begin moving around freely. The heat alters their structure, turns a solid into a liquid. I couldn't help wondering then if the heat on July Fourth had broken up my structure too, and that was why I went to the grid paper. To put myself into some kind of structure again.

When I thought about it some more I realized my structure had been broken up long before with those words from my mother, 'I wish you'd never been born.' Then the Oscar thing when she gave me away like that, and 'Frank Wait isn't your father, Milton is.' These were traumatic events but they didn't cause me to melt. With the power of will I escaped to another country and held it together by having a life where I was able to use my brokenness by playing other characters who had been shattered in some way. It wasn't a long term solution, not when there was just covering up the cracks and no healing was involved. By the time I realized the old cliché that love was the answer, it was too late. Love had passed me by because I didn't even know what love was. I wanted to escape again but was told if I died I'd only have to come back. This crack was too wide to cover up and the first shaft of light entered in. It got me back to New York again and gave me the strength to begin studying the light. I studied structures too. The solidity of 3D we take so for granted like the bone and muscle constructions of the body, and the structure of buildings that could be measured, copied and set down on paper. I painted 4D too, the world of dreams and imagination, and pictured love as a surrender of one flame to another. But where was the melting, the change in molecular patterning like when a solid becomes a liquid? Perhaps it was only a vibrational change. They had been wild those weeks leading up to July Fourth. Spirals pulsing and swirling and completely taking me over. I hadn't been afraid of them though, and maybe they were what brought on the heat July Fourth. Or brought on the change that enabled me to bear it.

Maybe all the events that occurred in those preceding weeks were about bearing it. The air-conditioner conking out in the middle of a heatwave and painting women melting. Thinking to cool off in a movie theater that ended up feeling like a tomb when Rosa was shot and tossed in the canal. Coming home and drawing a woman crawling away to the cool of the forest and being called back the next day when the phone rang and it was Gene calling. *For heaven's sake*, I'd said. The assignment was to paint an animal in a cage, but before I could begin I had to picture my willingness to allow the *sea* to enter in. Because once I drew the bear in a cage I was going to have to contend with the cage I was in too, simply by being a human who would die someday. There was no way out. Yet the very fact of the cage itself had created an opening. All I had to do was accept the bars, the trap where I was doomed, no different from the one in the No Exit dream, and surrender to it. It was like that night at Direct Centering when I tried to figure out what I was up against and the next morning I looked up and saw *Girl*

Under Water hanging on the wall. It made no sense because I didn't feel trapped at the time, and instead thought of surrendering to Gene. I was still doing it the following year, surrendering to his vision, but doing it out of love. Doing it *for heaven's sake*. I like to think the heat burned away the last remnants of my resistance, enabling a vision of the number five to come through. What I thought of as 5D, the unconditional love of Heaven.

EPILOGUE

MAKING THE UNKNOWN, KNOWN • 2024

Without a star to steer by,
without a map or charts,
You've reached your destination,
with the compass of your heart.

— JACK WILLIAMS

Until I counted the years I didn't notice that since the summer I was thirty-seven and told to write how I got here, thirty-seven more summers had come and gone. As if the time it's taken to retrace my steps had to be equal to the time it took to arrive there in the first place. When I did more counting I realized Petra died in '43 and lay at the bottom of the sea for 43 years until I painted her in '86, holding out a branch for me to pull her to the surface. Were these odd coincidences, or were they part of some mysterious cosmic scale seeking a balance?

Another double was six and six. Petra died June 1, 1943, six years and six months before I was born on December 1, 1949. I called the painting *Girl Under Water,* which made her initials GUW, sound like, 'Gee, you double-you.' It's the sort of thing that can make you wonder about a hidden world of mathematical harmonies playing out beneath the surface. The closest I've come to making sense of it has been to think in terms of frequencies. When the outer-self or the persona is aligned to the frequency of the inner-being, the soul, the light—and perhaps the heat of the light too—can come through.

Knowing this, I can see the answers were in front of my nose all along. Like the two sixes on my parents pale yellow bedspread when I was growing up. My mother had it custom-made with the two Fs for their initials, Frank and Frances circled in white-eyelet in the center.

All I saw as a child was the two Fs. It's only now I see them as sixes because F is the sixth letter of the alphabet. But it's also the number of Venus. Six in the tarot signifies the Lovers and means union. Union is "an act or instance of uniting or joining two or more things into one." One F faced forward and the other faced back, as if love and union could look back as well as forward in the circle of time.

Even GUW adds up to six. G=7; U=21=3; W=23=5. 7+3+5=15=6. My own initials, NLW, speak loud and clear to me now, what with N being the 14th letter making it a five, L for angle standing straight and tall in the middle, followed by W, the 23rd letter, which is also a five. All along, ever since I was born I'd had initials telling me, *Five, angle five.* I didn't notice this until I began looking at letters and the spelling of words and names, listening to how they sounded from another angle.

Juliet might say, "What's in a name?" and declare, "… that which we call a rose by any other name would smell as sweet." Gertrude Stein can go ahead and say, "A rose is a rose is a rose." But there is always more to it if you look deeper. There was more to 'Bob Dylan' once I studied his name and could read it as a particular vibration that had meaning for me, the reminder to be the angle from 4-to-5. Angling from the lower realm to the higher, the Fourth Kingdom of Humanity to the Fifth Kingdom of Soul. On July Fourth I vowed to stay as long as it took, and while it has taken a long time, I can readily see how everything that exists and everything that happens, occurs on more than one level.

You have to have a reason for that type of delving though, and mine went back to the psychic at Marble Arch. I was twenty-three when I asked her, 'Why couldn't my mother have married Milton?' I thought if only she'd married Milton she would have been happier then, and by association I would have been happier too. 'Oh no,' said the woman. 'You chose everything to be exactly the way that it was.' This was said in such a tone of quiet authority that I couldn't discount it. All I had to do was figure out the reason why.

It all makes sense to me now, even Chicago where I was born. Chicago was more than the name of a city, it was a bridge to the past. I had to be born there because we lived in the suburb of Skokie which didn't have a hospital in those days. The key was in the letters. C for 'see.' H for 'bridge' since it's shaped like a bridge. The next two letters, I and C, were 'I see,' and the last three letters, A-G-O, could be read either as 'ago' or 'a go,' as in 'it's a go.' And Chicago became, "See-Bridge-I-See-Ago," or "I see a go," as if it was green-lighted, the place where my soul saw a bridge to the past. The one that would lead eventually to Petra.

Skokie even had the sound of 'key' at the end. First came S for Ssss… like the hissing sound when you're trying to get someone's attention. Ssss…kokie, or 'co-key.' A key or a frequency that was shared. Like the light that was shared with me at the end of the Dream of '76 when Sharon, the future coffee-girl, appeared and held out a light when I needed it. Sharon, Share-on. The share was on. This light from the inner world was being shared with me so that I might bring my own inner world to light. It's been a long and drawn out process and it's taken a good part of my life. But I got my reward. A dream not long ago where I saw myself gleefully taking on the task.

I saw myself in some kind of holding area in the etheric, waiting my turn with dozens of other cherubs by the opening where the slide was. Waiting for the call it was time. I don't recall hearing anything—it was a very silent sort of place—but suddenly I made a dash for the opening as if there wasn't a moment to lose.

In time I've come to picture the scene in 1943 when German war planes followed an unarmed British civilian aircraft on its flight from Lisbon to Bristol. Maybe the call came when the Nazis opened fire over the Bay of Biscay, and I arrived in time to experience the shots and the fall to the bottom of the sea. Experiencing death on an energetic level. It was the memory that came back to me in the Dream of '76 along with the doorway that suddenly appeared. I didn't go through the doorway though. It wasn't yet time. In 1943 Frances Hawkins, née McCarthy was only eighteen, getting married to her first husband. She won't be looking to divorce him until the winter of '49 so she could marry her second husband, Frank Wait. Which was why she took the bus to Nevada to establish residency. The bus where she would meet Milton, the handsome veteran still in uniform on his way to a government job in a mining town called Tonopah. While she was falling in love with the Jewish man who was so different from the midwestern boys she had grown up with, I waited on the threshold in a timeless realm at the bottom of the sea.

In the Dream of '76 it seemed only a few moments before I was whisked back to the present in London. But having that dream was the first inkling I had some kind of knowledge within. Knowledge that would only make sense from the angle of a soul looking 'forward and backward in the circle of time' like the two Fs on a bedspread. It all makes sense now, why I chose everything that happened. It was so I would remember death.

If my mother hadn't wished me away I never would have had the No Exit dream. If she had married Milton there would have been no Oscar thing and I wouldn't have retreated back to the bottom of the sea to get away from him. I was shy like Milton, but my father had been an actor in his youth and gave us all voice and diction lessons in the living room when we were little. I became an actress to please him and got it into my head to study in London. I had to get myself back to England as if I'd known all along that Petra had been on her way home and I had to finish the journey. Then I had to finish my own. What began as a sense of irretrievable loss of a father from a different background that was foreign and mysterious, became the loss of the key to my soul.

The day it all came to a head was keyed to the number five. A Friday in May, the fifth day of the week, the fifth month of 1976, a year whose digits added up to five. (1+9=10; 7+6=13=4; 10+4=14; 1+4=5.) The date in full, May 28, 1976, the day I thought of driving my car off a cliff, adds up to 11, a gateway number. I wanted out alright, but that wasn't the way, not when I heard I'd only be sent back. The right way was to give up, surrender my will and be guided. After a week at St. Mary Abbots I experienced the memory of death in a dream when I was shot from five feet away, five days after the thirty-third anniversary of the downing of a plane called *Ibis*. When I woke up I smoked four cigarettes and put the fifth one back. Five had become scary.

I knew where I was with four. There were four sides to a window and four to a door, all meeting at right angles like the black and white checkered hallway in the hospital that helped me get my bearings. As soon as I got home I took note of the sofa shaped like a rectangle and the club chair like a square. Now that I think about it, the square was the first shape I noticed when I was four. We were still in Skokie then and I was sick with a temperature of 104°. I kept hearing them say, "A temperature of a-hundred-and-*four*," as if that was the limit. Apparently the fever wouldn't go down. I knew it was serious when my parents moved me from the top bunk in the room I shared with my younger sister and brother, and put me in their bed while they must have slept on the sofa bed in the living room. I probably needed to be in easy reach for sponge-baths and temperature-taking and doctor visits, but they gave me presents too. We never got presents unless it was Christmas or our birthday, and now I was given a toy-tool set I was too sick to play with, and *Madeleine*, the story about a little French girl with red hair who was sick and got well. But mostly I looked out the window. Lying on the bed I was too low to see anything but the changing color of the sky, so I looked at the window itself, a square with a line down the middle and a line across making four more squares. Though I think of it now as the first time I saw a grid, all I saw then was a plus sign. Plus means more.

And there was more. Five would always come next. I turned five, and in May of 1955 we moved to New York. I threw up on the plane, but when we arrived and I looked out the taxi and saw lights all the way up to the sky, I thought we'd moved to fairy land. Once you've seen fairy land it's hard to let it go. I found it again in the magic that took place under those gel-colored stage lights of the theater. And now I see it in the magic of the 4-to-5 angle between body and soul. I like this age-old symbol of counting to five, how the fifth line crosses out the other four.

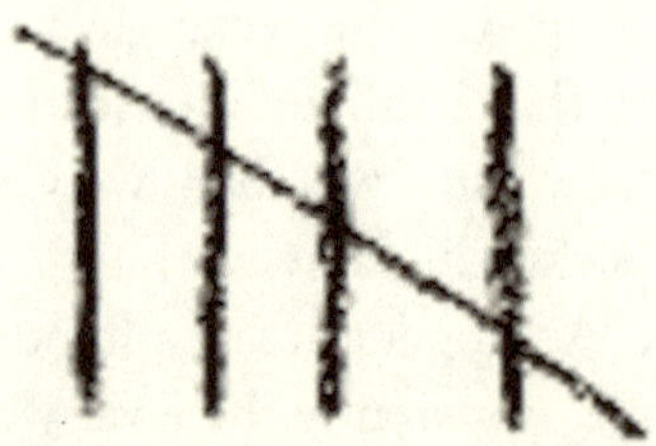

I like seeing the lines representing the five kingdoms of nature. First came the rocks and stones of the Mineral Kingdom. They were followed by the plants and flowers of the Vegetable Kingdom. Then came the Animals, and finally the Human Kingdom. We may be at number four but we're not where it ends. There's more. Those four lines won't be complete until the fifth line with its slant of finality crosses them out. I like it best when the angle starts on the lower right where four leaves off, and ascends on an angle towards upper left, suggesting a journey back, as in back home. Or back to spirit. Or back to source, the beginning of it all. But going back from a different starting place, now that it has passed through each of the four kingdoms. From what I hear, the Fifth Kingdom of Soul is as high as we can go while still in a physical body. It's the 4-to-5 angle. The angle home.

ABOUT THE AUTHOR

Nancy Wait was born in Chicago, Illinois in 1949 and grew up in New York City. She attended the Royal Academy of Dramatic Art in London and had a career in England during the 1970s acting in theater, film and television under the name of Nancie Wait.

She returned to New York and was a painter in the 1980s, as well as a freelance artist of architectural renderings. Since then she has been writing her story.

www.ingramcontent.com/pod-product-compliance
Lightning Source LLC
LaVergne TN
LVHW090545110826
845146LV00001B/30

* 9 7 9 8 9 9 1 0 2 0 0 0 8 *